D1188136

THE RUSSIAN FIVE

KEITH GAVE

THE RUSSIAN
FIVE

A story of espionage, defection, bribery and courage

KEITH GAVE

THE RUSSIAN FIVE

Library of Congress Control Number: 2017960389

ISBN: 978-1-947165-17-5 (hardcover)
ISBN: 978-1-947165-44-1 (eBook)

Printed and published in the United States of America.

This book is available in quantity at special discounts for your group or organization. For further information, contact Gold Star Publishing at (734) 717-8600.

The Gold Star Publishing Speakers Bureau can bring authors to your live event. For more information, contact the publisher at (734) 717-8600.

Visit our website at: www.keithgave.com
Contact the author at: keith@keithgave.com
Cover design: Amjad Shahzad
Interior design: reddovedesign.com

Gold Star
PUBLISHING
A DIVISION OF THE GOLD STAR FAMILY OF COMPANIES

100 Phoenix Drive, Ste 300
Ann Arbor, Michigan 48108
www.danmilstein.com/gold-star-publishing-

10 9 8 7 6 5 4 3 2 1

Table of Contents

For Jo Ann

On a visit to Russia as a graduate student, American author Elif Batuman spent all four days of a conference at Yasnaya Polyana, the estate of literary master Leo Tolstoy, wearing the same clothing.

Aeroflot, the country's state-run airline, had lost her luggage. Unable to purchase new clothing because the estate was far from any shopping centers, she phoned Aeroflot each morning to inquire about her suitcase.

"Oh, it's you," the clerk sighed. "Yes, I have your request right here. Address: Yasnaya Polyana, Tolstoy's house. When we find the suitcase we will send it to you. In the meantime, are you familiar with our Russian phrase *resignation of the soul?*"

This is the story of five men who refused to resign themselves to a life in a futile, sometimes brutal system – and forever changed their sport, and our world.

PROLOGUE

'That Night in Helsinki'

Inside the raucous Detroit Red Wings' dressing room the air was palpable, a curious concoction of mist from cheap champagne and a cloudy haze from several bootleg Cubans. The added scent of many freshly uncapped beers helped camouflage the ubiquitous odor of the sweat of several exhausted men celebrating like the champions they had become just moments before. They were joined by scores of family members, friends, reporters and an eclectic assortment of celebrities who always seem to find their way into once-in-a-lifetime events like these. Among them was Jeff Daniels, the Academy Award-nominee and Wings season-ticket holder. And Alto Reed, the sax player in Bob Seger's Silver Bullet Band who occasionally performed the national anthem before games.

Piercing voices and riotous laughter ruptured 42 years of pent-up frustration. Finally, the Stanley Cup had found its way back to Detroit. Here was a moment to savor – for everyone in this room and the tens of thousands still hanging around on the streets surrounding Joe Louis Arena on a sultry late-spring evening. Many of them had just witnessed the conclusion of a four-game sweep of the Philadelphia Flyers. Most fans had left the building, but refused to go home. Many more left their homes after watching this unforgettable moment in Detroit sports history on TV, wanting to be part of the excitement. They drove to the northern banks of the Detroit River to join in a spontaneous celebration that lasted until the wee hours of the morning.

Championship celebrations throughout professional sports were pretty much the same – at least until they started to be choreographed for TV, with players donning goggles to avoid the sting from the inevitable champagne showers. So it was on that pre-goggles night of June 7, 1997, when I inched my way into the crowded Red Wings' locker room. The first player I encountered was Vladimir Konstantinov, who for some reason was going the other way, toward the exit. He had taken his Wings jersey and skates off, along with his shoulder and elbow pads, but otherwise was dressed as he had been a few minutes earlier with his teammates, waltzing the Stanley Cup around the ice. His left hand gripped a bottle of bubbly along with an unlit cigar dangling precariously between his fingers. His right hand found mine through the crowd as soon as we made eye contact.

Here was a man as friendly and affable away from the ice as he was contemptible on it, now smiling wearily. At 30, he was in the prime of his career and one of the best defensemen in the world. And he played much, much bigger than his 5-foot-11, 180-pound frame. But the ferocity with which he played took a toll, and I understood at that moment why, even since his days as a teenager in junior hockey, teammates called him *"Dyadya"* – Grandpa. Even then, he was 18 going on 40. After a brutal two-month stretch of Stanley Cup playoff hockey, he appeared as though he might be pushing 60 the way he moved.

"Congratulations, Vladdie. *Molodyets,*" I told him, using the Russian word loosely translated to mean "attaboy."

Here was a man so colorful he needed more than one nickname. The Vladinator, fans loved to call him. But to his opponents who'd encountered the blade of his stick along the boards, he was Vlad the Impaler. To most of those who played with him, though, he was simply Vladdie, the guy who always had their backs.

"It was very hard," he said in barely a whisper, "so hard." As he spoke, he pulled me toward him in a one-armed embrace, soaking me with a mix of suds and sweat from the blue undershirt he wore still tucked into his hockey pants. "We win the Cup! We win! But it was so hard. Hardest thing ever."

As he spoke, he raised the bottle of champagne and poured the remnants over my head and laughed. Then he whispered the word *"spaciba."*

"Thank you," he said, repeating himself in English, looking at me in a way that made me wonder exactly what he meant.

Very slowly, I made my way around the room, shaking hands, asking a few questions, trying to take notes I'd never be able to read because the ink on the paper became illegible as it continued to rain champagne and beer. There was Steve Yzerman, the team captain, shaking hands, surrounded by reporters and patiently answering non-stop questions after his long-awaited waltz around the rink with the Cup over his head. Never again would his leadership be questioned. Nearby were Slava Fetisov and Igor Larionov, two aging former Soviet Red Army stars who had just won the only prize that had eluded them in their redoubtable careers. Alongside Larionov was Slava Kozlov, who grew up a few blocks from Larionov in their hometown of Voskresensk – nearly 5,000 miles to the east of Joe Louis Arena.

At various corners of the room, there were Kris Draper, Joey Kocur, Kirk Maltby and Darren McCarty, four-thirds of the Grind Line (the three-man forward unit the Wings deployed against the opposing team's top players) that meant so much to this team of superstars. And Nicklas Lidstrom, who would become known as "The Perfect Human" the way he conducted himself on and off the ice. I stopped to congratulate them all, finally making my way to a corner where the best hockey player in the world was surrounded by friends and family.

"Congratulations," I said, extending my hand toward Sergei Fedorov, the first of what would become Detroit's Russian Five, one of the most renowned units in the history of the game, and one that would forever change how it was played in the National Hockey League. He was beaming as our hands clenched. Then he leaned forward, lowering his voice to say something he didn't want others to hear.

"Hey Keith, you remember that night in Helsinki, long time ago?"

I nodded.

"I remember, too," he said. "And I don't forget that. But I never tell anyone, OK? Never. That was a big moment for me."

Only then did I begin to understand what Konstantinov might have meant when he whispered that "thank you."

Nearly two decades later, I ran into Vladimir again at Joe Louis Arena before a Stanley Cup playoff game in the spring of 2016. He was accompanied by his full-time physical therapist, Pamela Demanuel. She was guiding him along behind his walker, headed toward the Red Wings' locker room, when I approached them.

"Hi Keith!" he said, breaking into a wide grin as our eyes met. Then he grabbed my hand and squeezed it with the same authority and strength as that night moments after he and his team had become champions. I spoke a few words in English and a few more in Russian, and it was obvious he understood every word. It was a short conversation, but finally I was able to tell him what had been weighing on my mind since the night of the tragedy that ended his career and nearly ended his life.

"Thank you, Vladimir. Thank you for all the wonderful memories you gave us. We love you."

CHAPTER 1

A Special Assignment

A month or so after the annual National Hockey League entry draft, in mid-July 1989, a time when most folks involved in the league were enjoying some respite between seasons, my phone rang. Jim Lites was on the line inviting me to lunch. Strange timing, I thought, to hear from the executive vice president of the Detroit Red Wings, then the son-in-law of owners Mike and Marian Ilitch. I had a good working relationship with Lites, but I usually only heard from him like this after I'd written something he didn't like. He'd rant, I'd listen, we'd agree to disagree, and it was over. But I hadn't written anything in nearly two weeks. I was on vacation. I figured Lites wouldn't be asking to meet if it wasn't something important.

The next day, we were sitting across from one another at the recently renovated Elwood Bar and Grill, which at the time was across Woodward Avenue from the Fox Theatre. The Ilitches bought and, with Lites running the project, refurbished the Fox and turned it into a showpiece that would ignite the renaissance of Detroit's embattled downtown. We ordered soup and sandwiches. Lites began to speak.

"Just let me say right up front that if I cross any lines here or make you uncomfortable in any way, I'll stop and that will be the end of it," he said.

I raised my eyebrows. After a pause, Lites continued. A lawyer in his mid-30s with a quick smile beneath a prematurely receding hairline, he tended to speak quickly, but always choosing his words carefully.

While doing little to conceal his emotions, Lites was always in control of the conversation. He laughed easily, and when he did the whole room laughed with him. When he was angry, and I saw that side of him frequently enough, you knew it before he said a word. Now, he was serious – as though he was about to deliver some distressing news. And he got right to the heart of his subject as our sandwiches arrived.

"We're prepared to pay considerably – serious money," he said. "We can assure you exclusivity to any stories, book rights, you name it."

"Hold on," I said, using my hands to signal a time-out. "What are you talking about?"

"As you know, we drafted a couple of Soviet players in the draft a few weeks ago."

I nodded. Of course I knew. I had written about it at length in the pages of the Detroit Free Press. It had been a historic moment for a global sport when the 21 National Hockey League clubs gathered for their annual entry draft, taking turns selecting amateur players from junior hockey, colleges and universities, and European leagues. The Red Wings had chosen center Sergei Fedorov in the fourth of 12 rounds – the highest a Soviet-born player had ever been claimed. In the 11th round, they selected defenseman Vladimir Konstantinov.

"We've learned that the Russians are holding part of their training camp in Finland in August, the Soviet National Team," Lites said. "They're playing an exhibition game against one of the Finnish elite teams in Helsinki."

"And?"

"And you're the only person I know who speaks Russian."

I sat back in my chair. Stunned silent, I listened to his pitch. Lites explained that he and the ownership family were hoping I could use my cover as a sportswriter credentialed by the National Hockey League to attend that game in Finland. While there, I could "interview" Fedorov and Konstantinov, and perhaps covertly pass along the message that the Red Wings were interested in bringing them to Detroit as soon as possible, even if that meant an unlawful departure from a country that had no intention of allowing them to leave.

"We want you to contact Fedorov," Lites explained. "Konstantinov, too, though we think he'll be a lot harder for us to get out because he's married and has a child. "You could write a letter. . ."

That letter would provide some background about Detroit and the Red Wings. I could outline some important financial terms and provide contact information to help them begin the process, Lites said. When they were ready, the Wings would use all their power, political influence and money to bring them to North America – the sooner the better.

"You know hockey, you know the league, and you know us," Lites said. "And as a member of the media, you can get access to those guys when nobody else in the NHL can. All we're asking for is that you make that first contact for us. We can take it from there – if it's going to happen – but we can't do anything without that initial contact."

Though I tried not to show it, I was both excited and conflicted, flattered and at the same time offended. My heart was telling me one thing, that this could be the story with the potential to define my career. My head, however, screamed that I should be insulted that Lites would even broach a subject like this. But I was also more than a little intrigued. In six years in the intelligence business as a Russian linguist working for the National Security Agency, I never got close to such a mission. Here was, in every respect, a magnificent opportunity for an actual cloak-and-dagger assignment.

"Impossible," I said abruptly. "I can't do it. No way. Not a chance."

"Enough said then." Lites allowed the subject to drop after apologizing, insisting he hadn't meant to offend me.

We made small talk, finished our lunch and parted. I felt lousy.

A few weeks later I was on board a Northwest Airlines/KLM flight to Boston and then on to Helsinki, by way of Copenhagen, Denmark, with an important message for a couple of prominent young Soviet hockey players.

Since that meeting with Lites, my days were restless and my nights sleepless as I wrestled with the notion of accepting his offer. I had explained my dilemma, that it would be ethical suicide to enter into some sort of financial arrangement to do such a favor for the team I was assigned to cover. My allegiance was totally and completely to the newspaper that entrusted me with the challenge of a professional sports beat and paid me well to cover the Detroit Red Wings as thoroughly and as fairly as I could. And especially to its readers, who included some of the most passionate and knowledgeable hockey fans in the world.

This could cost me my job. But while I worried about putting my career in jeopardy, I also argued with myself, trying to justify my heart's position, that I would be doing my newspaper a great disservice if I didn't leverage as much of an advantage as possible over the competition in a city that prided itself in having two great daily newspapers. Besides, Cold War history cannot be written without stories of correspondents for the great Western news organizations occasionally used as pawns to send messages between covert agents representing the Soviet Union and the United States.

Indeed, entire books have been written about the roles American reporters have played, often unwittingly, as messengers, recruiters and sources of information and disinformation since the 1940s. In a 1977 article published by Rolling Stone, Pulitzer Prize-winning reporter Carl Bernstein wrote a groundbreaking piece titled "The CIA and the Media." In it, he wrote that journalists with the New York Times, CBS and Time Inc. were among the most valuable to the U.S. intelligence organization.

"In the field, journalists were used to help recruit and handle foreigners as agents, to acquire and evaluate information, and to plant false information with officials of foreign governments," Bernstein wrote. "Many signed secrecy agreements, pledging never to divulge anything about their dealings with the Agency; some signed employment contracts, some were assigned case officers and treated with unusual deference."

What I was considering doing paled in comparison, but I nevertheless agonized over the decision. I discussed it with the one person in my life I knew I could trust, my wife, Jo Ann, who had spent 14 years working on the newsroom's administrative side of the Detroit News. She understood my dilemma and said she'd support me whatever I decided. I knew I should discuss it with my editors at the Detroit Free Press – I could trust them as well – but I also had a pretty good idea what they would say: The only way I'd get to Helsinki was on an assignment for the newspaper, and there was no way it would pay to send me there for a story about two players who might not be in Detroit for many years, if ever.

But there was something about this offer, this opportunity, this mission, that I couldn't shake. In retrospect, maybe part of me was still fighting the Cold War. I remembered meeting those great players with the Soviet National Team in Quebec City for "Rendez-vous 87" – the two-game all-star series with NHL players. The Russians wore the same sober, unembellished faces as the conscripted Soviet soldiers I'd seen at Checkpoint Charlie at the Berlin Wall in the mid-1970s. Perhaps, I reasoned, I could do some good for a couple of those young hockey players, help change their otherwise miserable lives.

And so, I made the boldest decision of my newspaper career – one that defied every ethical instinct of my being and one that, in 15 years of teaching journalism later in life, I implored my students never to do: get so close to a source that, if discovered by readers or editors, it could call into question everything they ever wrote. I was certain that while so few people knew about it at the time – Lites, team owner Mike Ilitch, my wife, and me – eventually details of my involvement would become public and I would have to answer for it. This would be the worst decision I could ever make, or one of the best. History would determine that.

A few days after that lunch meeting, I called Lites at his office and told him I could go to Helsinki to try to make contact with Sergei Fedorov and Vladimir Konstantinov. He was surprised, but ecstatic. I assured him, however, that I would go on a strictly conditional basis: I could accept no money from his hockey club regardless of its generous, life-changing offer. Nor would I accept any subsistence from the Wings to pay for expenses. I would cash in a mountain of frequent-flier miles to cover airfare; the rest amounted to a few hundred dollars that I considered to be down payment on a future investment. Most important to me, as I told Lites, was that whenever these players were on their way to Detroit and however it happened, I wanted the stories first for readers of the Free Press. Also, I wanted the first opportunity to interview them on their arrival in Detroit. While I appreciated Lites' offer of exclusive rights to books telling their personal stories of potential defections, I felt I couldn't hold him to it because it seemed to me a promise he might not be able to deliver.

"Deal," Lites said.

Now the challenging part began. While awaiting my overseas flight out of Boston's Logan Airport, I dug out my well-worn English-Russian dictionary and began to write.

"Dorogoi Sergei. . . Dear Sergei. . ." I tentatively began the first message. It was a slow, laborious process, and I found myself digging into that dictionary far more than I'd anticipated. Once, I had been nearly fluent after spending a full year – six hours a day, five days a week – studying Russian at the Defense Language Institute in Monterey, California, at a time when nearly every other Army draftee like me was headed to Vietnam. That was 18 years earlier. And even though I'd spent three years at a state-of-the-art spy station on a hill in a forest of West Berlin, eavesdropping on the Soviets to gather intelligence for the NSA, those language skills had eroded significantly. Nevertheless, I was confident that I could communicate the message the Red Wings were desperate to send to Sergei and Vladimir.

"Welcome to Detroit," the letters continued, "a great industrial American city that loves hockey and adores its Red Wings. It is the team of Steve Yzerman and Gordie Howe, famous players from the National Hockey League club that selected you in its recent entry draft in Montreal, Canada. . ." The letters included some basic background about the Wings and how they were beginning to trend upward in the league standings under coach Jacques Demers after many years of futility. I explained how the team was interested in helping them – in any and every way possible – to get out of the Soviet Union to continue their careers in the NHL. In some detail, I let them know that the Wings had a history of helping players like them get out from behind the Iron Curtain, explaining how in 1985 they orchestrated the rather daring defection of Petr Klima from Czechoslovakia.

The letters, of course, included the important stuff, what Lites knew would get the players' attention: The Wings were willing to pay them $250,000 a year for their services – a salary that would have put them in the upper echelon of salaries in the NHL at the time. Moreover, so long as they were members of the Detroit Red Wings, the team would pay their families in Russia $25,000 a year – an exorbitant sum of money for a family in the Soviet Union at that time.

It took most of the seven-hour flight to Copenhagen to write those letters. I arrived in Denmark shortly before noon, and after a layover I was finally on the last leg of the journey, a 90-minute hop to Helsinki. Shortly before 4 p.m., local time, I arrived at the Finnish capital on the Baltic Sea.

The puck would drop within a few hours of my arrival in Helsinki. All I had to do was find out where the game would be played, talk myself into the arena, get access to some of the most closely guarded players in the world, get them to meet with me, pass along messages that could cause serious problems for these players if they were caught with them, and get the hell out without causing an international incident.

Cue the "Mission Impossible" theme song.

With a growing sense of urgency, I did what always served me well when I was in over my head on a newspaper assignment: I threw myself on the mercy of complete strangers. With my carry-on in one hand and my computer bag slung over my shoulder, I approached what appeared to be an information counter. It turned out to be a currency exchange office, so I traded some American greenbacks for some Finnish markkas. The woman behind the counter greeted me with a warm smile and spoke to me in English. I asked her if by chance she knew where in this city of a half-million people I might find a hockey game that muggy summer evening in August. She looked at me like I was visiting from another planet. But at the mention of the word "hockey," a man behind her looked my way and smiled.

"You are here for hockey?" he asked. I nodded.

"There is a game this evening at the Helsinki Ice Hall," he said. "The Soviets are here to play one of our top sports clubs."

I asked about hotels near the arena and he suggested the Radisson Blu, just a short walk across the park.

I thanked the man several times in English, Russian and German. He smiled again and said, *"Ole hyva,"* which I learned later means "you're welcome," in Finnish. "I might see you there," he added in English. The Finns love their hockey, too.

I hailed a cab and after a short ride arrived at the Radisson Blu Royal Hotel shortly before 5 p.m. I was tired, and that bed looked awfully inviting, but there was barely enough time for a quick shower and a change of clothes. Face-off, I assumed, was at 7 p.m. Before leaving, I carefully organized some important materials for a critical hand-off.

The Red Wings' media guide at the time was a small book, five-by-eight inches, less than a half-inch thick. It was easily portable and included everything reporters needed to know about every Detroit player and prospect, former players, the coaching staff, management and ownership, as well as a thorough collection of team and individual records. It was something a beat writer carried at all times, along with other important tools of the trade: a laptop computer, a hand-held voice recorder, reporter's notebooks, and plenty of pens.

The media guides served a dual purpose for this mission. They would tell these players much about what they needed to know about the team that, since the entry draft less than two months before, owned their NHL rights, and the books would serve as the perfect place to hide the letters I'd written. Or nearly perfect. When I tried to tuck them between the pages of the guides, I wondered if I'd erred. They were a bit bulky when folded; they weren't well-hidden. If the players were caught with them it could put them in a precarious, career-threatening situation. The iron-fisted leaders of the Soviet hockey system, even while the Communist regime was starting to crumble, had no sense of humor when it came to its star athletes – among the nation's most precious commodities – turning their backs and walking away. Bulky or not, I had no other plan. This would have to do.

It took me barely five minutes to walk from my room, across a beautiful, tree-dotted city park to the main entrance at the hockey arena a few hundred meters away. The weather, high 70s and a bit humid, was by Northern European standards as good as a summer day gets. My timing was perfect, too. I'd arrived just as the Soviet players were exiting a bus. A small crowd watched the players step off, all of them stone-faced and silent. Unlike scenes like this in Canada or the United States, no one bothered these marvelous athletes for their autographs, even though the team included Olympic and world champions – some destined for the Hockey Hall of Fame.

A mere flash of my NHL media credentials at the main entrance, and I was in the building. Just inside the door was an area I mistook for a press room so common in North American arenas. It was, in fact, a coffee and snack shop, and I was surprised to see so many representatives from various NHL clubs. There were several scouts, executives and even a coach. All were there to evaluate the talent the Russians had on the ice that night. Other teams had followed Detroit's lead in the draft earlier that summer and began claiming some of these Soviet players. Like the Wings, they were desperate to get them over to North America as soon as possible. I was the only newsman in the room.

They stood on either side of me, nearly matching bookends, both with wet blond hair shaped haphazardly by hand after being interrupted following their showers. Both were fair-skinned with the unmistakable high, pronounced cheekbones that proclaimed these young men to be sons of Eastern Europe. To my right was Sergei Fedorov, at 6-foot-1 slightly taller than Vladimir Konstantinov to my left. Both had bodies sculpted by year-around, and often-times brutal and punishing, physical training. Another thing they had in common standing there with remnants of their recent showers dripping to the floor: they were cold. A big sheet of ice was just a few steps away. Each had goose bumps on his arms and chests. And it was clear they were confused about why they were brought out to meet with me.

I needed to make this quick. But for an instant I marveled at all the good fortune that brought me to this point. During the game, I had wandered around the arena looking for someone, anyone, who might be connected to the event as a sponsor or a promoter. Once again, I felt that low-level panic bubbling to the surface, as it had at the airport a few hours earlier. What if I came all this way and failed to connect with the players? Finally, during the second period, after asking several friendly strangers, I found one of the organizers of the game. When I explained who I was and why I was there, he was more than eager to accommodate.

"We don't see so many journalists from North America here at our hockey games," he said in perfect English. "Especially in August. This must be very important."

I fibbed a bit, saying I had been vacationing in Europe, and when I learned that the Soviet team would be in Helsinki, possibly with two players recently selected by the Detroit club I covered for my newspaper, I made the short side trip in hopes of introducing myself and conducting brief interviews.

"Do you speak Russian?" he asked.

"I do, but I'm afraid my eroding skills might not be good enough to conduct a formal interview."

"I can try to help you. I speak some Russian. Many Finns speak a little bit, since we are neighbors. Sometimes not-so-friendly neighbors."

I wanted to hug the guy.

After the game, when the promoter entered the Soviets' locker room and brought out the two players, I was struck by how critical and, frankly, dangerous this encounter could be – especially for them. I stood with my back against the wall, across the corridor and a few steps from their changing room. Unlike in North America, it's unusual for reporters to have access to Russian players in their locker rooms. Not even the NHL media credential got me access there.

Almost immediately after the players came out, I noticed a man eight or ten feet to my left. Clearly Slavic by his features, wavy hair combed back, pronounced cheekbones. His clothing was disheveled chic, a bit rumpled and appearing to be straight off the rack of an American Goodwill store in the mid-1970s. His back was to the wall as well, but he kept stepping forward looking in our direction through several people between us. His cold eyes locked on us with obvious suspicion, looking as though he could care less what we might be up to but clearly wanting me to know he was there. Sergei Fedorov noticed, too, with an imperceptible glance. He remained stone-faced, turning his head casually back toward our conversation.

That the man was there hardly surprised me, and once again

I felt a bit lucky to have identified him just then. It was his job, I knew immediately, to make sure that all those players who left the Soviet Union for this preseason training junket to Finland returned home. He was an agent with the KGB – one of the "spies," as they were referred to by the players – who always traveled with the Soviet teams. There would be no defections on his watch, even if it meant a subtle display of intimidation to anyone from the West who showed the slightest interest in his players.

I call him Viktor. I never knew his real name, of course; he didn't bother to introduce himself. But I'd met him before – or rather someone just like him, I should say. A decade earlier, as a journalism student at Michigan State University, I was working as a part-timer on the sports desk at the Lansing State Journal when I was assigned to cover a Green-White basketball scrimmage at Lansing Everett High School, the alma mater of Spartans' sophomore Earvin ("Magic") Johnson. While I was talking with team members in the locker room after that game, MSU coach Jud Heathcote turned the interview around. He mentioned that he thought he'd met everyone on our newspaper's sports staff and wondered who I might be. I explained that I was studying at the university, hoping to get a newspaper career started after spending six years in the Army as a Russian linguist. His eyes widened, and he asked if I knew that the Soviet national basketball team would be visiting East Lansing in a few weeks for a game against his Spartans. I smiled. Of course I knew, and I told him that I was hoping to find a way to be part of our newspaper's coverage of that game, but that I didn't have enough seniority on the staff for that assignment.

"How good is your Russian?" Heathcote asked.

"It's not horrible," I told him, explaining that I'd spent a recent semester in MSU's Russian language graduate program before transitioning to journalism.

"Maybe you can help us. Work as an interpreter for the coaches and players, help out our media, too," Heathcote said. I told him I'd be happy to try, and he said he'd send a media credential to the newspaper with details. True to his word, the press pass arrived a few days before the game. I was there around noon when the bus carrying the Soviet team arrived. We went to lunch at a restaurant across the street from campus, where the Russians needed no help from me placing their orders. To a man, they ordered "beefsteak, medium. Salad." Players sat in fours, eating wordlessly. The coaches sat as far away as they could get, talking quietly among themselves.

After lunch, they dispersed for their pregame solitude – time traditionally used for a short nap. I met up with the team again well before the pregame warmups to help provide a few sportswriters with some background details about the visitors. The Soviets were led by Alexander Gomelsky, the coach of the team that won 85 percent of its games during his 22-year tenure. He is widely remembered as the father of modern Russian basketball. His team included several players who were on the 1972 Olympic gold medal team that beat the Americans in a controversial finish – when questionable officiating allowed the Soviets three opportunities to replay the final seconds of the game.

Now Gomelsky's club was on a tour throughout the United States, playing some of the finest collegiate teams. The results were fairly predictable. The Russians were veterans, grown men with NBA skills who had spent years playing together. They had little difficulty on this tour, beating several college basketball powers like Notre Dame, Indiana and Purdue. But they met their match against Michigan State that night.

I had one of the best seats in Jenison Field House – on the Russian bench next to Gomelsky. I was there in case a dispute arose and he needed help communicating with game officials. It would not be necessary. He rather calmly watched his team get dissected by the Magic-led Spartans, 76-60. Afterward, Gomelsky spoke admiringly of Michigan State's *"contra-attaka"* – a deadly transition game the Spartans rode all the way to an NCAA title the following spring. In fact, it was precisely the kind of transition strategy, that conversion from defense to fast-break offense as soon as a rebound fell into the hands of a Michigan State player, that the Soviets had perfected in the way they played hockey.

Following the basketball game, I attended a reception at the home of a Michigan State administrator. It was there, when I found myself alone for a moment, that I encountered a man who smiled as he took a beer out of my hand and replaced it with a tall glass of straight, cold vodka – just as the Russian's drink it.

"Na zdarovye," he said, and our glasses clinked before we drank. "I am Viktor. And who are you?"

We shook hands, and there, cornered away from anyone who might overhear, we began our little dance. Viktor was polite, his interrogation clearly purposeful. I had seen him earlier in the day, dining with the coaches and sitting at the end of the bench. I had assumed he was with the coaching or training staff. When I explained that I was a university student preparing for a career in journalism, he was skeptical. "Who are you really? Who do you work for? Where did you learn to speak such good Russian?"

Now I was beginning to understand why the Soviets had politely ignored me the whole day. They didn't trust me. I insisted that I was telling him the truth about my role for the day, that I was asked by the university team's coach to lend a hand, if needed, as an interpreter as a courtesy to the visitors from the Soviet Union. I also politely noted that it was no business of his where I learned to speak his language. I thanked him for the compliment, preferring the conversation to end right there.

Viktor, of course, persisted.

"Americans don't speak other languages, especially not Russian," he said. I agreed, then smiled, figuring the truth would best serve me in this increasingly uncomfortable confrontation. We were speaking in Russian, though I'd occasionally toss in an English word when my vocabulary failed me. I told him I had studied Russian at the Defense Language Institute in Monterey, California.

Now Viktor smiled and nodded. "Ah, I know this place," he said. "So, you were in the military, yes? And what did you do after you learned to speak our language?"

"Yes, I was in the military, the Army," I said. "But what I did afterward is none of your business, to be perfectly honest. And I couldn't tell you even if I wanted to."

In truth, I was barely a year removed from my service with the NSA. Those of us entrusted with the highest level of security clearances wouldn't dare divulge classified information for fear of winding up in prison, or worse. Viktor knew that, of course. But as I sipped from my glass, I could feel this universal truth serum working, and I thought I'd toy with him just a bit.

"After language training," I confided, "I was assigned to a duty station in West Berlin."

Again, his eyes brightened. "Ah, my friend," he said, "I was in East Berlin!"

We laughed, touched glasses and drank another toast to our shared, secret past, each having a better understanding of the other after a short but intense conversation. I then looked him straight in the eyes and, in English, said, "Look Viktor, I spent more than six years in the Army in service to my country. You served in the Red Army in service to your country – and now you're still serving your Party in a different role. You know very well what I was doing in Berlin just as I know what you are doing here. But now, I promise you, I am done with all that."

Once more I emphasized that I was a simple college student striving to build a career as a journalist, and that my goal was to one day be assigned to Moscow as a reporter, a member of the foreign press in his country.

"Perhaps we will meet again then," he said. We shook hands once more, and I wished him well.

"Right now," I said, glancing at my watch, "I must go. I am on deadline and must return to my newspaper and get some work done."

If I did that work well enough, he might just see the results in the next day's edition, I told him. We toasted once more, and I walked away. Back at the newsroom, I sat down at my typewriter. Bleary eyed and feeling as though I was typing with all thumbs as Viktor's vodka coursed through my veins, I wrote a feature story about how these visitors from the Soviet Union spent their time in East Lansing. In fact, their day was rather routine: arrive, have lunch, rest and play another game against another American college team. The story, of course, would be spiced with comments about the quality of competition the Soviets were experiencing in this 13-game tour meant to prepare them for the coming 1980 Moscow Olympics. Most of my story, in fact, came from events at the late-evening reception, highlighted by the parting toast by the Russian team's smallest player, Stanislav Eremin.

"This is the warmest feeling I've had in all the time I've been in this country," he told the East Lansing gathering. "It's hard to explain, but I really got to know the American people. I think I really made friends tonight."

My story, with the headline "After-game party lesson in détente," would appear on Page One, above the fold, the next day. It was my first front-page byline. That was the moment I fell hopelessly in love with journalism.

Outside that dressing room in the Helsinki arena, I tried to keep watch out of the corner of my eye on this other Viktor as I continued a disjointed conversation with Sergei Fedorov and Vladimir Konstantinov. My new friend and interpreter spoke Russian as well as he did English, and I was beyond grateful for having found him. After he explained who I was, I congratulated the players on a good performance. They shrugged. Just another rather meaningless game against another inferior opponent in a torturous eleven-month season that was only beginning. Besides, they were just doing what they were supposed to do in a system that didn't take losing lightly.

I showed the players the reason for my interest in wanting to meet and interview them – a copy of the list of players the Detroit Red Wings had selected in the NHL entry draft just six weeks before. Though neither spoke any language besides Russian, I was certain they'd be familiar enough with the English alphabet to recognize their names. I turned to Sergei and pointed to his, showing he had been selected in the fourth round by the Red Wings. His reaction? Nothing. Stone-faced. If he was the least bit interested or excited, his cold blue eyes refused to show it, even though, as I would find out later, this was his first inkling that he had been chosen by the NHL team from Detroit.

Then I turned to Vladimir and pointed to his, which was eleventh of twelve names on that list. He could barely contain his exuberance, like the boy who found the shiny red bicycle parked next to the Christmas tree. His green eyes danced; he beamed as he turned to face me, our eyes locking as if he were seeking absolute assurance that this was not some sort of ruse. Clearly, he was learning for the first time that he, too, was coveted by an NHL team.

Reaching again into my leather shoulder bag, I mentioned that I'd brought some other items from Detroit. I handed each of them, including the interpreter, a Red Wings lapel pin, along with my Free

Press business card. I explained in English – the interpreter translating – that I understood how this wasn't the best time for a formal interview, but I would be interested in arranging a time for that soon, by telephone. I promised I would work on my Russian so that we could have a decent conversation. I also gave them business cards of Detroit Red Wings officials, including Jim Lites and Jimmy Devellano, the team general manager. Finally, I pulled out the last of the items – two Red Wings media guides barely concealing the secret messages.

I handed them the books and asked if they had any questions of me before we parted. As the interpreter spoke, I nearly panicked when I noticed Sergei holding the book in front of him, thumbing through its pages. It didn't take long for him to discover the hidden envelope. Again, without the slightest show of emotion, he closed the book and casually held it behind his back with both hands. This guy would be dangerous at a poker table. Vladimir never looked at his book while we stood there in the hallway, keeping it in front of him with both hands.

To our left, Viktor was stepping out again and staring at us. I knew it was time for me to go, and I couldn't get out of there fast enough. I looked at all three men and, as I shook their hands I spoke in the best Russian I could muster: "Thank you very much. It was my pleasure to meet you. Best of luck and good-bye."

I told them I looked forward to speaking to them again soon Then I turned quickly and left without looking back to see what Viktor might be doing.

At nearly 10 p.m., Helsinki was wide awake. It was still broad daylight as my pace quickened to get me as far away from that arena as quickly as possible. I didn't know where to go, but I felt certain that heading straight back to my hotel room wasn't a good idea. Though I was exhausted after two days of travel with little rest, I was also too exhilarated to sleep. I worried about being followed, too. What if Viktor had confronted those two players and demanded that they turn over what I'd given them? What if he found the letters? What would happen to them? And would the Soviets then come after me?

I kept reassuring myself that I'd seen too many spy thrillers and read too many books by American journalists who wrote of being constantly shadowed and caught up in the middle of something they shouldn't have been involved in. But this was different. This was something of my own making. I was plagued by a sudden uneasiness, questioning my motives and wondering with no small degree of uncertainty whether I'd done the right thing by coming to Helsinki. So I walked, constantly looking over my shoulder to try to determine if I was being followed. By 1 a.m., it was more like dusk than dark, and after nearly three hours of wandering the chemical buzz that had my heart racing had begun to subside. Suddenly, I craved rest, so I hailed a cab and took a short ride back to my hotel. Still more than a little paranoid, I opened my door and entered slowly, every ounce of my being on alert in case someone was there to greet me.

I was alone and relieved as I reached for the telephone. I quickly did the math and figured it was about 7:30 p.m. back home. So I dialed. The phone rang twice before Jim Lites answered. I told him I had made contact and passed along the messages without apparent incident. By now, both players knew they were wanted in Detroit, the sooner the better.

"That's great news," Lites said. "I can't wait to tell Mr. Ilitch about it. And I can't tell you how excited we are that you were able to get this process started. Thank you so much."

I continued my briefing for several minutes: Sergei was difficult to get a read on, but there was no doubt that Vladimir Konstantinov was absolutely thrilled. Captain or not of his team, he seemed to me to be a prime candidate to defect, if given the opportunity. Then I told Lites I would be returning to Detroit the next day.

"Jim, I did what you wanted me to do, but now I'm out. The rest is up to you," I told him. "I just want you to remember that when you eventually get those guys out, the Free Press gets the story first. And we're the first to interview them, as well. Total and exclusive first access. That was our deal."

"Absolutely," he said. "You'll be the first to know. We'll take it from here, and as far as I'm concerned, from this moment forward, this never happened."

I returned to Detroit the next day.

Nearly a full year later, on July 22, 1990, my telephone rang as I was having dinner at home in Dearborn.

"Keith, it's Jim Lites," the caller said. "I'm on Mr. Ilitch's plane heading back from Portland, Oregon to Detroit."

He asked if I was ready for some news, said he was sitting next to somebody pretty important. I pushed my plate away and grabbed a pen and paper, ready to take notes for a story that would break above the fold on Page One of the Detroit Free Press the next morning. It would soon become a major international news story.

CHAPTER 2

Made in Detroit

The first thing Mike and Marian Ilitch did after they bought the Red Wings for about $8 million in June 1982 was to hire an architect of one of the last great true dynasties in all of American sport. Jim Devellano – "Jimmy D," as he likes to refer to himself – showed up in Detroit wearing three Stanley Cup rings. The New York Islanders would win a fourth straight Cup after he left, further evidence that Devellano knew how to build a lasting winner. His task as general manager in Detroit, however, was greater than he ever could have imagined.

"The team I took over was in the Detroit River, quite frankly," he said somberly, as if recalling a horrific tragedy. In fact, through the entire 1970s to midway through the '80s, the Detroit Red Wings had been a punch line in hockey circles throughout North America.

"At the time, the Red Wings were a bankrupt franchise in every sense of the word," Jim Lites would recall more than 30 years later. Married at the time to the Ilitches' eldest daughter, Denise, Lites was an attorney appointed as a Wings executive upon the 1982 sale. "They were beaten down, playing in a bad facility, Joe Louis Arena."

In fact, the Joe was only three years old when the Red Wings changed hands. Built haphazardly and on-the-cheap by the City of Detroit, it was never completed. When it opened, locker rooms weren't finished. It had no press box. Fluorescent lights hung from bare wires through the facility. Concessionaires set up card tables in barren concourses to sell souvenirs and refreshments.

The Red Wings were the perfect metaphor for Detroit. In too many ways to count, the once-great dynastic franchise personified the demise of the city. In 1950, when a young Gordie Howe was emerging as the dominant player in the NHL, Detroit was one of America's great cities. With 1.85 million people living within its sprawling city limits, Detroit was the fifth-largest city in America, and one of its most affluent with a thriving middle class that had attracted workers from throughout the Deep South and Appalachia to work in its auto factories, steel mills, and plastics and parts shops that supported the giant auto manufacturing industry. From 1950-55, Howe led the Red Wings to the Stanley Cup championship four times. Detroit was runner-up in 1956.

But it wouldn't last. A labyrinth of freeways from downtown eviscerated several prominent neighborhoods, at the same time making it easier to get from work in the city's factories to the suburbs, where a growing number of workers and their families, predominantly white, were moving. The jobs would follow them; from 1945-57, the Big Three automakers, General Motors, Ford and Chrysler, built 25 new manufacturing plants in the metropolitan area – none of them within Detroit's city limits. By the mid-1960s, Detroit was in a visible state of deterioration, and racial tensions – simmering for two decades – and began to make worldwide headlines. A five-day riot on the city's near west side in July 1967 resulted in 43 dead, 1,189 injured, more than 7,000 arrests and more than 2,000 buildings destroyed. It was finally quelled with the help of not only the Michigan National Guard but the 82nd and 101st Airborne Divisions dispatched by President Lyndon B. Johnson – at the height of the Vietnam War.

More troubles were predicted for the following hot summer, but the city's residents were distracted – and many insist unified – by the Detroit Tigers' run to a World Series title over the St. Louis Cardinals. By the early 1980s, global pressure on the auto industry from foreign carmakers and the Big Three moving plants and thousands of jobs away from Michigan to places like Mexico, resulted in the loss of tens of thousands of jobs. By 1982, when Mike and Marian Ilitch bought the Red Wings, Detroit's population had dipped below 1.2 million. Within a few more decades, it was below 700,000.

The once-powerful Red Wings also had been in a state of severe decline. Founded as the Detroit Cougars in 1926, the National Hockey League franchise played its first season in what was then called the Border Cities Arena, across the Detroit River in Windsor, Ontario, until the Detroit Olympia Arena opened in 1927. Like the city's auto industry, there were growing pains. The hockey club struggled in its early years. There followed a name change from Cougars to Falcons in 1930, and in 1932 – when the team was bought out of receivership by James Norris – it became the Red Wings. Their emblem was a winged wheel, an homage to the city's auto industry. It is now one of the most iconic logos in sports. Norris, who at one time controlled four of the "Original Six" clubs in the NHL, built a powerful club in Detroit. After his death in 1962, his heirs struggled for control. It eventually ended in the hands of Bruce Norris, who also had inherited his father's vast grain business. It deteriorated steadily under the younger Norris; the franchise's final hurrah was a Stanley Cup Finals appearance in 1966, followed by a 24-point decline in the standings. It got worse: During the period from 1967-82, when Ilitch rescued it, the team was so bad it was known throughout hockey as the "Dead Wings."

Meantime, rising oil prices continued to cripple Detroit's auto industry, which reacted slowly when the demand rose for smaller, more fuel-efficient vehicles made by foreigners. By the late 1970s, only a federal bailout saved Chrysler. At about the same time, Detroit destroyed yet another of its great neighborhoods, Poletown, to make way, ironically, for a Cadillac plant – built with millions in government subsidies.

While Ilitch's team had a relatively new building that had replaced Olympia, it had no practice facility. That made it difficult to book concerts and other money-making events to the downtown arena because the Wings needed it for their off-day practices. Frequently, though, they were displaced by concerts, circuses and skating shows, left to find places to practice in various suburban rinks from Lincoln Park downriver to Oak Park in Oakland County. Worst of all, however, the Red Wings had a woeful roster of players.

"When Mr. and Mrs. Ilitch bought the team, it had 81 players under contract, if you can imagine that," Lites said, "and there weren't eight of them that were capable of playing in the NHL."

On the business side, the club was bleeding money. The season-ticket base was below 2,500 fans. That's when Detroiters began to see exactly how committed Mike Ilitch, who had made his fortune through his Little Caesars Pizza chain, was to creating something that would make his hometown proud.

"It started with Mike's energy, his commitment, his financial resources and the love he has for the city of Detroit," Lites said. "It was a love affair right from the beginning, and he fueled it with marketing ideas like giving away automobiles every home game that first season. He gave away an American car in a downtrodden Detroit auto market at every game. Everybody thought he was crazy."

Crazy like a fox, because soon the Wings were among the NHL leaders in attendance despite still being one of its weakest teams. Fans liked their odds of driving off in a new car even if they had to sit through another horrendous Red Wings loss. "It was Mr. Ilitch's way of reminding people that the future would be better," Lites said, "because at the time the team wasn't very good."

Against that backdrop, Devellano began to rebuild Detroit's beleaguered franchise. A short, rotund man who battled with weight issues under a mop of dark, unkempt hair, Devellano was a guy who spoke in two voices. When he was holding court with reporters, which he seemed to rather enjoy, his voice could be deep and bombastic, coming from the depth of his diaphragm. When pressed on an issue he wasn't comfortable with, he could sound whiny, with a voice that rose in pitch and seemed to escape from the front of his throat. He could have used either in what must have been a rather uncomfortable conversation with the new owners over dinner shortly after he was hired.

Marian Ilitch, with characteristic candor, asked the question that immediately put Devellano on the defensive. A striking, petite woman who preferred her hair blond and her talk straight, she was not shy about letting people know that she was an equal partner in the ownership of what she called "my little hockey team." She, more than her husband, was the lifelong hockey fan. She, every bit as much as her husband, ran their business empire. Mike Ilitch was the former Marine; Marian Ilitch could talk like one, and she didn't care who was within earshot. So, it was with the kind of bluntness that has been her trademark in corporate boardrooms throughout her career that she began the conversation over dinner.

"Jimmy, how long do you think it will take us to win the Stanley Cup?" she asked.

"Marian, it's going to take us eight years," Devellano said. "We're going to win it in our eighth year."

She exploded. "Eight years! Oh, my God. I'm going to be an old lady by then. I won't be able to go out on the ice!"

Devellano wasn't quite sure how to respond just then. Being at a loss for words was out of character for him. But in retrospect, he admitted, he wished winning the Stanley Cup had taken just eight years.

"It actually took us fifteen," he said, confessing, too, that he was lucky to hang around long enough to see it finally happen. "But to be very fair, to be candid and honest, we had some very good teams before we won the Cup."

The first thing Devellano did as he began the rebuilding process was to deliver a pledge to fans, the media, and his ownership that the franchise was done trading draft picks and young prospects for NHL has-beens who came to Detroit to put their careers in hospice care. That had been the Red Wings' way for a generation of futility before the Ilitches salvaged the team.

But building through the draft is a painfully slow process, and it comes without a guarantee. It takes immense patience and more than a little luck – borne through years of scouting and stockpiling and developing players who were teenagers barely shaving when they were drafted onto their NHL teams. Aside from the few sure bets (some of whom turn out to be not-so-sure after all), the NHL entry draft is little more than an organized talent lottery, with teams claiming young men they can only hope will evolve into serviceable players. In Devellano, the Wings felt they had the right man at the head of the draft table. In scouts like Neil Smith, Ken Holland and Alex Davidson, among others, they had the right people providing the GM with reliable guidance and advice. But in Mike and Marian Ilitch they had owners with great expectations – and precious little patience.

That was apparent when the Wings were barely settled in at the draft table on that June 8, 1983, at the Montreal Forum. According to virtually unanimous opinion around the NHL, there were three "can't-miss" stars among the best prospects that day. Detroit drafted fourth, which was the kind of luck Red Wings fans had come to expect. Among those three young stars was Pat LaFontaine, the 1983 Canadian Major Junior Player of the Year who grew up in the Detroit suburb of Waterford Township. He was slated to be drafted third by the New York Islanders, after Minnesota took Brian Lawton, who starred at Mount St. Charles High School in Massachusetts, and after Hartford selected Sylvain Turgeon, out of Hull in the Quebec Major Junior Hockey League. Stephen Gregory Yzerman, an undersized center-iceman with Peterborough of the Ontario Hockey League, was the best of the rest. But Ilitch didn't want to settle for fourth. He coveted LaFontaine, as someone around whom he could build a formidable marketing campaign.

Before the draft began, Ilitch put his hand on Devellano's arm and said, "Jimmy, go see your buddy Bill Torrey over there at the Islanders' table and offer him a million bucks just to trade draft picks." Devellano didn't flinch. He put his hand on Ilitch's and said, "Mike, save your money. This is going to turn out all right for us."

The process went exactly as predicted. The Wings selected Yzerman, a slender, frail-looking young man who wore a red tie when he showed up at the Detroit table that day. He looked more like a kid arriving to pick up his junior prom date than a professional hockey player. Nevertheless, the Red Wings would soon put the franchise on his shoulders. Devellano was right. He knew from purely a scout's perspective that there was little separating Steve Yzerman from Pat LaFontaine. Both had prodigious upsides. Yzerman, however, turned out to be the best player taken in that draft, by far (although a series of concussions suffered by LaFontaine prevented him from career statistics that might have otherwise rivaled Yzerman's). Both would be inducted into the Hockey Hall of Fame. The two drafted before them had disappointing careers in the NHL.

That 1983 draft was momentous for the Wings. After Yzerman, the Wings drafted: right wing Lane Lambert, who logged nearly 300 NHL games before his career was cut short by eye problems; left wing Bob Probert, who combined scoring talent and toughness that had never been seen before – or since; and right wing Joe Kocur, who with Probert formed the most feared fighting tandem in NHL history, a tag team known as the Bruise Brothers. In between Probert and Kocur, however, the Wings showed the kind of creativity at the draft table that would help them build the foundation of a dynastic franchise. With the 86th pick overall, two spots ahead of Kocur, Detroit selected Petr Klima, who had risen to stardom behind the Iron Curtain in Czechoslovakia. There was no guarantee Klima would ever be able to leave his country. But Ilitch personally authorized spending a fairly high draft pick on the talented young Czech.

"He had as much talent as any young player in the world at the time," Lites recalled. "That's when the concept of 'we're-going-to-do-whatever-it-takes-to-get-better-as-soon-as-we-can' began. That's what started the whole process. We're going to use foreign players. We don't care where they come from. If they're good, we're going to find them and we're going to bring them here. That's the dynamic that Mike Ilitch brought."

But how, exactly? That was to be determined. And it was up to Lites to get it done.

"We were really flying by the seat of our pants," he recalled. "You know, there's no book that explains how you make contact, how you get a guy to defect. There was no place to go. It was all common sense and capital, meaning we used cash. But we learned pretty quickly that these guys, the Czech players especially, for sure wanted to play in North America. They hated the system, hated the Russians, hated being there. They wanted out, wanted to make money, to play in North America. They wanted to play in the National Hockey League."

None of them more than Petr Klima.

The Wings fell in love with Klima, a 6-foot, 190-pound right-hand shot left wing, after then-coach Nick Polano first saw him play with the Czech National Team in the world championships in 1983. Several other team scouts concurred. This was one of those high-risk, high-reward moments.

"We thought we'd take a chance, even though we knew we'd have to get him to defect," Devellano said. It was risky because it was far from certain any Czech player at the time would get through the Iron Curtain into an NHL locker room.

But Polano had done his homework. With the help of team scout Alex Davidson, Polano arranged a meeting with Klima in June 1983 in Nykoping, Sweden. Through an interpreter – Czech teammate and trusted friend Frantisek Musil -- Klima acknowledged he would be interested in defecting, but only after his military service.

A few weeks later, at the NHL entry draft, the Wings had an extra fifth-round pick and Polano did some fast talking.

"Minnesota took Musil in the second round, and after that I figured there was no way Klima would last," Polano said. "Finally, we had that extra pick and I talked Jimmy into taking him."

After he announced the pick, Devellano turned to Polano and said, "OK, I did it. Now you go get him."

Polano was optimistic, because he knew how badly Klima wanted out of what was then Communist Czechoslovakia for the freedom to play in the NHL. And Polano's gut told him Klima had the perfect temperament for a would-be defector.

"We knew from talking to some people that he had a reputation as being kind of a bad kid. He was always in trouble," Polano recalled. "We liked hearing that because we figured maybe he wasn't such a good Commie. Maybe he's more like the typical American or Canadian kids, fun-loving and happy-go-lucky. Maybe he just wanted to come over and play hockey, make some money and live a good life."

Polano knew the Czechs, like the Soviets, seemed to prefer their players to be stoic at all times, showing little emotion. And most of them were, perfecting that sober, dead-eye facial expression that made them hard to read. Not Klima. He wore an ever-present smile, his eyes seeking mischief wherever he went. If he couldn't find any, he'd often create it.

But he wasn't so much of a free spirit that he would walk out on his military obligations to the Czech Army. That was why he didn't accompany his best friend, Petr Svoboda, when in 1984 the talented Czech defenseman defected to the Montreal Canadiens. Montreal general manager Serge Savard had orchestrated such a brilliant and discreet defection that it shocked the hockey world when the Canadiens chose Svoboda with the fifth overall selection in that year's draft – then introduced him moments later when Svoboda strode to the podium.

"We wanted to defect together," Klima would recall after he came to Detroit, "but we couldn't because I was in the Army. I would never go AWOL."

Klima had two years remaining in the military when the Wings drafted him, and Klima knew he could face the death penalty if he deserted. Even worse, like every player who considered fleeing for freedom and a career in the NHL, he worried about his family if he left the Army before his discharge.

Polano and the Wings persisted, however. He met with Klima several times when the Czechs competed in the 1984 Canada Cup, first in London, Ontario, again in Buffalo and once more in Vancouver, British Columbia. The Wings convinced Klima to sign a 10-year contract divided into two equal segments, allowing the club a second five-year option if Klima lived up to its expectations. It was very good money, averaging about $250,000 a year at a time when the typical player was paid about $150,000. The 10-year length was extraordinary for the time, but it was designed to provide some security to a player who might never be able to return to his homeland.

But it wasn't for another year, when Klima's military obligation was coming to an end, that he finally committed to leaving Czechoslovakia for a new life in Detroit. By then, Polano had been elevated to assistant general manager. His first big assignment was to continue courting Klima while Devellano went on an unprecedented shopping spree, signing three NHL veterans and five undrafted college players in an attempt to beef up the lineup. The ownership's patience already was wearing thin. So they were elated when, in a clandestine meeting with Polano at the world championships in Prague in the spring of 1985, Klima re-pledged his commitment to the Red Wings, saying he would begin the process to escape the Iron Curtain.

In mid-summer 1985, Polano received a telephone call from his Czech contact who told him Klima was ready to defect. Klima would accompany his team to Rosenheim, West Germany, located about 50 minutes south of the Bavarian capital, Munich. The Czechs were staying in a hotel in nearby Nussdorf. Polano, Jim Lites and the translator were soon on their way to West Germany, where they first met Klima in a wooded area behind the team's hotel.

"We had no clue who was going to walk out of those woods," Polano recalled. "It was scary."

Polano and Lites urged Klima to leave with them right then, but Klima wasn't quite ready. Moreover, he surprised them by raising two final demands: He wanted the Wings to get his girlfriend, Irena Zelenak, out of Czechoslovakia, too, since he was certain he would never return to his home country; and he asked to renegotiate the terms of his contract. He wanted more money. While the financial terms were quickly resolved, the Wings weren't thrilled with the burden of choreographing another, potentially more difficult, defection.

"We kept telling him, 'Petr, there are plenty of girls in America. You don't have to bring your girlfriend,'" Polano said. "But he kept insisting."

Once Klima was assured that the Wings would facilitate his girlfriend's escape, as well as pay him what he wanted, he agreed to leave. The defection was set for a Sunday, two nights later. Wearing a T-shirt and jeans, Klima met them as planned, but at the last minute he decided to return to his hotel room for some items, mostly mementos.

"Longest five minutes of my life," Polano said.

"I've never been more scared in my life," Lites recalled. "I mean, those Czech teams were accompanied by the Russian military when they traveled. There were guys with guns around him."

After what felt like an eternity, Klima slipped out of a small hotel window in the middle of the night and ran to the waiting car with Lites at the wheel, Polano riding shotgun, and the interpreter in the back seat.

"It was wild," Lites said.

With the would-be defector in the back seat of the rented Mercedes, the car sped off. Klima looked around the interior of the rented Mercedes 500, the car sped off. Klima looked around.

"Nice car," he said to the interpreter. "How fast can it go?"

Within seconds, he found out as Lites put the spurs to the luxury sedan, quickly hitting speeds that coaxed the needle past 120 m.p.h. on the autobahn, Germany's superhighway with no posted speed limits. The idea, Lites said, was to put as much time and distance between themselves and Klima's former team, especially because Czech officials would know what happened when Klima was a no-show for the 11 p.m. curfew. They headed to the Bavarian hinterlands. Fast.

For nearly five weeks, the trio hid out in hotels throughout what was then West Germany, staying mostly in the country's southern region. They spent time in Stuttgart, Frankfurt and Koblenz among other places, according to Polano. A sixth week passed before they dared to visit the U.S. Embassy, figuring it was being monitored by Czech officials. Thanks to some political influence wielded by Mike Ilitch, then well-connected to the Reagan Administration in Washington, U.S. Immigration officials eventually granted Klima what it called "a parole for humanitarian purposes."

Growing restless while keeping a low profile and fighting relentless boredom, Klima eventually convinced his handlers to let him take the rented Mercedes for a spin around the West Germany countryside. He didn't hold a valid driver's license, even in his home country, but he told Lites and Polano he'd had plenty of experience behind the wheel. A self-described speed demon, Klima managed to return from his drive in one piece. The car did not. He totaled it.

"Petr just laughed when he said the car had been wrecked," Polano said. "But the lady at Hertz didn't think it was very funny."

Lites was just thankful that Klima survived unscathed. "Thank God it was a Mercedes," Lites said. "It was built like a tank."

Klima got his visa on Sept. 22, 1985, and immediately he was on his way to Detroit with the interpreter. Polano stayed behind. While they were killing time in Germany, Lites had arranged for operatives to smuggle the girlfriend out of Czechoslovakia into Austria. Polano was to meet her in Vienna after her dramatic escape choreographed in part with the use of a hotel laundry hamper.

"That was scary, too, because I didn't know who I was meeting, what kind of people I was dealing with or what they might try," Polano said. "Petr told me to look for a birthmark on her eyelid 'to make sure she was the right one.' Turned out she was, and Polano brought her to West Germany to begin another visa application.

Klima arrived in Detroit in time to join his new teammates at training camp in Port Huron, about 60 miles north of Detroit and across the St. Clair River from Sarnia, Ontario. He was eager to get his NHL career going, and more than a little nervous. I was among a few other reporters at Detroit's Metro Airport, and when I met him I made a horrendous mistake. I shook his hand and welcomed him in Russian.

I figured that like most people who grew up when he did in countries controlled by the Soviet Union, Russian was his second language. I was right. But the look of terror that flashed through Klima's eyes as his smile disappeared told me I'd made a grave error. He let loose of my hand, put his head down, and walked away quickly.

"I thought you were bad guy for sure," Klima said later. "I was scared you were KGB."

It took weeks to gain his trust. Eventually, he figured out I was relatively harmless as a local sportswriter he'd see at every team practice and game. In time, Petr Klima became one of my most trusted sources among players in the dressing room.

More importantly, the Wings had developed a blueprint for getting a high-profile athlete beyond the Iron Curtain. The Klima affair would prove invaluable for three more remarkable "departures" from the crumbling Soviet Union just a few years later that would change forever the trajectory of the downtrodden franchise.

"What we learned from Klima was how to get a guy out," Lites said. "Before we could even start thinking about drafting Soviets, we drafted this great young Czech player and we had to find a way get him over here. We cut our teeth on that. We learned how the political process worked to get a visa. We learned everything we needed to know on how to get the Russians out years later. That was very important. It set the stage for everything that followed."

Devellano, encouraged by the result, wanted more. The Red Wings needed more. And the Ilitches were all in, willing to do anything necessary to build a winning franchise.

"Petr Klima was really our first big European we got," Devellano said. "That gave us an appetite."

And a scouting staff with an increasing presence in Europe was putting constant pressure on him to import more players through the NHL's entry draft.

"We knew there were more like him," Devellano said, "and we knew they were in Russia."

Petr Klima was the most celebrated new arrival in Detroit that memorable summer of 1985, but he was hardly the only one. After three years of ownership and two playoff appearances, each ending in a first-round knockout, Mike Ilitch was ready to ratchet up the process. Clearly losing patience, he directed Devellano to do whatever necessary to fortify the lineup with players who could orchestrate a serious run in the post-season. Devellano wound up spending Ilitch's money on eight more players. They included five undrafted collegians and three from other NHL teams. All three clubs filed tampering charges against the Red Wings, who were later found guilty in all three cases.

Detroit's unprecedented spending spree sparked national attention. Even Sports Illustrated, which at the time was run by editors who had little regard for hockey – and therefore gave it precious little space – sent a reporter and photographer to training camp in Port Huron. The result was a multi-page feature spread about how a little-known pizza magnate was spending all his dough in moves designed to propel the Detroit Red Wings to the top of the NHL standings.

The Wings, who had managed to reach the playoffs just four times in their previous 19 seasons – never reaching the second round – were suddenly being touted as Stanley Cup contenders. "It was almost like it was too easy," recalled Colin Campbell, then a first-year assistant coach who was looking for more of a challenge behind the bench. The infusion of all that new talent had given Detroit a formidable roster. At least that's how Campbell and a lot of other people saw it.

But the results were startlingly, humiliatingly bad. Detroit opened the season against Minnesota and raced to a 6-2 lead. One of the college kids, Chris Cichocki scored twice, and Klima scored once as the new guys put their fingerprints on a new era in Motown. Joe Louis Arena was rocking to the rafters. It would be the highlight of the season. The Wings allowed four unanswered goals and settled for a 6-6 tie, then lost the next eight games. They finished with the worst record in a 21-team league at

17-57-6, the worst season in their checkered history. They went through two coaches – the charismatic comedian Harry Neale (8-23-4) and the colossally inept Brad Park (9-34-2). Their roster was a revolving door of players, most of whom struggled to compete in the NHL. By season's end, two of the three NHL players the Wings had signed the previous year had been traded away, and only Adam Oates remained of the five college players Detroit had signed.

Oates signed what was then the richest-ever rookie contract worth $1.1 million over four years, and he proved he was worth the investment. He scored nine goals among 20 points in 38 games with Detroit that season, ending it in Glens Falls, N.Y., where he helped Adirondack, the Wings' top minor league affiliate in the American Hockey League, to a Calder Cup championship. Oates went on to a Hall of Fame career. He would have his best seasons for other teams, however, after the Wings traded him to St. Louis in one of the worst deals in NHL history. In June 1989, Oates and high-scoring winger Paul MacLean went to St. Louis for aging, ineffective forwards Bernie Federko and Tony McKegney.

"No question, that was the low point for us," Devellano would often say about that 1985-86 season. "Lucky that I can look back on it now and laugh."

It wasn't funny to an embarrassed ownership, though fans hardly held a grudge. Hungry for a winner on the ice, they were grateful that Mike Ilitch was at least trying. The proof: The Wings averaged nearly 18,000 fans a game, second in the league in attendance. But soon Devellano was off tampering again, this time luring coach Jacques Demers away from St. Louis.

The Demers era in Detroit proved to be a rollicking roller-coaster of a ride up and down the NHL standings. In his four seasons behind the bench, the Wings created the illusion that they were close to being a Stanley Cup contender, but in the end they proved only how far away they really were. Thanks to Demers' motivational magic and, more likely, Detroit's residency in the Norris Division, by far the weakest of the NHL's four regional groups in those days, the Wings made a stunning reversal in just one year. After nearly doubling their point production, from a franchise record low 40 to 78 and a second-place finish in the Norris, the Wings turned a city starved for hockey success on its ear with a four-game sweep of the Chicago Blackhawks in the first round of the 1987 playoffs.

In the next round, to this day one of the most memorable post-season series in franchise history, Detroit lost its first two games at home in the best-of-seven series and fell behind, three games to one, in the division finals to archrival Toronto. Fans and media had the Wings buried. But Detroit stormed back with three straight victories over the Maple Leafs, including a pair of 3-0 shutouts by Glen Hanlon, and success-starved fans were delirious. Now the Wings were in uncharted territory, playing beyond the second round of the playoffs for the first time in franchise history. In their Original Six heydays, four teams competed in just two playoff rounds to determine a Stanley Cup champion.

It didn't matter to Detroit fans that the opponent in the Campbell Conference finals was the Wayne Gretzky-led Edmonton Oilers, who had won the Stanley Cup in two of the previous three years. Detroit fans were just happy to be there, and their team lost the series after stunning the Oilers with a win in the series opener at Edmonton and providing stiffer competition than anyone expected.

After another run to the Campbell Conference finals the next season, and a similar end at the hands of the Oilers, who went on to win their fourth Cup in five years, the Wings started to backslide. The defining moment of the Demers era came on the final day of the 1988 season. The night before Game 5 in Edmonton, several of his players were caught breaking curfew at a club called Goose Loonies. Among them were Bob Probert and the injured Petr Klima, two of the team's most prominent players. Detroit Free Press sports columnist Mitch Albom overheard players talking about it during breakfast the following morning, and Mitch and I decided to confront Demers back at the team's hotel following the morning practice. We asked the questions and the coach didn't hold back.

"Jacques, who was probably worried about his own ass, should have shut the hell up and said, 'There's no truth to that.' But no – he threw us under the bus," Probert wrote in his book, *Tough Guy*, which was published shortly after his death of heart failure at age 45 in July 2010. "That way, if we lost, it's not his fault, because the guys were out drinking, right? He called a meeting and he says, 'Guys, if you win tonight's playoff game, it might be on the back page. But if you lose, it'll be front page.' Sure enough, we lost, and it was front-page news. And Jacques was all over it. Of course, I was the ringleader, right? Jacques said we cheated our fans."

Probert wasn't the only player fed up with Demers heading into his third season in Detroit. The Wings played uninspired hockey that season, but even going through the motions they were able to win the Norris Division with a .500 record. This time, however, it was clear they had no inclination to raise their game in an effort to make another long post-season run. The Wings lost to Chicago in the opening round in six games, including a 7-1 rout that ended their season. The following year, they failed to make the playoffs (something that wouldn't happen again until 2017). Mike Ilitch decided to make a change. Shockingly, Demers was so out of touch with his team by then that when he was summoned to the owners' home he thought he was going to be promoted to general manager.

After a short search that included a flirtation with the polarizing Mike Keenan, Ilitch signed off on the hiring of Bryan Murray to the dual role of coach and general manager. He was introduced in mid-July, 1990. It was under Murray's watch that the Wings began seriously importing Europeans, who would change the club's fortunes forever.

CHAPTER 3

Putting Some 'Red' in Red Wings

Jim Devellano's greatest legacy throughout his 51 years in the NHL may be the people he developed in his front office and his scouting staffs that have gone on to realize enormous success with other clubs. In those early years in Detroit, he had two young protégés – Neil Smith, who rose from part-time scout to assistant general manager, and Ken Holland, who was elevated to chief scout when Smith became assistant GM. Smith eventually left to win a Stanley Cup as GM of the New York Rangers. Holland would rise to GM in Detroit, and it was on his watch that the Wings won four Stanley Cups. But it was the late Alex Davidson, the most trusted and experienced scout on the Wings' staff in those early years, who deserves credit for sparking the intrigue regarding Soviet players in Detroit.

"I remember Alex Davidson coming to me and saying he saw the best 18-year old player in the world, a guy named Fedorov," Devellano said. "And I listened to him."

Devellano dispatched Smith, who came to Detroit with him from the New York Islanders. A Toronto native, Smith had played hockey at Western Michigan University followed by several seasons in the minors. He was in his early 30s when the Wings made a commitment to finding more players from Europe. Smith recalled his first trip abroad, to Stockholm, Sweden, with no contacts and little idea how to get around on a foreign continent. He contacted the NHL's Central Scouting Bureau for advice, and was given the name of a taxi driver who was a part-time scout. That was Christer Rockstrom, and the two of them became fast friends. Rockstrom gave Smith the lay of the land not only in hockey circles around Sweden, but Finland and Russia as well. Rockstrom was a few years younger than Smith. Both were single and they began to spend a lot of time together away from the rinks as well.

"I was young, free. It's Europe, you know? It was fun," said Smith, who began spending a lot of time across the Atlantic. Time that paid off. By then he had seen many of the best prospects in Europe often enough to speak with authority about their chances for success in the NHL.

By 1989, his hockey club was desperate to upgrade its roster. The Wings were upset in the first round of the Stanley Cup playoffs by the Chicago Blackhawks, who had finished 14 games below .500, and all the progress Detroit seemed to have made in the previous two seasons felt like a mirage. After two decades of futility and six years of trying to build a team as Devellano had promised – by drafting primarily North American players – the Wings felt themselves falling behind in the competitive arms race. The quickest way to catch up, Devellano was now convinced after numerous briefings from Smith, was to begin drafting Europeans, especially those groomed behind the Iron Curtain. The Soviet Union was recognized worldwide – at least everywhere except in Canada – as the dominant hockey-playing nation, but its players were still toiling as inexpensive, disposable pieces in what was then the final days of the republic, the CCCP (USSR) as it was known on the sweaters of the Soviet athletes.

The Iron Curtain still stood, but it had begun to show signs of rust and decay. There were some hockey players on the other side – notably Slava Fetisov and Igor Larionov – helping to knock it down by standing up to a brutal Soviet regime, starting with a tyrannical and legendary coach, Viktor Tikhonov. At the same time, Mikhail Gorbachev, the general secretary of the Communist Party of the Soviet Union, began to introduce terms like *glasnost* and *perestroika* to the Western vocabulary. *Glastnost* is translated to mean "openness," a term referring to political and social reforms leading to more rights and freedoms for the Soviet people, allowing them more access to the political system through freedom of expression, which included less censorship and more rights for the media. *Perestroika* (restructuring) was a term that referred to the overhaul of the political and economic systems established by the Communist Party, leading to actual contested elections and a more democratic system widely practiced in Western societies.

In other words, massive change appeared to be coming – quickly. The smartest NHL executives sensed that. They were betting that the floodgates eventually would open and the exodus of all that talent to North America would begin. Except nobody knew exactly when. Which made building a consensus difficult – even in Detroit as eager as the Wings were to upgrade their talent. While Smith and Holland also had seen Fedorov and absolutely agreed with Davidson's analysis and recommendation, they were apprehensive about spending an early draft pick to secure his rights.

"We needed players," Devellano recalled. "Remember, when I got to Detroit in 1982, I had promised the media and the fans that I wouldn't trade our draft picks, that we'd hire a good scouting staff and build through the draft."

Devellano made that pledge knowing people were tired of seeing Detroit trade its future in draft choices and young players for aging stars who accomplished little on their arrival. That resulted in a perpetuating downward spiral over two decades without anything remotely close to a decent playoff run. "Build through the draft" was Devellano's mantra from the beginning. Acquire the best young players available in the league's annual entry draft and develop them into NHL regulars.

"And that's what we did," Devellano said, "but after so many years, and especially that '85-86 season, my plan was getting a little bit frustrating. There just weren't as many top North Americans coming through."

It would get worse. In 1986, after finishing last among the NHL's 21 teams, Detroit drafted Joe Murphy, a Canadian-born center out of Michigan State with the first overall pick, leaving Wings management open to criticism for not taking home-grown Jimmy Carson, from the Detroit suburb of Grosse Pointe Woods. Carson played junior hockey in Verdun, Quebec. Murphy was a colossal bust, his first weeks with the Wings highlighted by a suspension after he missed a team plane. He showed up at the wrong airport for his first road trip as a professional, he said. Meantime, Carson was enjoying spectacular success with the Los Angeles Kings, becoming only the second teen-ager in NHL history to score more than 50 goals in a season. The other was a guy named Wayne Gretzky.

The obvious question is why did the Red Wings select Joe Murphy over Jimmy Carson? And the obvious answer is that their management thought Murphy was a better player at the time than Carson. But it goes deeper than that. Truth be told, the Wings simply preferred Canadian-born players over Americans. They would never admit it, nor would they do anything but dismiss it without comment if they were ever questioned about it. But it was an open secret that if it came down to selecting a Canadian or an American on draft day, Detroit would always take the Canadian. That would change over the years, but that's how it was in the early days of Devellano's stewardship.

As his frustrations mounted, however, Devellano was willing to the point of desperation to take some risks at the draft table. At the rate his team was progressing, the Wings wouldn't be close to challenging for the Stanley Cup in the eighth year, as he had promised the new owners. Devellano had a problem, and the solution, his scouts insisted, lay behind the Iron Curtain.

"We knew there were some great Russian players, some great Czech players," he said. "I also knew there was the Iron Curtain, but when we get into the second and third rounds, there are very few really great North American players left. So, I talked to Neil and I talked to Kenny and said maybe it's time we start to draft more Europeans."

Smith, Rockstrom and Holland had seen the best of them, including Russians like Sergei Fedorov and Pavel Bure and the equally dominating Czech Jaromir Jagr in world tournaments.

As much as the scouts raved about these players, there was some skepticism about committing precious draft picks. "They're great players, sure," the scouts assured Devellano. "But what if we can't get them out? We don't know if they'll ever be able to get over here to play."

That was the risk, Devellano conceded, but it carried a great reward. He was willing to at least reconsider his blueprint for building a successful team – take a great risk for a greater reward.

"I figured we've got one thing in our corner: Mike Ilitch," Devellano explained. "He has a little money. He has some political connections. And we also have Nick Polano and Jim Lites, who have some experience with this sort of thing, like getting Petr Klima out of Czechoslovakia. That's where it all started, really. So I went to Mr. Ilitch and explained to him what I was thinking. He said, 'Jimmy, if there's a superstar there that you can get in the third or fourth round, do it.' I said, 'Mike, we might be able to get the best player in the world in the fourth round. The trouble is, how the hell are we going to get him out?'"

Leave that up to me, Ilitch told him in so many words. So Devellano went to the 1989 NHL entry draft with a mission. He even tipped his hand a few days before at a luncheon of the Detroit Sports Broadcasters Association.

"Maybe it's time for us to start drafting some Russians," Devellano declared. This was a rather dramatic revelation, since revealing any part of a plan within a few weeks of the draft was unthinkable. And here was Jimmy D. declaring publicly that Detroit was committed to putting some Red in Red Wings.

Despite Devellano's pronouncement, there were considerable anxieties at the Wings draft table that June 17, 1989, at the Met Center in Bloomington, Minnesota.

"There was a certain amount of feeling that if we don't start taking these players earlier, other teams are going to start to do it," Jim Lites said. "Nobody had ever used anywhere near a high pick on a Russian – and if you listen to the scouts, anything higher than a six was a high pick."

That draft began routinely enough for Detroit. In the first two rounds, the Wings selected gritty center Mike Sillinger and hard-nosed defenseman Bob Boughner. Both would have substantial NHL careers, though each would do his best work with other NHL teams.

Getting two players of their caliber in any draft is enough to satisfy most hockey executives. But as it turned out, the Wings were just getting warmed up when Devellano turned to his top scouts in the third round and said, "OK, take your European." Surprisingly, however, that pick was not a Soviet player. With the 53rd overall selection, they took a slender Swedish defenseman, Nicklas Lidstrom. Devellano, according to Lites, was satisfied. He had drafted his European, and now he was ready to return to North America for his players. But Smith and Holland where pushing, despite their concerns, to select a prominent young Soviet player.

"We were all at the table. I was just an observer – but I ran the business," Lites said. "And the scouts kept asking me: 'If we use these higher picks on Russian players, can you get them out? You've got to give us some comfort that you think you can get them.'"

At Mike Ilitch's command to draft the best players no matter where they came from and leave the details to management to deliver them, Smith and Holland went to work on Devellano.

"I remember Neil and Kenny imploring Jimmy Devellano to take Fedorov with the fourth pick," Lites said. "They kept telling him that this was a top-three forward in the world."

Devellano conceded, telling his scouts he didn't want to hear about any more Europeans for the remainder of the draft. With their 74th pick, the Detroit Red Wings began their own Russian revolution, taking a gifted center from the Central Red Army Club of the Soviet Union. As soon as Smith announced Fedorov's name, a murmur swept the arena. Heads turned at several of the nearby tables filled with scouts and executives from the 20 other NHL clubs. What were the Red Wings doing? A Soviet in the fourth round? Were they crazy wasting a pick that high on a player from behind the Iron Curtain?

At the time, the NHL draft consisted of 12 rounds. Teams typically burned only late-round picks to select the occasional Soviet player or a few others from Soviet-controlled nations like Czechoslovakia, Latvia and Lithuania. Suddenly, the Wings had made history by spending the highest-ever draft pick on a Soviet-born player. And they were willing to quickly double-down with their next pick.

Smith and Holland kept the pressure on Devellano. With the team's fifth-round pick, they wanted to draft yet another Soviet, Pavel Bure – Fedorov's Red Army linemate. But the team was advised by then-NHL Vice President Gil Stein that Bure wasn't eligible. Rockstrom, the chief European scout, however, was adamant, arguing vociferously that he could prove Bure was, indeed, eligible to be selected. In the heat of the moment, and with time dwindling, the Wings decided to draft Shawn McCosh, a center from Oshawa, Ontario. But they vowed in the moments after the pick to take Bure with their sixth-round selection and worry about eligibility issues later.

As it turned out, however, Rockstrom wasn't the only scout who had done his homework. Mike Penny, then chief scout of the Vancouver Canucks, also had felt strongly that Bure qualified to be drafted in the later rounds because of his participation in some international games. The Canucks had planned to select Bure in the eighth round, but after learning what Detroit had done by selecting Fedorov in the fourth round and trying to take Bure in the fifth, they changed strategies. Just three picks before Detroit's turn in the sixth round, the Canucks claimed Bure – and the NHL-Soviet arms race commenced.

McCosh went on to play nine games in the NHL over two seasons with the New York Rangers and the Los Angeles Kings, retiring from hockey to become a middle school teacher in Phoenix, Arizona. And after winning his freedom in a federal courtroom in Detroit, where a judge deemed Bure's contract with Red Army was invalid because it was signed under duress, Bure went on to have a spectacular career with the Canucks. Known as "The Russian Rocket" for his speed and flamboyant play, he scored 437 goals and 779 points in 702 NHL games in route to his induction into the Hockey Hall of Fame in 2012.

It's remarkable enough that the Red Wings were able to acquire two eventual Hall of Fame players on consecutive picks in the third and fourth rounds in Nicklas Lidstrom and Sergei Fedorov – both inducted in 2015. If the Wings' scouts had had their way, however, they would have drafted three straight Hall of Famers by taking Bure when they wanted him in the fifth round.

Nevertheless, when the 1989 draft had ended, Devellano was beside himself with unabashed – and unabridged – joy.

"I'm fucking ecstatic," he said. "You want to know why? Because today we drafted the best young hockey player in the entire fucking world. And we got him in the fourth fucking round. His name is Sergei Fedorov, and wait until you see him play."

Later, in the eleventh round, Detroit used the 221st pick among 252 overall to select defenseman Vladimir Konstantinov, the captain of the Red Army club. But drafting these players was the easy part.

"Now all we have to do," Devellano said, turning toward Lites, "is figure out a way to get them over here."

That's where I came in, though I didn't know it at the time.

CHAPTER 4

Sergei Fedorov:
'Get Me Out of here'

The truest measure of a player in the National Hockey League, at least according to his peers, is twofold: How does he perform when the stakes are highest, and how much does he sacrifice himself for his teammates by playing through injury and illness?

The important numbers that describe Sergei Fedorov as a playoff performer with the Detroit Red Wings are indisputable. In 162 Stanley Cup tournament games, he scored 163 points, including 50 goals and 113 assists. In one four-year stretch that culminated in back-to-back Stanley Cup titles, Fedorov appeared in 78 games and produced 84 points. His 24 points in 17 games through the Cup Finals in 1995 remains a club record. His 10 goals in 1998 and 18 assists in 19 games in 1996 are also team records.

But for as good as he was, Fedorov was also dogged, largely through a whispering campaign emanating from his own locker room, by allegations that he wasn't "tough enough" to play through a hangnail. People saw Wings captain Steve Yzerman limping on a bum leg after earning five points in a victory at Los Angeles and wondered why Fedorov was inclined to take a night off if he wasn't feeling 100 percent.

At least that was the *perception*.

Not until 2012 – about when Fedorov's professional playing career was ending after three seasons with Metallurg Magnitogorsk of Russia's

Kontinental Hockey League and nine years after he left Detroit – did we learn exactly how resilient, how *tough*, Sergei Fedorov really was. And we have the late Dr. John Finley, a Wings physician for almost five decades, to thank for that. In the prologue to his book "Hockeytown Doc," Finley described a moment in the 1997 Stanley Cup playoffs that highlighted Fedorov's valor:

"Sergei Fedorov lay on his side on the trainer's table struggling for every breath and fighting off the immense pain that came with it. Moments earlier, one of the game's brightest stars, a former league MVP, sustained a severe costochondral rib injury after being checked by an Avalanche player early in the second period of a critically important playoff game at Joe Louis Arena. What happened as he lay there was something I'd never experienced either before or since in a career of nearly 50 years caring for NHL players – and what followed was something straight out of a Hollywood movie."

Finley then described how, as he and other medical personnel were tending to Fedorov, Yzerman left the Detroit bench and stood in the doorway of the trainer's room imploring Fedorov to get back on the ice. This was unprecedented, in Finley's experience; never had he seen a player leave the bench in the middle of the game to appeal to a teammate to get back on the ice, as Yzerman was doing. "C'mon, Sergei. We need you!" But Fedorov could hardly speak. "I can't breathe," he said in barely a whisper, wincing as he spoke. Returning to play in Game 3 of this tied best-of-seven Western Conference finals series against the archrival Colorado Avalanche seemed remote, at best. Without Fedorov, the team's best player, the odds of Detroit winning the series and advancing to the Stanley Cup Finals dropped sharply.

After evaluating Fedorov and determining how severe the injury was, Finley turned to Dr. David Collon, the team's orthopedist, and concluded that Fedorov needed a rib block. Fedorov had suffered a serious rib injury, a tearing of the tissue where the rib had joined the cartilage.

"I've never done one," Collon said of the common but extremely delicate procedure that called for injecting a small amount of local anesthetic to help diminish the pain. One false move, though, and the procedure could compound the injury. If the injecting needle is passed too deeply, it could easily cause the lung to collapse, Finley explained in his book. And though he had performed many of these procedures in his career, never had he tried it on a patient who was awake. All the others were immobilized under anesthesia. Yzerman had returned to the Detroit bench as Fedorov lay there in intolerable pain while Finley described what he was about to do.

"'Just hold your breath,' I told him, explaining that there could be no unusual movement. I prepared the combination short- and long-acting local anesthesia, surgically prepped the involved area and made a skin weal with some quick-acting local. With Dr. Collon and Wings physical therapist John Wharton holding onto Sergei to steady him, I passed the needle through the weal until it struck the involved rib, slid the needle just inferior to the bony edge of the rib, injecting the previously prepared local (anesthesia) safely into the area of involvement."

Within a few minutes, Fedorov was off the table, breathing normally and, miraculously it seemed, ready to play. Or not. Despite the doctors' reassurances that he could play without worsening the injury so long as it was well-dressed and protected, Fedorov decided he was done for the day. During the intermission, word had spread quickly among his teammates in the locker room that Sergei was finished. He had taken himself out of the game. He was peeling off his uniform and equipment when one of the quietest guys in the dressing room stood up and strode to the trainer's room.

"We have no idea what he said because he was speaking Russian, but none of us had ever heard that tone of voice from Vladdie," teammate Brendan Shanahan recalled. "He was loud, and when he was done he came back into the room, sat in his stall and never said another word."

Vladimir Konstantinov had spoken. Doctors dressed Fedorov's injury with a splint and once again cleared him to play. All this occurred within about 15 minutes after Fedorov was helped into the trainer's room. When the Wings returned to the ice after the intermission, Fedorov was with them. Big time. Slava Kozlov scored both goals in a series-turning 2-1 victory over the Avalanche. Each goal came with assists from his Russian Five teammate, Sergei Fedorov.

Detroit took a 3-1 series lead with a 6-0 victory in Game 4, but the

Avs responded with a victory of their own by the same score in Game 5. Game 6 at the Joe was much more closely contested. It was finally decided on Shanahan's empty-net goal, 3-1. But it was Sergei Fedorov, still hurting and still requiring that delicate shot before each game to anesthetize the injury, whose goal at 6:11 of the third period stood as the series-winning goal.

Only then, Finley pointed out, could Sergei and all his Red Wings fans finally take a decent breath and exhale a sigh of relief. They were on to the Stanley Cup Finals for the second time in three seasons. And only then did the whispering campaign and the questions about Sergei Fedorov's courage finally end.

After months of meticulous planning, the moment of reckoning was approaching quickly, and Nick Polano was getting nervous. Worried about being recognized by the wrong people – and the Portland, Oregon hotel was crawling with them – he and an accomplice ducked into the back of their waiting limo parked in a dark corner on the side of a hotel. Polano told the driver that they'd soon be joined by two more men, and he should be ready to leave immediately, heading in the direction of the airport. Now the driver was nervous. He studied Polano in his rear-view mirror and saw someone straight off a Hollywood set – 6-feet-3, 210 lean pounds, a guy casually dressed wearing a mane of thick, black hair combed high and back, and a chiseled, ominous expression that suggested he may soon be joined by Mafia hitman.

"Look man," the driver said, turning in his seat toward Polano, "I don't want to be involved in anything like this. I don't want any trouble. I've got a family. . ."

Polano burst out laughing. "He thought we were going to whack somebody," Polano said. Quickly and calmly, he explained that nothing bad or illegal was happening, but that the driver was playing a key role in a story that would make headlines around the world the next day.

"Don't worry. You're going to be fine," Polano assured the driver as he pointed to the hotel lobby. "And the guy sitting in there right now is going to give you a real big tip."

That guy, Jim Lites, who had spent nearly a year orchestrating this elaborate escape plan, was sitting there waiting. And waiting. Drinking coffee after coffee as he read and reread a newspaper, trying to blend into the furniture in the lobby of the Shilo Inn – and not rouse suspicion. As Polano was talking the chauffeur off the ledge, a bus pulled up to the front of the hotel. It emptied quickly. A few dozen hungry young men sprinted to a dining area where a late meal was being served. Last off the bus was the guy who would be making those headlines.

Sergei Fedorov spotted his man sitting there reading a USA Today newspaper and walked calmly up to him.

"Ready to go, Jim?" Fedorov asked, in practiced English, as casually as if he were commenting on the weather. Lites rose and they headed out a back door toward the waiting limo. But just as they were about to leave the hotel, an elevator door opened and there stood one of Fedorov's Soviet Red Army teammates, a tall, older man. Fedorov stopped. Lites' heart sank. Busted.

"I be right there, Jim," Fedorov said.

"Sergei, let's just go, right now," Lites implored.

"Thirty seconds," Fedorov said, and he walked toward Sergei Tchekmarev, one of his closest, most trustworthy friends in a society where trust was rare and fragile. Tchekmarev was a massage therapist and equipment manager for the Soviet National Hockey Team – and Fedorov's roommate.

"Let's go have dinner," Tchekmarev said.

"I can't," Fedorov said. "I gotta go."

"Where are you going?" Tchekmarev was now laughing.

"I'm going to Detroit."

"Yeah, yeah, yeah. Let's go," Tchekmarev said. "We can talk about it over dinner."

"No, there's a gentleman here right now. I'm going."

"No, no, no!"

Fedorov turned and walked away, not sure what might happen next. He didn't look back.

"I knew he might grab me and drag me to the coaches," Fedorov recalled. "He was twice bigger than me. I had no idea what would happen. It was kind of a nervous moment. But eventually I would be able to get to his mind for him to understand: I was really going."

Fedorov walked his friend to the elevator. Before a hasty, emotional departure, he reached into his pocket and took out all the money he'd saved after four years of playing hockey as a professional in the Soviet Union, about $1,500, and put it in Tchekmarev's hands.

"It was a small token of my appreciation if he gets in trouble for me leaving and being my roommate," Fedorov said. He knew well that in those days in the Soviet system even innocent people were persecuted just for being in the same circle as someone who was perceived to be a troublemaker.

Fedorov rejoined Lites and they jumped into the idling limo. Twenty minutes later, the four men were sitting in owner Mike Ilitch's plush Gulfstream G2, which was fueled-up and ready for take-off. The defection of one of the Soviet Union's most prominent young hockey stars was under way. On July 23, 1990, nearly a year after our first meeting in Helsinki, Sergei Fedorov, five months shy of his 21st birthday, arrived in his new hometown to begin his career in the National Hockey League.

"We had him in Detroit before the Russians knew he was gone," Polano said.

In an interview shortly after his induction into the Hockey Hall of Fame in November 2015, Fedorov admitted he didn't quite know what to make of that meeting in Finland when I showed him the list of Detroit Red Wings draft selections and handed him the media guide stuffed with the letter I had written inviting him to Detroit as a defector.

"I still didn't understand what the draft is, who the Red Wings are, nothing really about the NHL," he said. "I just say, 'OK. Great. So what?' That was my attitude. I had no idea that in a year I could have gone anywhere."

The letter, though, eventually created some anxiety. "It was a nervous time, an uncomfortable time," he said. "Later, I read the letter and understand. It was exciting kinds of thoughts."

Exciting enough that Fedorov put the brakes on an offer from his

Red Army coach and commander, Viktor Tikhonov. The Red Army club was intent on promoting Fedorov from private to lieutenant, a significant advancement in prestige, pay and other perks. But it also came with substantial strings attached. He would be asked to sign a 25-year contract. Fedorov's father, Viktor, had urged him to sign it – and Sergei was tempted. But the dollar signs the younger Fedorov saw in that Helsinki letter prompted him to reconsider. On arriving home in Moscow, he turned to the one person outside his hockey circle and his family that he thought he could trust: Valery Matveev, a sports writer with Pravda, one of two national newspapers in the Soviet Union at the time. The other was Izvestiya. (Pravda, in English, means "truth"; Izvestiya means "news." A popular axiom among Russians was: There is no truth in the "news," and no news in the "truth.")

Matveev, a slight, bespectacled man approaching his 30s, had chronicled the young Fedorov's rise to stardom during his four years with CSKA Moscow. He was the first journalist to write a lengthy feature story about Fedorov. In the process, the reporter earned the player's trust. And I eventually earned Matveev's trust over a series of lengthy conversations in Moscow about five years after the fall of the Soviet Union.

"He was maybe 17 then, playing in Minsk," Matveev recalled. "I don't remember much about it, other than I wrote he was a nice person and a very talented guy. And I quoted Tikhonov, who told me he was thinking of the future of the Red Army club, and how Fedorov, with Alex Mogilny from Khabarovsk and Pavel Bure in Moscow, would one day replace the great line of Igor Larionov, with Sergei Makarov and Vladimir Krutov ('the KLM line').

"Tikhonov paid much attention to the young guys, and when he brought Sergei to Red Army, Fedorov was the coach's favorite guy on the team. He was quiet, worked hard and he was big and strong. Tikhonov knew it was unusual to find so many good things in one person.

"After he got that letter, Sergei started thinking for the first time seriously of his future in the NHL," said Matveev, adding that he immediately advised Fedorov to seek a release from the Red Army so that he could play in the United States.

"Oh, no," Fedorov responded. "My parents would be very upset with me if I change my mind now and try to get a release."

Viktor Fedorov was pressuring his son, advising him that the Red Army offer was best for his future. On Sergei Fedorov's other shoulder was Matveev, who had reported on the defection of Mogilny, Fedorov's closest friend, the year before. Matveev knew better. He understood the machinations of the military police state and, more important, the shifting political winds in the collapsing Soviet Union.

"I knew there would be great changes in our nearest future," Matveev said. "I told Sergei it would be a stupid thing to sign with Red Army. Then it becomes very hard to get a release. It's not comfortable to play hockey for a man who is also your commanding officer. If he did something to anger the coach, Tikhonov could sign an order sending him to the Chinese border for 25 years."

About the same time, something was happening within the Red Army club that mirrored what was happening with the weakening Communist system. It also underscored how important Fedorov was to the future of the powerful Red Army Club. The stars in its first unit, including center Igor Larionov and defenseman Slava Fetisov, the team's captain and a major in the Red Army, began feuding with Tikhonov. Drafted several years earlier by NHL clubs, they wanted their release to pursue careers in North America. That coincided with Pravda's publishing some of the most controversial work by Matveev and others regarding the unofficial rules that Tikhonov adhered to in building his club and commanding loyalty. Pravda reported that if a player is not an Army officer it was much harder to become a member of the Soviet National Team or even to maintain a regular position with the Red Army team.

"We wrote that there were big changes in our lives right now in Russia, and maybe it was necessary for the Red Army club to make some changes, too," Matveev said.

By now, Fedorov was beginning to think the NHL was indeed his best bet. But Tikhonov was no dummy; he knew the Red Wings would press Fedorov to leave for Detroit. What he didn't know was that Matveev, who also had earned Tikhonov's trust, was prepared to be a willing middle man.

About the same time in Detroit, Jim Lites found someone else willing to facilitate a defection. In October, early in the 1989-90 season, Lites was in the Wings' locker room when he was approached by Phil Myre, the team's goaltending coach. Myre mentioned that he had a good relationship with renowned Soviet goalie Vladislav Tretiak, and Tretiak had a good friend in Montreal, a photographer, who had nearly unbridled access to the CSKA and the Soviet National Team's players. Within minutes, Lites was on the phone with the photographer, Michel Ponomarev. Within a few days, the two were meeting in Montreal.

There, Lites met a man pushing 50, a Russian ex-pat who had left his country when he was in his 30s. Because he spoke Russian, French and English, the Soviets used Ponomarev as their official photographer whenever they were in North America or Western Europe. "I can talk to the guys for you," he told Lites, who was beginning to feel like he could make the kind of deal that would pay enormous dividends for the Red Wings.

"As Mike Ilitch told me over and over, always close," Lites recalled. "So I sat there and said, 'Let's talk. If we do this, you have to work for me. I have to know your loyalties are to us." Their handshake deal was followed up with a written contract that said the Detroit hockey club would pay Ponomarev $35,000 for a successful defection of Sergei Fedorov or Vladimir Konstantinov.

"And Michel, from that day on, was my guy. That's how all this started."

Not long afterward, Fedorov's representative, Valery Matveev, and Lites' rep, Michel Ponomarev began to communicate. Both understood that Fedorov was reluctant to leave the Soviet Union, even when his military service ended. He worried about his family, his parents and brother, and what might happen to them if he defected like his best friend and linemate Alexander Mogilny, whose family was harassed and faced some minor reprisals after he left.

But Fedorov was still willing to listen. With Ponomarev facilitating, Fedorov agreed to meet Lites in Chicago, just before Christmas in 1989, when Fedorov's Red Army club was competing in the Super Series of exhibition games against NHL clubs. Lites was well-prepared, and he was confident that he could get Fedorov to walk away right then.

He booked a suite at the luxurious Drake Hotel, a favorite shelter by Detroit hockey clubs when they were barnstorming around the NHL. The Soviets were staying at a hotel nearby. Ponomarev, who had flown in from Montreal, arranged to have dinner with Fedorov. The dinner would be served by the Drake Hotel's room service.

"Sergei walks in and he's dressed in his best suit," Lites said. "It was a good Russian suit, especially for a 20-year-old kid. But really it looked like something he had gotten out of the Goodwill. It was shiny. But it didn't matter. He was a handsome guy, really good looking. And he was confident."

They talked for hours, during and after dinner. Lites showered him with all manner of Red Wings gear, including home and road jerseys with his name on them. Then he got serious.

"I armed myself with all the things I thought would matter to the Russians," he said. They included:

- A standard NHL player's contract, although Lites took it a step further. He brought a contract that was identical to the one captain Steve Yzerman, the team's best and highest-paid player, was working under at the time. He had learned in previous telephone conversations with Sergei that Yzerman was someone Fedorov greatly admired. So he brought Yzerman's contract and he was prepared to give Fedorov the same deal.

- A stack of $50 bills that totaled $10,000. If Lites had learned anything at all from Mike Ilitch, his mentor and father-in-law, it was that cash was king. The stack of bills would serve as a little seed money – part of a six-figure signing bonus.

- Some literature about the Riverfront Tower Apartments, a new high-rise right next to Joe Louis Arena, where the Wings housed several of their players. They were willing to pay Fedorov's rent in the nicest apartment available for up to three years.

- Finally, and what Lites thought might clinch the deal, a brochure from a Detroit Chevrolet dealership showing all the new Corvettes. "A whole catalog!" Fedorov would remember "I don't forget that. Jimmy Lites knew what he was doing."

But it was the Yzerman contract that most impressed Fedorov. Lites understood that it was important to him that he would be making as much as the team captain. The Wings' executive thought for sure he'd be leaving Chicago right then with the newest Detroit Red Wings star. Instead, Fedorov stood up, shook Lites' hand and, with Ponomarev interpreting, thanked him for his generous offer and declined.

"I cannot leave now," Fedorov said.

"But Sergei, all this is yours if you leave right now," Lites pleaded. "You never know what is going to happen in world politics. Russia could change. You never know when you will have an opportunity like this again. It might change politically. It might all go away. If you do this now, I have lawyers here who can make everything good."

Incredibly, considering how frustrated he was at toiling in conscripted servitude and kept in what he called "a cage" by the Soviet hockey system, Fedorov still resisted.

"My military service is going to end soon," Fedorov told Lites through his interpreter. "I do not want to desert from the military. I will be out the first week in January, and I am not going to continue my service. I want to play in the NHL and I will come out in the summer. You can count on it."

Lites was disappointed, but he left feeling good about what had transpired. Fedorov left the meeting feeling confident, too. He told Matveev about the contract Lites had offered him, the same one the Detroit club captain had signed.

"It was an official document with dollar figures that had lots of zeroes," Matveev said. "Sergei starts to understand that he is an important person."

Not so fast. Fedorov's military service was to end on Jan. 1, 1990, but Tikhonov arbitrarily extended his term of service until the Super Series ended to guarantee he would return with the team to Russia. In

April, while Fedorov helped the Russians win the gold medal at the World Championships tournament in Bern, Switzerland, Matveev and Ponomarev placed another call to Lites with a plan to help Fedorov go to America.

"I would never call from Russia because I never know when the KGB might be listening," Matveev said. "We thought the best way would be to find an American girlfriend for Sergei. But Mr. Lites explained that that would be very difficult and take a lot of time. He said maybe Sergei should leave like Mogilny did, especially since he wasn't a soldier anymore, with no military obligation and no contract with the Red Army.

Fedorov refused, but soon he changed his mind. He had finally lost patience with the Soviet system when he nearly landed in jail while trying to vacation at a Black Sea resort.

"Sergei and I and a couple of my friends decided to spend a few weeks on vacation at a nice Intourist hotel near Sochi, one of the nicest cities on the sea," Matveev said. When they checked in, they had to show their passports. Fedorov's passport listed no home address.

"Every person in Russia has to have a home address stamped in the middle of his passport," Matveev said. "If you don't, it's like you are a street person, a beggar, and the hotel wouldn't let him stay there. We tried to explain that Sergei Fedorov is a very famous hockey player, and that he was born in Pskov, but living in Moscow with me while the Red Army is promising to get him his own apartment very soon. But Red Army wanted Sergei to sign the (military) officer papers first."

The hotel referred Fedorov to the police for help.

"But the young officer at the desk in police headquarters didn't want to even talk with us," Matveev said. "He took Sergei's passport and said the best place for him to stay is in jail at the police station. Sergei got very angry, and we tried to relax him.

"We went to the store and bought a lot of beers, Heineken, and a carton of Marlboro cigarettes. We came back to the police station and gave the beer and cigarettes as a present for the police officer, and he gave us the paper that Sergei needed immediately.

"We had a nice vacation, but that's when Sergei started thinking: 'Get me out of here.'"

Back in Detroit, Jim Devellano, the Wings' general manager, ran into Yzerman in the team's workout room. The captain was pumping his legs furiously on an exercise bike, though the start of another hockey season was months away. Yzerman had competed for Team Canada in the World Championships, and out of curiosity Devellano asked for a scouting report.

"So, what did you think of the Soviet kid we got on our list?" Devellano asked.

"Sergei Fedorov? Oh, he's real good," Yzerman said.

"But how does he compare to you?"

"Oh, he's better than me."

"Say that again."

"He's better than me."

"Stephen, come on. You're just being nice, aren't you?"

"No, no. He's bigger and a stronger skater. He's better than me."

Few players competed with more pride and courage, earning more widespread respect from his peers in a career that spanned more than two decades, than Steve Yzerman. He knew his place in the game and he didn't mince words. Nor did he sprinkle his comments with clichés or false praise. What he said to Devellano about Sergei Fedorov had the GM dreaming in high definition long before the technology was even available.

"Oh, that's all I needed to hear," said Devellano, who tended to dramatize certain words when he was excited. "My *gosh*. I couldn't wait until we got him over here. If Sergei Fedorov is as good as Steve Yzerman, OK. Never mind *better!* If he was as good as Yzerman, we were going to be strong, *strong* down the middle."

As much as Fedorov wanted out of the Soviet system to play in the National Hockey League, and as desperate as the Detroit Red Wings were to have him, he was relentlessly tormented by the prospect of leaving his family behind. Those feelings began to haunt him in the spring of 1989, more than a month before he was even drafted by the Wings. After the Soviet Union won its 21st world championship title in

Stockholm, the Soviet players were rewarded with two "shopping days" before their scheduled departure. On one of those days, Fedorov took a walk with his closest friend and linemate, Alexander Mogilny.

While the Red Wings are widely given credit for starting the NHL's Russian revolution, it was the Buffalo Sabres selecting Mogilny in the fifth round in 1988 and convincing him to defect that triggered it. Mogilny, 20, and Fedorov, 19, combined with 18-year-old Pavel Bure to form the most dynamic young forward line in the world. Their coach, Viktor Tikhonov, counted on them to provide many more gold medals in world and Olympic competition in the years ahead. But Mogilny had other ideas. On a park bench that May day in the Swedish capitol, Mogilny confessed that he would be leaving, defecting to play in the NHL with the Sabres.

"Come with me," Mogilny pleaded with Fedorov.

"Oh, no. I can't. No way!" Fedorov responded. "What about my mother, my father, my little brother?"

A few days later, on the sunny morning of May 4, Mogilny was gone.

"I had no idea what would happen. I felt very responsible for my family. No way I'm going to do something like that, to leave on my own, without thinking through everything," Fedorov said in a wide-ranging interview at his Central Red Army Club headquarters in December 2015, when he was in his fourth year as general manager of the team he defected from a quarter-century earlier. "Everything was great in my young mind. You're 19. The Red Wings want you. They show you catalogs, give you money. But in the back of my mind, I knew I had to think about my family."

Sergei Fedorov left that Christmastime meeting with Lites in Chicago feeling, in his words, "worried, but happy worried. . . I was always thinking about it. Those things were on my mind constantly. Only hockey took me away. When I was able to play, I could relax a little bit."

Compounding the problem, he said, was that he had no one to share those immeasurable, tangled feelings with, no one to help him make sense of it all. Not even his parents. Perhaps least of all his parents because he didn't want to put them in harm's way in what was still a dangerous time for dissidents – whether in politics or athletics – in the Soviet Union. This was a few weeks after he turned 20, the average college sophomore's age. He needed guidance, wanted it badly, but didn't know where to turn.

"Maybe one or two friends I spoke to, but very carefully," he said. "I didn't want to get anybody in trouble. In the Soviet Union, people get in trouble even though they are not involved in any process – just standing right next to you. I was very careful about that."

Fedorov wasn't sure what to think regarding the fate of his parents, who lived in the Murmansk region, more than 900 miles north of Moscow. He took some comfort in simple geography. Maybe the distance isolated his family enough so that the authorities wouldn't seek retribution on the parents if their son left.

"I was hoping nothing would happen," Fedorov said. "My mom, my dad, they never really spoke about it even though I asked a couple, three-four times. I got the feeling that it's not a very comfortable subject. I still wanted to ask, but there was not much information."

In retrospect, Fedorov came to believe, his parents were being guarded in the extreme. There were times, he said, that they felt someone had been inside their apartment when they were away. Other times, they heard distinct clicking sounds on their home telephone, especially when their son was calling when his team was competing in North America. This was life in the Soviet Union, and a young Sergei Fedorov was getting sick of it.

Fedorov lived with his Red Army teammates at an estate remindful of old tsarist Russia. "It was 20 minutes from Moscow – without traffic. A two-hour ride with traffic," he said. "It was beautiful, no doubt. Very secluded. It provided for us great food, great accommodations."

The problem for these men, including experienced, older players who were married with children, is that they were there for 11 months of the year, training hard.

"Eventually, it became like a cage on a secluded island," Fedorov said. "Mentally, it got tougher and tougher"

In conversations with journalists, Fedorov said, he began to understand what was happening in his country, and he worried what life would be like in Russia with the fall of the Soviet Union. He understood that hockey may not have the same kind of support from a new regime forced to rebuild the nation's political and economic infrastructure. He also began to realize that for all the success the world's most dominant hockey club enjoyed for more than a generation, it wasn't doing all that much for him.

"I'm not making anything," he said. "I was already a two-time world champion with Alex and we didn't have − I know it's funny to say − but we couldn't even buy a car for some kind of reason. It was like having money and not being able to do something. It kind of gets you down. You start thinking different. You just want freedom."

He would find that in America, he knew. And with what the Red Wings were offering he would have the resources to enjoy it more than even most Americans.

"We start to think outside of the box, and eventually it led us to leaving," Fedorov said. "Leaving the system. Leaving the country. Leaving our families. We start thinking about a more exciting life. But hockey was still definitely the No. 1 reason. That's why we left. We want to play."

So not long after his return from Sochi, Fedorov − through a phone call from Ponomarev − let Lites know he was ready to make his break. Fedorov knew the stakes. He knew he had to be careful. He knew someone was always watching, someone whose job it was to make sure every player who traveled with the Soviet teams returned home.

"We have a guy," Fedorov explained. "We always have a guy. KGB. He was just an everyday guy, our friend. But we understand why he was there: to 'protect' us."

In other words, defecting wasn't going to be easy. Nevertheless, Fedorov was certain that once he and his Soviet teammates crossed into the United States in July 1990, he wouldn't be going back. Curiously, his passport − still with no address − worked just fine when he passed through U.S. Customs. Now the plan was under way.

"We knew this would be the best chance for Sergei to leave and join the Detroit Red Wings," Matveev said. "He planned to leave at the end of the tournament, but we found out that another player, Dmitri Khristisch (drafted by Washington), had decided to leave, too. If one player left, it would be almost impossible for another player to go."

Here was a high-stakes game of defection being played like musical chairs.

Lites called an audible, changing his plans on the fly.

"We're literally making it up as we went along," he said. "We checked into the hotel. We got a room for the three of us, which seem kind of odd, three men checking into one room. I remember the hotel guy kinda looking at us funny, like, 'What are you doing?'"

The Soviets were playing a game that night in Portland, an exhibition against Team USA before the teams left for Seattle, where the Goodwill Games would be played. Lites told Ponomarev to contact Fedorov to see if he would leave immediately. The car was waiting. So was the plane. Fedorov refused.

"I want to play in the game," he said. "It's my last game to play for my country."

"We said, 'Come on, Sergei. We're all here. The game is meaningless. Let's go. We can get a head start on this!'"

Fedorov's response: "No. I want to play in the game."

So Lites crafted another plan. He wanted to make the break immediately after the game, as soon as the players returned, with no possibility for a delay. He told Fedorov to pack his suitcase and place it on his bed. Then, before leaving for the game, he was to place his room key under Lites' hotel room door. Ponomarev would use it to retrieve the luggage and it would be in the limo by the time Fedorov returned.

Since Fedorov insisted on playing, Lites and Polano decided they might as well go watch. The performance didn't last long, at least for them. "On his second shift of the game, Sergei Fedorov just buries Kevin Miller," Lites said. "Sergei cross-checks him right in the head and gets kicked out of the game in the first period. Now we're thinking maybe we can find him and get going sooner."

No luck, so they returned to the hotel and waited. As the hour of the team's return grew closer, Polano and Ponomarev sought refuge in the limousine with the nervous driver. Lites read and re-read the newspaper, pounding caffeine.

"Longest half-hour, 45 minutes of my life," Lites said. Finally, the bus pulled up. "I'm sitting there trying to act nonchalant while these Russian players come running off the bus to get something to eat.

They're dressed in jeans, T-shirts. A bit of a mess. The last guy off is Sergei Fedorov, wearing a suit – the same suit he was wearing when he met with me at the Drake Hotel in Chicago – with a nice white shirt. He looked like a million bucks."

More than 26 years later, Lites remembered every detail of the moment. Remembered Sergei recognizing him. Remembered him casually walking over. Remembered the eye contact, the smile, the cool, casual question.

"Ready to go, Jim?"

With the wheels up and Mike Ilitch's Gulfstream G2 headed to Detroit with a freshly minted Detroit Red Wing, Jim Lites could finally exhale. The hard part – the potentially dangerous part – was over. They were safe, and nothing could harm them now.

"In the back of your mind, you're always thinking: 'Will there be a physical confrontation with somebody?'" Lites confessed. "In '85, if you went to Prague, there was a Russian soldier on every corner. Prague was occupied by the Soviet Union. The Russians traveled with the Czech team that Petr Klima defected from. They were there. They traveled with them. They had guns."

With that in mind, he couldn't help but worry that the Soviets were just as protective with their players.

"But I never saw that with the Russians when they were traveling," Lites said. "They came to North America. They played in that Super Series. But there wasn't that fear that they were going to shoot you. There was just that fear that there might be a confrontation, where someone gets in your face and says, 'He can't leave.'"

That's why Lites was especially nervous when the elevator opened and a big burly guy stepped out – and Fedorov began talking to him. When they were finally on the plane headed to Detroit, a spread of food in front of all four passengers on the plane, Lites asked.

"Who was that guy, and what did you say to him?"

"That was my best friend and roommate," Fedorov responded. "He is a trainer on our team. I said to him: 'I am leaving for Detroit and the NHL. No matter what they tell you, I am not being kidnapped. I am doing it of my own free will, and I will see you down the road.'"

That wouldn't be the last time Fedorov would have to testify that he was leaving of his own volition. Immediately on arrival in Detroit, the group went to the team's executive offices at Joe Louis Arena, where Nancy Beard, the administrative assistant to the general manager, could begin the process of filing the necessary papers with the U.S. State Department, including Fedorov's application for a work visa. That evening, Fedorov and Ponomarev were at the home of Denise and Jim Lites, and Sergei said he wanted to watch the Goodwill Games, the brainchild of billionaire Ted Turner, who owned, among other things, CNN, the 24-hour cable news network.

That's where the news broke that Fedorov had disappeared, with network anchor Larry King butchering the player's first and last names while reporting the Soviets' claim that Fedorov had been kidnapped.

That's about when Liteses' home phone rang.

"Mr. Lites, do you know the whereabouts of Sergei Fedorov?" a man on the other end asked.

"Yes, I do," Lites said. "Who is this?" The man identified himself by name and title, saying he was with the State Department.

"You have created an international incident, sir. My boss is going to call you."

Five minutes later, the phone rang again. Lites listened for a moment and said: "Look, the boy has not been kidnapped. He is in Detroit. He's willing to talk to the Russians and tell them he has not been kidnapped. It's not a problem. In fact, why don't you have the Russians talk to me?"

The next caller was a Russian who did not identify himself, but he spoke English with urgency.

"Sergei Fedorov does not want to go with you," said the man, who seemed to be connected with the Red Army Club or the Soviet Hockey Federation. "He cannot go. He is under contract!"

"Well, that's not my understanding of the situation," Lites responded. "He doesn't have any intention of going back to Russia, and he's certainly not going back to play in the Goodwill Games. It's done. It's over."

So was the conversation. Lites hung up the phone. There were about a half-dozen more calls that night between Lites, the State Department and Soviet officials. During each of them, Sergei Fedorov was on a nearby couch, casually watching TV. Eventually, a bilingual State Department bureaucrat was on the line, and he asked Lites to hand the phone over to Fedorov.

"Do you have any intention of going back to Russia?" the man asked Fedorov.

"No. *Nyet*," Fedorov responded, handing the phone back to Lites.

The next day, yet another high-ranking official from the State Department called. He, too, was bilingual and asked to speak with Fedorov. It was a fairly one-sided conversation. This time, Fedorov did most of the talking.

"I am not going back to the Goodwill Games, and I am not going back to Russia," Fedorov said. He spoke bluntly, in Russian. "I have applied for a work visa. I am going to play hockey for the Detroit Red Wings."

When Fedorov hung up the phone, the issue was over.

"There was a little bit of tension there," Lites recalled. "The calls were nasty, but quite fun to be honest with you."

Fedorov made one important call himself. It was hard to hear the other end, and it lasted just a few minutes, just long enough for him to say: "Mom, Dad, I am OK. I'm safe. I'm happy. Nothing to worry about."

Well into his 40s, Fedorov remembered the moment as feeling like he was lighting a stick of dynamite: "Boom! That was it," he said. "Hopefully, they understood."

And there began the most memorable time of Sergei Fedorov's young life.

"Best summer ever," he said wistfully. "Every day was like California."

But Fedorov had come to Detroit to play hockey, and he couldn't wait to get to the rink.

"No," Lites said. "We don't have training camp for almost two months."

"Two months?" Fedorov said, wondering what he might do with

all that free time. All that freedom. He figured it out quickly.

He spent much of it in the Liteses' backyard pool, swimming with their kids. Brooke was 6 and swam like a fish. Sam was a year old, getting around the water with inflatable floaties. The three played for hours in the water, oblivious to what quickly became a kind of neighborhood spectacle.

"He's an Adonis," Lites said of Fedorov. "An unbelievable athlete, and the best body you've ever seen."

"I didn't know what was ahead of me, but I knew I was in such great shape," Fedorov said. "I have these pictures of my body then, and I was ripped, you know? I was ready to play hockey then."

The women of Bloomfield Hills could offer supporting testimony.

"All of a sudden, all my wife's friends, these 30-something-year-olds, are coming over," Lites said. "Just stopping by. Ones I've never seen at the house before are coming over all the time just to get a gander at this kid. We laughed about it. Sergei was very popular."

And he hadn't touched a puck yet in Detroit.

The next few weeks were a blur. Ponomarev spent three days at the Lites' home serving as an interpreter before leaving for home in Montreal. He was $35,000 richer for his help in a successful defection. By then, Lites had hired another interpreter, Michael Chovich, whose family had emigrated from Yugoslavia. Chovich was just a few years older than Fedorov and enjoyed athletics as well. The two became fast friends, working out together at nearby Cranbrook, the exclusive private school in Bloomfield Hills.

"Sergei said he wanted to go for a run, and I'm thinking it's going to be a nice jog," said Lites, describing the scene he watched unfold. "But he ran 82 laps in full sprint without breaking into a pant. You can't imagine the shape this player was in. He ran. He lifted weights. It was fun to watch. You could tell right away the kid was disciplined. He took care of himself. He worried about what he was eating – and this was before that was the norm in professional sports."

Before training camp began, Lites moved Sergei into his new high-rise apartment next to Joe Louis Arena, where Fedorov finally began meeting his peers during informal, pre-training camp workouts. In his idle hours, Fedorov had other worries, like decorating his new apartment, buying things like draperies and pillows. And a badly needed new wardrobe.

During training camp, new Red Wings coach Bryan Murray made his first brilliant decision, rooming Fedorov with Shawn Burr and thereby providing the young Russian with a crash course in English. Burr, a fan favorite and one of the most likeable and funniest men ever to step foot in an NHL dressing room, never shut up.

"He took me under his wing," Fedorov said. "He was my teammate, my linemate, my roommate and an amazing host. He showed me from day one. He would teach me so many things, many funny jokes. Shawn Burr was an amazing, amazing guy."

Burr was fond of telling a story from Fedorov's first day at training camp with the Wings.

"Sergei comes up to me and says, 'Shawn, I need love.'"

"Yeah, Sergei," Burr responded. "We all need love."

"No. Love. Love! I need love!" Fedorov kept saying, pointing to his hand.

And Burr finally figured it out. He took Fedorov to the team equipment manager and got him a pair of hockey *gloves*.

When the Wings returned from training camp, they had a surprise for Fedorov. Some serious love, you might say. His new Corvette, the one he picked out of that catalog he'd first seen in Chicago, had arrived.

"A burgundy Corvette, and it was right inside the arena," Fedorov said. "Oh, my God! It was the shiniest car I have ever seen. So, I drive it to my new apartment – 500 yards away. That was the longest trip ever. I'm 20, don't forget. I was just happy getting it in the parking structure without an accident. It was an exciting time. Very cool time."

With a new car, his contract signed and a six-figure signing bonus in the bank, Fedorov set about immersing himself in the best America had to offer. With Chovich at his side, he quickly learned the geography around Detroit. He found there were four main expressways leading out of a downtrodden inner-city to some of the most affluent suburbs in the world – and he discovered a shopping mall just off each of those highways. They made a big impression.

"Those stores are just huge and happening," he said. "The people are happy, just walking around, relaxed. I say to myself, 'Wow, this is nice. All that just to play hockey?' When you are happy outside the hockey rink, you can go and just do your best there. I was like swept away. It was an amazing feeling. Like I come to Disneyland."

CHAPTER 5

Vladimir Konstantinov: Surviving 'Terminal Cancer'

Professional hockey coach Barry Smith spent much of his career working behind the bench in hockey rinks throughout Europe, including stops in Sweden, Switzerland and Russia, and all over North America. Wherever the game took him in his nomadic career, he tried to get to know the people and their histories, which helps in part to explain his fascination with whatever biological influences went into creating Vladimir Nikolaevich Konstantinov.

"Imagine the gene pool that went into that guy," said Smith, a former Detroit Red Wings associate coach under Scotty Bowman. "He's from way up there in northern Russia, by the Arctic Circle. There must have been some incredible warriors up there because he's one of the most ultimate warriors I've ever seen. The more they go after him, the more he raises his game level."

Konstantinov grew up in Murmansk, a port city of about 300,000 souls in the extreme northwest part of Russia – the largest city north of the Arctic Circle. Once a strategic hub of submarine and icebreaker activity of the former Soviet Union, it's now home port to *Atomflot*, the world's only fleet of nuclear-power icebreakers. It's also an important fishing and shipping destination.

"There must have been some Mongols up there, some Swedish influence," Smith told me in an interview for a story in the Detroit Free Press. "Who knows what else?"

A little Cossack, perhaps. Equal doses of Peter the Great and Ivan the Terrible, emperors of all the Russias. And definitely more than a pinch of Rasputin, the mad monk whose spell over the last remnants of the Romanov Empire inspired a royal conspiracy to kill him. And that wasn't easy. When bullets and massive quantities of poison failed, Rasputin's murderers finally succeeded in drowning him beneath a sheet of thick ice on the Malaya Nevka River in St. Petersburg, Russia, in 1916.

A few generations later, Vladimir Konstantinov personified the best kind of elite Soviet athlete produced by a society bent on proving Communism's superiority in the world through sports. After he escaped the system, he quickly established himself throughout the National Hockey League as one of the game's fiercest competitors and most hated opponents. Another seemingly superhuman muzhik, a Russian peasant like Rasputin, Konstantinov was also among the world's best defensemen destined to become one of Detroit's best-loved sports icons.

Buoyed by their success getting Sergei Fedorov to defect, the Red Wings immediately turned their attention to freeing Vladimir Konstantinov from his contractual obligations in what would soon become known as the Russian Federation, an emerging fragile democracy embracing capitalism after more than 70 years of communism. The Iron Curtain had crumbled; the Berlin Wall was knocked down. Some elements of the Russian society, however, like its sports programs, still stubbornly clung to time-tested Soviet-Marxist traditions. None more successfully than the country's ice hockey federation, which continued to treat its players like indentured servants. It restricted their movements and decided when, if ever, they could enjoy some of the perks of the new system – like spending more time with their families, buying a car, finding a better apartment or, heaven forbid, freedom to travel, a right that other Russian citizens were starting to enjoy.

When I first met Konstantinov and Fedorov in Helsinki less than two months after the Wings selected them in the 1989 NHL entry draft, I shared my impressions of the two youngsters with Wings executive vice president Jim Lites. While Fedorov seemed ambivalent and hard to read, Konstantinov clearly was thrilled to see his name among the list of Detroit's draftees. After he defected to Detroit, Fedorov confirmed that Konstantinov was also eager to leave Russia to play in Detroit.

"We found out from Sergei that Vladdie absolutely wanted to come, and he'd come in a minute if he could find a way to get out of the military," Lites said. "He was dying to get out of there, but he's got a wife and kid, and he's captain of the Red Army team."

The greater obstacle, however, Lites would soon learn from the team's immigration attorneys, was that Konstantinov also held the rank of captain in the Russian military. If he deserted, he'd be considered a felon in Russia. That would render him ineligible for an H-1B work visa needed to play in the National Hockey League. Worse, the Russians had documents signed by Konstantinov committing him to the Army for 25 years.

Lites remained undaunted. In fact, opted to intensify his efforts regarding Konstantinov after Fedorov brought his friends, Valery Matveev and his wife, to Detroit. The couple lived with Fedorov in the months after he moved into the Riverfront Apartments adjacent to Joe Louis Arena. Fedorov introduced Matveev to Lites as Konstantinov's agent, and it didn't take long before the two of them began scheming.

"I immediately liked Valery," Lites said. "He was a pretty cool guy, a journalist in Russia, so he had really good access. He was a college graduate, articulate and intelligent. And he said, 'I can help you get Konstantinov out.'"

Lites was in. He offered the same deal to Matveev that he had made to Ponomarev, who facilitated the Fedorov defection: The Wings would pay him $35,000 if he helped orchestrate a successful transfer from the Red Army to the Red Wings. Technically, Konstantinov's departure wouldn't be considered a defection given the new freedoms in Russia that its hockey players didn't yet enjoy. Russian citizens may have been free to leave. Its soldiers, however, as in any military in the world, were not.

Curious about how Matveev could orchestrate Konstantinov's exit, Lites suspected that it involved bribery of high-ranking hockey officials. He wondered if that would include Valery Gushin, the Red Army general manager.

"Is he corruptible?" Lites asked Matveev. "Is there a way to get Gushin on our side to get Konstantinov out?"

"No, never," Matveev responded. "He's a Communist. A true believer. He's going to say no."

"Then how are we going to get this done?"

"I don't know," Matveev said. "I have to think about this."

Months passed in that season of 1990-91. Matveev had gone silent. Then the National Hockey League made a surprise announcement that had the Wings feeling that they had won some kind of lottery. Vladimir Konstantinov would be coming to Detroit after all, to play in Joe Louis Arena, albeit as captain of his Red Army team that was scheduled to play an important game against the Red Wings.

Jim Devellano reached down on either side of his chair and grabbed two heavy duffel bags, tossing them onto the desk that separated him from his visitors – an anxious young Russian hockey player and an interpreter commissioned by the club. Devellano, the senior vice president of the Wings, had arranged for a clandestine meeting in the early hours of Christmas Eve, 1991, in his office in the bowels of Joe Louis Arena. He was prepared to do anything he could to get Vladimir Konstantinov to walk away from his Russian teammates to join the Detroit hockey club. If Devellano was successful, it would be the second defection of a prominent Soviet-born hockey player to Detroit in 16 months.

Konstantinov, then 23, was the leader of the most dominant team in the Soviet elite league. As luck would have it, the NHL and Russian Federation sports authorities agreed to a series of games between various Russian clubs and NHL teams. If the NHL team won its game, the two points for the victory would count in the overall regular-season NHL league standings. To Devellano's delight, Detroit drew Red Army, Konstantinov's team, as its opponent.

The previous year, Sergei Fedorov – Red Army's brightest young star – had defected to join the Red Wings. Out of respect for their Russian adversaries, the Wings kept Fedorov out of that game. As Lites explained it, "We didn't want to rub it in – and we didn't want him to get hurt if they decided to take any cheap shots." The Wings lost the game, 5-2. But the two points they failed to add to their standing paled in comparison to the opportunity presented by this game.

"Can you believe this?" Devellano thought to himself when the series was announced. Here was a chance not only for the Wings to evaluate Konstantinov's play in several games against NHL competition – and they sent two scouts to each game – but they also had an opportunity to court him in their own building. A remarkable opportunity the Detroit club would not squander.

"Their team was staying at the Pontchartrain [Hotel], right near the arena, so I hired a guy who could speak Russian and told him to find Konstantinov there and tell him that Jim Devellano wants to meet him in the Red Wings' offices," said Devellano, never shy about referring to himself in the third person. "We set the time for 1 a.m., well after the game. I told them to go down the back stairs at the Pontch so they wouldn't be seen, and I'd be in the parking lot. I was there at 1 a.m. sharp, and there stood Vladimir Konstantinov."

By now, the Wings knew Konstantinov could compete at an elite level from the moment he stepped onto an NHL rink. Devellano had seen enough in the game just a few hours earlier. They wanted him badly, and they didn't want to wait for Russian authorities to give their consent, if ever that might happen. So Devellano made his play.

"We got to my office and I had two big fucking bags," he recalled. "I picked them up and threw them on my desk and I told Vladimir Konstantinov they were filled with money for him if he wanted to play in Detroit. "'I'm going to make you rich!' I told him. 'This is all yours! All you need to do is defect right now to play with the Detroit Red Wings in the National Hockey League.'"

Devellano pronounced Detroit in three syllables, like many Canadians: De-TROY-it.

The Wings were ready to sequester Konstantinov in the Riverfront Apartments, just down the street from Joe Louis Arena. He would be Fedorov's neighbor. All Konstantinov had to say was *"Da."* Instead, he looked crestfallen. He turned to the interpreter and said, "Please tell Mr. Devellano I would love to, but I cannot. I have a wife and daughter back in Russia, and I just cannot do it. I cannot leave them there alone."

Devellano was not at all surprised by this. In fact, he expected it. He knew of Konstantinov's commitment not only to his family back home in Russia but to the military, making a successful defection improbable. But Devellano's primary mission had been accomplished. Vladimir Konstantinov now knew in no uncertain terms that the Detroit Red Wings were serious about their intentions. Devellano nodded to the player and spoke to the interpreter: "Please tell Vladimir that we will find a way to get him and his family here with us."

As midnight tried to assert itself, the medieval city of Turku, Finland, grew distant in the review mirror. A small car carrying four Detroit Red Wings officials on a covert mission traveled well past the stores and homes on the edge of town, onto narrow roads and into thick, opaque forests. It was mid-May during the 1990 World Hockey Championships, a time of year when the sun couldn't quite drop far enough off the horizon. It would remain a permanent state of dusk until the sun began to rise again a few hours later.

Lites, the executive VP, and Bryan Murray, the team's coach and general manager, were at the tournament to meet with Swedish hockey representatives. Their goal was to negotiate the release of defenseman Nicklas Lidstrom from his club. Earlier that morning in the lobby of their hotel, Lites was surprised to run into Michel Ponomarev, the Montreal photographer who had played a critical role in the Fedorov defection. Ponomarev told Lites he could arrange a meeting with Konstantinov that night. Nick Polano, who was scouting the tournament for the Wings, arranged for a car, which was a bit small for the driver and his four passengers. "It was like a clown car," Lites said. And it wasn't a short ride.

Weary of losing players to the NHL – after Fedorov bolted for Detroit, Dmitri Khristich left for Washington and Alexander Godynyuk left for Toronto – the Russians had developed a bunker mentality, going to greater lengths to shield their players from Western influences at these world events. Murray had little experience in these covert operations, and when he was invited to a meeting with Konstantinov that night he assumed the player would be joining Wings officials for dinner at the hotel. Now he was in the back seat of a compact car nearly 30 miles away on increasingly isolated roads. Finally, he turned to Polano and asked, "Nick, do you know where we're going?" Polano shook his head, but he assured everyone that the driver knew their destination precisely.

They arrived close to midnight, and Murray remembered the scene vividly.

"The driver took us out into the country, into this wooded area," Murray said. "It was drizzling. It was cold. And I'm standing there looking over my shoulder both ways wondering, 'Are we going to be in big trouble out here?' And all of sudden I see this figure running out of the compound the Russians are staying at, cutting across this field and onto the road to meet us: Vladimir Konstantinov. And then we had a discussion about getting him to Detroit to become an NHL player."

The conversation was intense, with Ponomarev interpreting. Konstantinov left the Wings' officials with no doubt about his intentions.

"Yes, I'm coming whenever I can – as soon as I can," Konstantinov said. "Please get me out. Do whatever you can. I'm coming. I don't care what you pay me."

Murray worried the entire time. "Every five minutes I was looking around, nervous that he was going to get caught, or we were going to get caught doing something wrong in relation to the Russian team," he said. "But in the end, we made an agreement and Vladimir obviously held up his part of the bargain."

Konstantinov had been ready to leave ever since his Christmastime meeting with Devellano, when he left Detroit not with two duffel bags full of money but with a Red Wings sweater with his name on it – and a promise. After the meeting in a forest of Finland, the Wings were more committed than ever to their promise to free Konstantinov from his Soviet shackles. Lites reassured him of that; he just didn't know how yet.

"We still had this dilemma: What do we do to get him out of the military?" Lites said. Several weeks later, Valery Matveev showed up in Lites 'office at Joe Louis Arena. They hadn't met in two months, but Matveev hadn't been idle.

"I've got it set up," he told Lites. "I can get Vladimir Konstantinov out of his military obligation in Russia."

"How?" Lites asked.

"I've got an idea. I need about $30,000 in cash. I'm going to get him a medical release from the military. I have one month. Don't ask me questions."

Lites couldn't help but wonder, though he didn't press the issue when Matveev told him: "I have to work with some doctors."

In an interview years later, Matveev told me that he knew if he had any chance of getting Konstantinov out he'd have to get creative. "The only way I thought we might be able to do it was pay lots of money to somebody in the Russian Army to try to get his release," he said. "Jim said, 'OK, go to Moscow and start working on it.'"

Lites didn't hesitate to get him the cash. "I had a really good feeling about Valery," he said. "And Sergei did as well. Everything he ever told us would happen happened."

Armed with a stack of team owner Mike Ilitch's American greenbacks, Matveev left for Russia intending to attempt to bribe military generals. But he soon concluded this was risky business and probably wouldn't work even at a time when nearly everyone in that country had a hand out. Somebody might end up in a gulag that way, and Matveev wasn't interested. Cancer, he decided, was a better idea.

"I was having dinner with a good friend of mine who was a doctor when the idea occurred to me," Matveev said. "I decided to find a bad disease for Vladdie. I would put him in the hospital and get the doctors to diagnose cancer and get his release from the Army."

Besides, Matveev acknowledged, bribing doctors was a lot less risky. "I had a good connection in this clinic," he said, "and they told me it was possible to prepare all the papers for Vladdie so he could get his release. I returned to Detroit and told this to Jim Lites, and he could not believe that was possible."

But Matveev remained hopeful, partly because Konstantinov always looked like a wreck anyway. Even as a teenager who was an elite athlete on the soccer pitch as well as on a big sheet of ice in a European hockey rink, Vladimir looked and acted far older than his years.

"He came to the Red Army school when he was 15, and even then we called him '*Dyadya*,' "said Igor Larionov, a teammate in Moscow and Detroit. It was a term of endearment meaning "Grandpa," the kind of old man forever screaming at kids to get off his lawn. "Always grumpy, always serious, never smiles. That's why we called him Grandpa."

Matveev was most optimistic about the scheme, though, because he had a pile of American money to spread around. In the two weeks that Konstantinov spent at the medical clinic, doctors concluded that he was suffering from a rare form of cancer. Worse, the Russian doctors knew of no medical protocol to treat him. The captain of the Red Army club and Russia's national team was dying, the doctors concurred.

When the new hockey season began, Konstantinov was still in the hospital. His wife, Irina, approached Red Army general manager Valery Gushin and coach Viktor Tikhonov. She explained tearfully that her husband was seriously ill and unable to play. She pleaded with them to allow him to travel to the United States to seek the best possible medical treatment.

"Everybody knows Russian medicine is not so good as in the U.S.," Matveev said. "But Tikhonov didn't believe us. First, he wanted to see the papers from the clinic. Then he decided to put Vladdie in *Burdyenko*, the best military hospital in the Soviet Union. Now it was necessary for me to find the right connections again. And pay again. But I know everybody in Moscow wants some money. Everybody wants a nicer place to live, a better car. And working for a newspaper, as I did, gave me lots of connections to many different fields of life."

Matveev indeed had excellent connections at *Burdyenko*. His grandfather, a retired army general, spent months there before his death. "I knew exactly with whom it would be possible to discuss this situation," Matveev said. But he would need another $30,000 or so in bribe money. And more. One of the doctors Matveev approached wanted a car. But not just any car.

"He wanted a big American car, the biggest," Matveev said. When he returned to Lites asking for more bribe money – and the car – Lites didn't flinch. He got another wad of Ilitch's money, bought the big sedan and titled it in Matveev's name. Matveev shipped it to Moscow, and that was the last Lites ever saw or heard of it.

"We were able to get him a Chevrolet Caprice, the biggest car in the U.S. market," Matveev said.

The doctor was apparently happy. While his team held its training camp, Konstantinov spent another couple of weeks being prodded and probed by military physicians, who could neither confirm nor dispute the diagnosis of the doctors at the cancer clinic. They did conclude, however, that with such an illness it was impossible for Konstantinov to continue his military career. He was battling terminal cancer, after all. They recommended he be discharged from the military.

The Red Army hockey club, however, defiantly disputed the authenticity of the conclusion by both groups of doctors, and Konstantinov was forced to appeal up the military's chain of command for his release. He met with some influential bureaucrats while Matveev spread even more bribe money around until Konstantinov was finally released from the military. Free at last from his Red Army obligations and no longer worried about being arrested as a deserter if he defected, he and his family were preparing to leave the country immediately. It was late August when Lites' phone rang.

"He's out," Matveev reported. "Vladimir has gotten his medical release from the military. We are flying out of Russia, and we will be there in Detroit on September 2, right before training camp."

Lites was thrilled. "This is great news," he said. "What do I have to do?"

"Nothing," Matveev said. "He will arrive with all his documents. We can then apply for his work visa and he will be ready to go. . ."

Now Lites was beyond delirious. But on the day of departure, Lites' phone rang again. On the other end, Matveev was frantic.

The old Soviet establishment that still ran Russian ice hockey with absolute power, refused to capitulate so easily. Amid growing political unrest, the shrewd Red Army GM Gushin, still suspicious about Konstantinov's sudden illness and inexplicable release from the military, used his own vast connections with border soldiers at the Sheremyetevo International Airport – the ones at Passport Control. Matveev had learned that Gushin ordered Konstantinov's name placed on a list of people who were to be detained if they tried to leave the country. He would not let go of his captain without a fight.

"So, we decided to leave by train," Matveev said, noting that by now Russian authorities had begun to loosen travel restrictions for its citizens. That wouldn't be so easy either, as it turned out.

Fate intervened in that late summer of 1991, when a group of Communist activists attempted a coup, taking Mikhail Gorbachev, general secretary of the Communist Party of the Soviet Union, hostage in his own home. Hundreds of thousands of Russians who had quickly adapted to new freedoms under Gorbachev's reform policies took to the streets to protest. Generals who supported the hardliners rolled tanks and other military equipment into the streets in a show of force that threatened to reverse the dramatic changes that were taking place throughout the country. Among the faces in the crowd: Irina and Vladimir Konstantinov and Valery Matveev, cheering Russian President Boris Yeltsin when he stood atop a tank during his defiant speech against the Communists.

"We were afraid they would close the borders immediately," Matveev said. "If Yeltsin would win, it would be possible for us to go. If not, we knew we would be staying in Russia all our lives. Some people were killed in these demonstrations, but any one of us would have stood in front of the tanks to try to stop them."

Yeltsin eventually prevailed. The coup collapsed. Konstantinov and his family were free to travel. But again, providence would intervene, and the best-laid plans many months in the making were in shambles. Suddenly, Vladimir Konstantinov faced his greatest hurdle yet in his path to Detroit and the National Hockey League. During the uprising in the streets, Matveev's car was vandalized. Someone broke a window, stealing the radio and, worse, a briefcase containing all of Konstantinov's critical medical documents, his military release papers, his passport and the remaining few thousand dollars of the Wings' bribe money.

The outrageous fake cancer plan that had worked so brilliantly was shattered by random larceny. Now Matveev worried that somehow all that "doctored" medical paperwork might wind up in the hands of the still powerful KGB. If it did, their problems were certain to multiply.

"We were very upset," Matveev recalled. He was sitting with the Konstantinovs at their kitchen table, all of them panic-stricken as they contemplated what they should do next, what they possibly *could* do next with their options suddenly so limited. No medical paperwork. No papers showing a medical military discharge. No passports. No money. Nothing. Their dream of starting a new life in North America, with Vladimir

Konstantinov playing for the Detroit Red Wings? Done. Finished. They were devastated, distraught, angry and scared. Konstantinov's playing career in Russia certainly was over, too. More likely, he could be headed to prison.

Then the telephone rang.

"The guy said he was a big hockey fan, and that he found all these documents," Matveev said. "But, of course we knew it was bandits who stole it. He said he would call back to arrange for us to meet him and pick it up."

Matveev was wary. Events like these could go from bad to worse in a society growing increasingly lawless as the government eased its control over the people. He immediately called a friend who had a gun "to help us with this situation," Matveev said. "We didn't know if the bandits would want more money from us – or something else."

The hour was approaching midnight when the phone rang again. The caller said to meet him near the Kosmos Hotel in northwest Moscow to get the documents. Armed with some hockey sticks, a helmet and some other trinkets – the only things they had left that might work as a bribe – Matveev and Konstantinov went to the hotel to make what they hoped would be a quick and uneventful exchange, without the need to use the gun.

The man they met was indeed a fan. He seemed genuinely delighted to meet Konstantinov, and he was thrilled with the hockey gear. So, of course, he held out for an autograph, too. And after CSKA Moscow captain Vladimir Konstantinov scribbled his name, the man returned all the missing documents. There was no mention of the wad of money that also had been in the briefcase.

Immediately, Matveev was on the phone to Lites again to synchronize a new plan. If Communist hardliners somehow gained control, the military surely would seal the borders.

"Just get him out of Russia," Lites said. "Can you get him across the border?"

"I can get him to Budapest," Matveev said.

"I'll meet you in two days. I'll have Mr. Ilitch's plane. I'm going to pick up our immigration lawyer in Washington first, then we'll meet you in Budapest."

The next day, the Konstantinovs and their three-year-old daughter, Anastasia, with Matveev, were on a train rolling toward Hungary. They were in Budapest when Lites arrived, right on schedule. As soon as the plane landed, Lites called the number he was given by Matveev. Lites, the Wings' lawyer and Nick Polano, Lites' longtime sidekick on these covert escapades, were on their way to a hotel. Immediately, the attorney began the paperwork, applying for Konstantinov's work visa in Budapest.

"We had two frantic days in Budapest, with the lawyer and Vladdie going with the family to apply," Lites said. "But these guys, the Washington lawyers who work for Mike Ilitch, they make magic happen. Vladdie has his papers and he was ready to go. His wife and daughter would have to stay two extra days, and they were able to fly over commercially."

The ink was barely dry on the immigration paperwork before Mike Ilitch's plane was in the air, carrying the Wings contingent and their newest world-class asset, Vladimir Konstantinov, to Detroit. At last, Lites could ask the question that had been gnawing at him for weeks. He turned to Matveev. "OK, how'd you do it?"

"I gave the money to six Russian doctors," Matveev said, explaining that three of the doctors were at the cancer clinic where Konstantinov was first diagnosed. The other three, he said, were the Soviet Red Army doctors – and one of them demanded the car. "All of them swore he had an inoperable sarcoma, and he was dying of cancer."

The money (and the car) changed hands, and with the flick of a pen all six doctors lied to a powerful, though crumbling, regime that could have sent them to a gulag forever. Or worse. But Konstantinov got his discharge from the military. He was free to leave his country without being labeled a deserter, a criminal. Lites figured the Wings' total investment in bribes, including the car, was about $100,000, a bargain considering the Soviets were demanding $300,000 in transfer fees – and that was for older players the Russians no longer wanted in their system.

As eager as he was to get to North America to begin his career in Detroit, Konstantinov was an emotional wreck about leaving his family behind, even for a few days. His wife, a native Muscovite and more sophisticated than her hockey-playing husband, understood the delay.

She was grateful for the arrangements the Red Wings had made for her family, especially when Lites put a roll of cash in her hand to pay for two nights in a nice hotel and enjoy a shopping spree while she waited for her Detroit-bound flight.

"That was a major thing for Vladdie, leaving his wife and daughter behind like that," Polano recalled. "He was a real family man."

Konstantinov nevertheless managed to enjoy the plane ride to Detroit. Polano had fallen asleep on the flight back, and when he awoke, somewhere over the Atlantic Ocean, he noticed nearly everyone else was sleeping, too. But when he looked forward to the flight deck, he had to rub his eyes and look again. Sure enough, Konstantinov was in the cockpit, seated at the controls.

"I thought, holy cow!" Polano said. "I can't believe it. He can't be flying the airplane."

He rose, walked to the front and addressed the flight crew. "What's going on? He's not a pilot."

"Mr. Polano, nothing is happening," the captain said. "Everything is on autopilot. He's not hurting anything."

As scheduled, Konstantinov's wife and daughter arrived in Detroit two days later. Konstantinov was already skating with his new teammates, getting ready for a training camp that would launch a memorable career.

In his prime as a barely 5-foot-11, 185-pound defender, Konstantinov quickly established himself as a player who would do anything, sacrificing his body and using every ounce of power in his physical force to help his team. He also had considerable offensive skills, having developed in his formative years as a playmaking center-iceman. He wasn't at all shy about leading a rush out of his own zone, and he had breakaway skills that many forwards would covet.

Konstantinov first appeared on the radars of scouts throughout the NHL at the World Junior Championships in 1987, known widely in international hockey circles as the famous "Punch-up in Piestany" in the former Czechoslovakia, now Slovakia. On the ice, the Soviets and Canadians had a long and notoriously virulent rivalry, and it hit a new low when players on both teams spilled over the boards in a bench-clearing brawl. The three on-ice officials were no match to control 40 players squaring off to throw punches or wrestle an opponent to the ice.

The melee lasted several minutes, and it was brutal at times. It got so out-of-hand that Czech tournament organizers finally ordered the lights to be turned off, throwing the arena into total darkness. At that instant, Konstantinov, the Soviet team captain, was rolling around the ice with Team Canada's captain, Steve Chiasson.

Ironically, just a few years later, Chiasson and Konstantinov were teammates in Detroit – and defense partners. They formed the Wings' top shutdown tandem, always competing against the other teams' best players, in no small part because they both had bona fide mean streaks. They were almost impossible to score against, but as any opposition forward would confess: It's difficult to unleash an accurate shot at the goaltender when you're constantly looking over your shoulder.

Naturally, the NHL media took some creative liberties describing Konstantinov and his style of play, and eventually he seemed to lead the league in nicknames: Vladimir the Terrible, Bad Vlad, Vlad the Impaler, The Vladiator and The Vladinator, a persona he adopted merely by slipping on a pair of stylish eye shades and promising -- like Arnold Schwarzenegger in the "Terminator" movies: "I'll be back."

Opponents, likewise, had their own names for Konstantinov, none of them remotely close to Mr. Congeniality.

At that first training camp in 1991, Konstantinov's recovery from "terminal cancer" may have seemed miraculous. But he wasn't an instant success; he struggled occasionally in his first few months in the NHL. That was quite apparent to his old boss. Gushin, the Red Army GM, happened to visit Detroit that November for a federal court dispute with the Vancouver Canucks over Pavel Bure's Red Army contract. (The Canucks went to court to free Bure from his playing contract with Red Army, arguing that it was signed under duress. The court agreed, and the Russian deal that paid him about $300 a month was torn up. Within a few years, he would be making $8 million a year.)

While in Detroit, Gushin attended a game at Joe Louis Arena in which Konstantinov didn't play very well. When he left the ice following the game, he didn't look so hot either. His face ashen, an ominous shade of green. And as always, he limped like an old man toward the Detroit dressing room. Gushin was standing nearby, and when he got a good look at his former star defenseman, he turned to Matveev and said, "It looks like Vladimir Nikolaevich is still pretty sick."

After he adjusted to life in Detroit and a different brand of hockey in the NHL, however, Konstantinov quickly established himself as one of the most popular Red Wings players. Despite language issues, he also quickly endeared himself to his teammates. None of this, of course, surprised Wings scouts and management, who fell in love with Konstantinov long before that. Murray first saw him play at the World Championships in Finland, when the Wings arranged that midnight rendezvous at the edge of a forest.

"This guy was so competitive. He was running around hitting Canadians, hitting Americans, whoever he was playing against. It didn't matter," Murray recalled. "And every time he came to the bench, he took his sweater off, his shoulder pads off, so obviously he had an injury. But he went right back out and battled again. He competed like crazy. And he had the big smile on his face any time he hit anybody, so you just knew: That's a guy you want on your hockey team if you could get him. He was the ultimate warrior."

In Detroit, Konstantinov was all that – and then some.

"You could tell he was willing to do whatever was necessary to be successful," Murray added. "And obviously it worked out really good for the Red Wings. After a short time, getting to know him and coaching him, I knew that every time I put him on the ice he was going to compete like heck."

That's what his teammates loved about him.

"Vladimir Konstantinov, to me, was the ultimate defenseman," said Gerard Gallant, who was well-established on captain Steve Yzerman's left wing when the young Russians started to blend into the team. Gallant, no stranger himself to hard-nosed hockey, adored the way Konstantinov played the game.

"He was one of the toughest players I ever played with," Gallant said. "Not fighting-wise, but just the way he played the game, the battles, the hitting, finishing checks. He could do it all. He had good puck skills. He could pass the puck, and he joined the rush all the time. He played a very tough game, a physical game. He wasn't cheap, but he could be dirty – and he knew how to back it up.

"He was a guy that every team feared, because when you crossed the blue line he made you pay a price. He definitely changed the way we all thought of Russian hockey players."

Igor Larionov, a former Red Army teammate who later would join Konstantinov in Detroit, put it more succinctly: "Vladimir was a tough sonofabitch. He was always trying to be in your face."

As Konstantinov grew accustomed to his new life in North America, a new side of his personality emerged. He wasn't always the grumpy guy in the room, though he still limped around like a man in his 80s. And perhaps because he had a comrade on the team who spoke his language in Sergei Fedorov, Konstantinov was slower to master a new tongue.

"Vladdie had some trouble with the English language," Gallant recalled, "and we always had fun trying to talk with him. He would more or less just grunt."

What teammates and coaches also deeply admired and respected about Konstantinov was that he had no patience for anyone not trying his hardest, even in practices. And he wasn't shy about letting people know about it – especially those closest to him.

"He would get mad at his own Russian players," Gallant said. "Vladdie was a guy who came to work every day. At practice sometimes, when he'd see the other Russian players slack off a little bit, he was the guy who got in their faces and pushed them really hard. He didn't like that stuff."

Character goes a long way toward making a great hockey club, and Konstantinov had it in spades. His teammates recognized that immediately, and they gravitated toward him. His character was contagious, and because of it the Red Wings were suddenly emerging as one of the NHL's elite teams.

"He was a real outgoing guy and very quickly all the other guys in the room took him under their wing," Murray recalled. "And before long, he was taking them under his wing, too, on the ice. Very definitely Vladimir Konstantinov was a big guy in the room. He made a tremendous difference on our hockey club."

CHAPTER 6

Vyacheslav Kozlov:
New Life in Detroit

In the rear of a luxurious white limousine the likes of which may never have been seen on *Ulitsa Novaya* (New Street) in the modest neighborhood in Russia's "secret city," Slava Kozlov turned to his friend, Alexei Melnyk, and whispered, "The people are going to think Boris Nikolayevich is visiting." They chuckled at the reference to the first president of the Russian Federation, Boris Nikolayevich Yeltsin.

The limo – then the second-longest in all of Moscow, according to Igor, its driver – eventually pulled up in front of a row house not unlike all the others lining both sides of the narrow, potholed street in Voskresensk in November 1994. Kozlov's boyhood home was just a short walk from the local hockey rink, as proud and prominent a welcoming gathering place as any of the city's Orthodox churches. Not far away on the horizon stood some of the city's most formidable structures, the hulking monoliths that produced the chemicals that sustained a way of life in this city and prompted Communist officials to close it off from the rest of the world. (The massive I.V. Stalin Chemical Combine, according to the Center of Ecological Policy of Russia, produced prussic acid, also known as hydrogen cyanide, a colorless, extremely poisonous and flammable liquid that has multiple uses – including chemical warfare. Today, the Russians say, the plant produces agricultural fertilizer.)

Anatoly Kozlov's business in that city was hockey. He was a career coach, an honored profession in Russia. And that fall, his son, Slava, should have been in Detroit, playing hockey at Joe Louis Arena. But because of the NHL's first lockout of its players over a labor dispute, Slava was returning home for a visit and bringing a Western journalist along with him – something that could never have happened just a few years earlier before the collapse of the Soviet Union.

During the league's four-month shutdown, NHL players did a variety of things to keep busy, stay fit, make a buck or promote the game. Two of the league's most prominent former Soviet stars, Igor Larionov of the San Jose Sharks and Slava Fetisov of the New Jersey Devils, organized a team of prominent players from the former USSR who had left to play in the NHL. Now they were returning for a kind of homecoming series of several games played throughout Russia. Larionov secured the financial backing from a Silicon Valley company; Fetisov greased the political skids, arranging for two famous young defectors, Detroit's Sergei Fedorov and Buffalo's Alexander Mogilny, to be received in a ceremony at the Kremlin, where they were presented new Russian passports. That was a much better outcome than could have been expected just a few years earlier, when a Communist regime might have tried them as traitors and sentenced them to long prison terms – if they were lucky.

Slava Kozlov was not among those NHL players invited on the junket. Instead, he returned with little fanfare to Moscow and began working out with the same Central Red Army club he walked away from three years before, the club that sued him in a federal court in Detroit for breach of contract. When Kozlov graciously invited me to his home in Voskresensk to meet his family and show me around one of Russia's preeminent bastions of hockey, I leapt at the chance. I met his parents, Anatoly and Olga, and his grandfather, the patriarch of the family who offered several toasts (*Na zdarovye!*) of fine Russian vodka in emotional tributes to his son, a renowned coach, and his grandson, a rising star in North America. We enjoyed a feast fit for a tsar, with Slava's mother serving plate after plate of Russian delicacies, smoked fish, cheeses, homemade breads and pastries prepared in her tiny kitchen. Between dishes, Anatoly took me into another room in the small house, Slava's former bedroom, to speak privately. He grew rather emotional telling me how proud he was of his son.

"I remember being a little disappointed when our first child was born and it was a girl," Anatoly said. "I was hoping for a son who would one day perhaps follow in my steps. When Slava was born, I wrote a note and sent it to my wife. I said I would carry her in my arms her whole life long for the gift of a son."

Anatoly spoke of how proud he was that Slava was playing in North America, in the best hockey league in the world. He was grateful that his son was so well-received, like the other Russian players, by the people of Detroit. Then he took me by the arm and led me outside on that cold, gray November day. Winter was coming fast, as usual, to this part of Russia. We walked to the side of the two-story house behind a tall fence separating it from the crumbling road. Anatoly – with gestures as much as words – pointed toward a low-lying space between two apple trees. The space wasn't very big, maybe 15-feet-by-10-feet tops. But it was big enough. For when the autumn rains came and the ground froze, they created a smooth little sheet of ice.

Perfect, as Anatoly Kozlov described it when he smiled and said, "Here, right here. This is where Slava learned to skate." I smiled, too, at the thought of a little boy with blades beneath his feet, falling down, getting back up and trying again, laughing at the sheer joy of gliding along on that little patch of frozen rainwater. Soon, the father would hand his son a wooden stick and a black, hard-rubber puck. A whole new world opened to the boy, and his joy grew exponentially. I could see it in my mind's eye.

"Here, right here," I thought to myself standing near that low-lying freezing ground just waiting to cradle a decent rainfall, "a star was born."

Slava Kozlov lay critically injured in a Soviet hospital, somehow clinging to life. Anyone who had seen the twisted wreck that remained of the car he was driving understood that for the Detroit Red Wings' most prized young prospect to still be drawing a breath after surviving the crash was nothing short of a miracle. Kozlov, then 19, had suffered massive head and facial injuries that were so severe it was difficult to even look at him.

"It was impossible to find his eyes, his nose or his mouth on his face. It looked like the moon," said Valery Matveev, who visited Kozlov a few days after the mid-November 1991 accident. Kozlov was Matveev's latest project, hoping to find a way to help deliver another young hockey star to the Red Wings as he had previously with Sergei Fedorov and Vladimir Konstantinov. Suddenly, all bets about Kozlov's once-certain future of NHL stardom were off.

He was in a coma for four hours. He would spend nearly three months in the hospital. But he was alive. His passenger and teammate, Kirill Tarasov, did not survive. The two were in a rush to return from Voskresensk to their Central Red Army hockey club. Their trip covered just 50 miles or so, but along poor roads around Voskresensk funneling into snarling Moscow traffic; it could easily take up to two hours from the Kozlov home to the CSKA rink. Kozlov, an aggressive driver who learned the basics by driving rental cars when Wings executive Nick Polano came to court him, knew the shortcuts on the way back to the rink. That morning, though, his route took him into the path of a bus that had just turned a corner.

Both young men were ejected through the windshield. Kirilov, a defenseman with NHL potential, was pronounced dead at the scene with a broken neck. Kozlov somehow survived. Investigators surmised that his strong hands on the steering wheel helped to catapult him out of his seat before the wheel could crush his chest. The little Lada 2106, which cost Kozlov the equivalent of $500 when new about five months earlier, was beyond recognition. "You could not even tell what kind of car it was before," Matveev said.

One of the most talented young players the Wings had ever scouted, Kozlov became part of NHL history in June 1990, when the Wings selected him with their third-round pick (45th overall) in the NHL Entry draft. At that time, it was the highest a Soviet-born player had been drafted, breaking the record set the previous year when Detroit took Fedorov in the fourth round.

Kozlov was a player general manager Jim Devellano had coveted since first seeing him at a youth tournament in Lake Placid, New York, several years earlier.

"I got on my phone to my ownership, Mike and Marian Ilitch, and I told them, 'I've just seen the best 15-year-old hockey player I've ever seen in my lifetime – and I saw Wayne Gretzkty play at that age,'" Devellano said. "This boy, Kozlov, was fabulous."

Understandably, the Wings were eager to get Kozlov in a uniform as soon as they could. But Kozlov stubbornly resisted Detroit's overtures. He had a pretty good thing going in Russia, and he knew it. At age 15, he was starting to play some games with his hometown's professional club, Khimik Voskresensk. He was that league's rookie of the year in 1990. And cocky, too, he admitted.

"I was a big star in Russia," he said years later. "But I did some stupid mistakes."

He acknowledged not getting along with his Khimik coach, which prompted his decision to play for the Red Army club, where discipline was the cornerstone of the program. It was what he knew he needed. But he also was influenced by the $120,000 CSKA promised to pay him, a factor in his reluctance to leave for the NHL.

Emboldened by the success in getting their other two Soviet draftees out of Russia and into the Detroit lineup, and recognizing Kozlov's enormous potential, the Wings put a full-court press on him even though their scouts were telling him he wasn't quite ready for the NHL. If the Wings managed to get him out, he'd probably need to spend a season or so in the minors before he was ready. At 5-feet-10 and barely 170 pounds at the time, Kozlov was on the small side, his body still maturing. He would need to add about 15 pounds of muscle to withstand the punishment that NHL players endure over an 82-game season.

Nevertheless, six months after they drafted Kozlov, the Wings put together a contingent that, again aboard owner Mike Ilitch's private plane, traveled to Regina, Saskatchewan, for the World Junior Championships. Their group included Jim Lites, Nick Polano and a rather boastful "agent" the Wings hired when Matveev was unable to attend.

"He was going to be my interpreter and introduce me to Kozlov," Lites said. "But this agent guy is all talk. He keeps saying, 'I'm like Don King!' He's crazy. Says he'll negotiate for Kozzie right away and he

(Kozlov) will leave Regina right from there. So, I'm rarin' to go. I lined up a rental car in case he doesn't have the right papers, so we could drive him across the border if we had to. You've got to make sure you do that correctly."

Except for one important thing: Slava Kozlov had no intention of leaving. In fact, at one point he felt like he was being kidnapped. Like all prominent young Soviet players coveted by NHL teams, Kozlov was worried about two kinds of people constantly around their teams: "spies" and "agents."

The spies were the KGB types assigned to all Russian teams that traveled outside the Soviet Union. They collected all the passports on arrival at their destination, and they were responsible for making sure all those players who made the trip returned home again.

"There were always spies traveling with us, and on the other side were the agents," Kozlov said.

The agents were like talent bounty hunters, always with designs on delivering players to their NHL teams and signing them to big contracts that would allow them to collect staggering commissions.

They would always be around the hotel, whispering to players in the elevators, Kozlov said. If they could get a player alone, they would give him gifts, including expensive skates. It was all very pleasant and flattering, though Kozlov knew the limitations.

"It was still the Iron Curtain," he said, "so you didn't know if you were going to leave or you were not going to leave."

The guy who was boastfully certain he could deliver Kozlov to the Wings was Vitali Shevchenko, a brash young entrepreneur. A Ukrainian introduced to the Wings by Matveev, Shevchenko was with Lites and Polano on that trip to Saskatchewan. He had established himself as a credentialed NHL agent when he managed to negotiate a contract with the Vancouver Canucks on behalf of Vladimir Krutov, one of the prominent older Soviet players who were among the first to be released to the NHL. Shevchenko went on to have short but sordid business relationships with several Russian players who wound up suing him. Kozlov was wary of how Shevchenko tried to represent him. But in the agent's defense, Kozlov conceded he led him on a bit.

The two had met in the fall of 1990, when Shevchenko turned up in Voskresensk, telling Kozlov that Detroit wanted him to defect as soon as possible, that the team representatives would be at the world junior tournament and that he could leave from there to the NHL.

"I should have said 'no' right away," Kozlov told a reporter for thehockeywriters.com. "But I just mumbled something pretty vaguely. I kind of let him imagine that it was OK to me."

When the two met again in Saskatchewan, Shevchenko approached Kozlov and told him, "A man from Detroit is waiting for you in the car."

Kozlov panicked. He rushed out of the dressing room, without a wallet, without any documents and, not knowing what else to do, he got into the car.

"Sit down," Shevchenko said, trying to get the young man to relax. "The plane is ready to go."

Now the Wings were nervous.

"We're all prepared to go. We've got everything arranged," Lites recalled. "And all the kid wants to do is drive the rental car. It's literally 30 degrees below zero in Regina. We're there for two days just before Christmas, and it's clear the kid has no intention of leaving right away. He just won't come. He wants to go home to Mom.

"By circumstance, a lot of guys who come through the Russian system are 19 going on 25. Slava was 19 going on 16 when I first met him. He was still a boy, and he wasn't ready to go, emotionally. I always kind of appreciated that about him."

Recalling that moment in the car with the Wings officials in Regina, Kozlov doesn't dispute that perception.

"I wasn't ready to be in such a rush," he confessed. "I said, 'I won't go anywhere. I can't let the team down. I don't even have my passport!'"

Kozlov told the Wings he would defect after the tournament perhaps, or during the summer. The Wings had no choice. As badly as they wanted the player, they weren't about to kidnap him.

"They drove me back to the hotel," Kozlov said, admitting his relief. "I was really afraid for my parents. Russia was still Communist at the time. I thought my father would get fired from his job, and my parents would be persecuted. So I decided I still have time, that I'm not going to defect."

The uncertainty about what the Soviet regime might do to his family, Kozlov said, was the single most important reason he did not leave immediately. It's also why he kept secret what had transpired in Saskatchewan.

"I didn't even tell my parents that I had contact with representatives of Detroit," he said. "At that time, there was very small amount of information about the NHL."

In fact, he didn't even learn he had been selected by Detroit until months after it happened. "That was the situation in our country," he said.

When the world junior tournament ended, with the Soviets winning silver, Kozlov returned home with his teammates. The Wings didn't press the issue, despite what Kozlov had told them earlier. But neither would Polano give up. He met with Kozlov three other times over the next year or so, trying to woo him to Detroit.

"It was always, 'No, no ready yet. No ready. We drive your car now?'" Polano recalled, chuckling. That's how Kozlov's recruitment went. They would hop in Nick's rental car and Slava would drive around and around the block while Polano talked to him about how good life was for a player in the National Hockey League, and how he could drive any kind of car he could imagine with what the Red Wings were willing to pay him.

Instead, Kozlov signed a rather lucrative contract with the Red Army club and bought himself a cheap Lada, which he wrecked after playing just 11 games with CSKA in the fall of 1991. Suddenly, he was on life support in an intensive care unit.

As soon as the Wings heard about the accident, Polano packed his bags and headed to Russia again, intent on offering any support the Red Wings might be able to provide.

On his arrival, he spent some of the club's money in the duty-free shops on gifts for Kozlov's family.

When we met in Moscow for an interview 26 years later, Kozlov still resisted talking about the accident. "I turned that page," he said, adding that there was much he still could not remember about the hours leading up to and immediately after the crash. "I don't want to remember it.

"I know I was very nervous about my career after it happened. What kept me going and helped me to recover the most was the fear of never playing hockey again, because that is the meaning of my life. And the situation with my parents, putting all their hopes on me, that helped me to come out of the situation and recover from the accident and keep moving."

The kindness Polano showed in representing the Red Wings went a long way as well, Kozlov added.

"I remember Nick came and he offered medical help – offered to take me under medical observation in Detroit," he said. "Detroit was really hoping and willing to help me in every way. They weren't going to throw me aside."

It wasn't just talk or moral support, either. Matveev immediately began working on doctors in much the same way he did to secure Vladimir Konstantinov's release from the military. Rather than fake cancer, however, which worked for Konstantinov, the Wings spread around enough cash so that doctors concluded that Kozlov had suffered permanent brain damage and a loss of peripheral vision stemming from head injuries sustained in the crash. It worked.

Over the strenuous objections of military officials, Kozlov ultimately was released from his Red Army enlistment, despite showing clear signs of recovery. Within two weeks of the crash, he could walk around for 15 minutes or so and eat solid food again. Meanwhile, Matveev had hatched a plan to bring Kozlov to Detroit – for purely medical purposes, of course. The Wings arranged for Kozlov to seek the help of medical specialists at Henry Ford Hospital.

"Of course," Polano said with a wry smile, "if we got him to Detroit, he was never going back."

That's about the time Red Army general manager Valery Gushin was beginning to smell a rat. He reacted by transferring Kozlov to a secure Red Army hospital in Moscow for a second opinion that, likely, would dispute the earlier prognosis of a serious brain injury.

"That made real problems for me," Matveev said. "For a couple of days, I couldn't find the way into this hospital." Finally, a connection in the Soviet military provided Matveev a pass – for a fee, of course – and soon he was visiting Kozlov every day. Matveev even managed to get a very nervous Polano to Kozlov's military bedside by bribing an armed guard with 25 rubles (about $2 at the time) and two packs of American cigarettes. "It was so easy," Matveev said.

By then, Kozlov's sizable paychecks from the Red Army hockey club had stopped coming. No longer was he one of the highest-paid players in Russian hockey history. His inability to play because of the accident was just part of it. The club had fallen on hard economic times. It was essentially bankrupt, and it couldn't pay big salaries anymore.

"At that time, for the first time, Slava started thinking of the NHL," Matveev said. "He figured that the Red Army team was just jerking him around."

Eventually, Kozlov turned to Polano and said, "I am ready now." Polano immediately began arranging the necessary travel documents. Though it was still unclear whether Kozlov would ever be able to play again at the elite level required to succeed in the NHL, the Wings were still all in. It was also uncertain whether military doctors could be persuaded to agree with the diagnoses of brain damage by the previous doctors. Matveev found himself in a test of wills with Red Army officials.

"Mr. Gushin believed it would be impossible for me to get the necessary findings that would get Slava his release," Matveev said. "He had promised these doctors they could travel to Western Europe, to Germany and Switzerland with the team at hockey tournaments. But I – well, the Red Wings – gave them lots of money, around $25,000. And I paid cash immediately.

"Gushin couldn't match that. After that, he just gave up. He told everybody it was impossible to compete."

With his release from the military, Kozlov was free to travel to Detroit to see more medical specialists and continue his rehabilitation.

"I am very grateful for Detroit, the leadership of the team, to Mr. Ilitch, that even under the circumstances they invited me to Detroit," Kozlov said. "They still believed in me. They were not afraid, and they still signed me.

"But I wanted to go, first and foremost, for medical reasons. At the time, I could only get the right medical attention overseas – in order to understand whether I will be able to play hockey, or do I need to retire? This was the most important thing. No matter what they (the Soviets) offered me – apartments, cars – there's nothing they could have done to keep me."

Kozlov still faced legal ramifications stemming from the accident.

Criminal charges could have been filed, but the Red Army intervened and pulled some strings on his behalf, Matveev explained. The hockey club could have been culpable, too, because it had allowed a young soldier to have a car and live away from his barracks. And a civil suit against him disappeared when the Red Wings paid an unspecified sum of cash to the Kirilov family.

So Kozlov was released from the hospital in January, and by mid-February he was on his way to Detroit. In fact, the Wings were committed to bringing over Kozlov and his father, Anatoly, at least temporarily, while Slava recovered and adjusted to life in North America. But Anatoly Kozlov was a devoted youth hockey coach who had no intention of interrupting his duties. He understood, however, that Detroit was a better place for his son than Moscow or Voskresensk. Slava Kozlov arrived in Detroit with his new agent, Paul Theofanous, who quickly reached a contract agreement with Lites. Shevchenko was long written out of the picture by all involved after the Saskatchewan fiasco.

Matveev remembered the player's warm reception at Joe Louis Arena. "The Wings were playing San Jose, and we arrived during the game," he said. "Slava met with Mr. Ilitch and Jim Lites in their private box."

Wings coach Bryan Murray, however, wasn't sure what to make of the new kid – hailed as the next great player to hit the NHL.

"It looked like he just got out of his sick bed. He had the damaged face; he was disfigured a little bit," Murray said. "He was frail-looking. Strength-wise, he was a little affected by the accident. Maybe we should have put him in the minors and let him play a little bit, get a little stronger."

But the Wings were in a hurry to build a winning team and Kozlov was in a hurry to play in the NHL. Within a week of his arrival, he was skating in practices with the Wings, and Murray knew one thing right away: No matter how he looked physically, Slava Kozlov had a big heart – and some serious hockey skills. By March, Kozlov was strong enough to make his NHL debut; Murray put him in the lineup in a game at St. Louis. The results were astonishing.

"He had the puck the whole game," Murray said. "I remember

saying to the other coaches, 'We have another Wayne Gretzky here.' This guy looked like he might be a dynamite player in the NHL – which turned out to be the case, although it took him a little while. I don't know if anybody is ever going to be another Wayne Gretzky, point-wise, but Slava sure had the ability to get points."

In that first game in St. Louis, Kozlov registered two assists on goals by Sergei Fedorov. With Vladimir Konstantinov on the blue line, the Russian Five was 60 percent complete. Two weeks later, however, Slava Kozlov's NHL career in Detroit was in doubt again. The Red Army hockey club re-staked its claim to Kozlov in a lawsuit filed in U.S. District Court in Detroit, arguing that the Wings had interfered with a long-term contract Kozlov had signed with Red Army. Once again, the Red Wings threw every available resource at Kozlov's defense.

"The story got real complicated," Lites said. "We got an injunction immediately to stop the Russians from stopping him from playing in the NHL."

The courts allowed Kozlov to continue to play while the legalities proceeded.

That case was heard by U.S. District Judge Gerald Rosen, who had been appointed to the federal bench in 1990, and the way he presided over the case made the Wings feel as though they had anything but "home-ice advantage" in the trial.

"He was a mean little bugger," Lites said of the judge. "The Russians had nothing really in their lawsuit other than that these people from Detroit are rich and they're a poor country losing their players. They used money as their argument. But he (Rosen) seemed convinced that the Detroit Red Wings were the evil empire and we had done all these things to get these Russian players over here. . . and of course we did."

It was worrisome and costly. Lites testified for three full days. Kozlov also took the witness stand for hours, telling the court through an interpreter that he went into the army in May 1991, signed his playing contract under duress in August and didn't get paid until November, shortly before his auto accident. He said he signed the contract because he was still a soldier, and if he didn't he wouldn't be able to get the exposure that could lead to an NHL career.

"It cost us a couple hundred grand in attorneys' fees," Lites said. "But basically, the judge couldn't really find a reason why this player shouldn't be playing for the Detroit Red Wings."

Eventually, however, the case ended without a ruling. After a week of testimony, the Russians said they planned to return a week later to present more testimony, Lites said. But the American attorneys representing the Russians never got paid, so they asked to be relieved of their obligation.

"The Russians had promised these lawyers all kinds of dough, but the Russian Hockey Federation was broke," Lites said. "They didn't have the money to prosecute this lawsuit. And basically, we had big-time lawyers. We were paying. They were greased. And the case just literally went away."

With that, Lites brushed his hands together like a dealer at a Vegas blackjack table getting ready to take a break. And the punchline, he added with a sardonic laugh: The American lawyers who had sued the Wings on behalf of the Russians approached Lites and the Wings' attorneys wondering if they knew any lawyers in Moscow who could represent them in a lawsuit to recover their legal fees in the Russian courts.

Gushin had a different version of the events. The Russians dropped their suit, he said, "after I decided it was unwinnable."

Finally and completely free to pursue his career on his terms, Kozlov went on to play nearly 1,200 NHL games, scoring 356 goals among 853 points. But success wasn't as immediate as Murray had suspected after watching him in that first game in St. Louis. Those two assists against the Blues were his only points in seven games. The next season he spent mostly with Detroit's top minor-league affiliate, Adirondack, in Glens Falls, New York. By his third professional season, however, Kozlov had established himself as one of his team's most productive players on the league's most powerful offensive team. He also developed a reputation for scoring important goals at crucial moments. He was a clutch player.

But as good as he was, we were all left to wonder how much better Kozlov could have been. The car crash took a lot out of him, he admitted.

"Could I have played better?" he said, repeating my question. "I think yes. But the car accident, it changed my life. After that, I don't care about being a star or scoring goals. I just play hockey."

The Wings thought so, too.

"He never turned into a superstar," Devellano said, "but he was a real good, above-average NHL player. And I think one of the reasons he didn't turn into a superstar was the car accident. It might have had more than a little of an effect."

Off the ice, Kozlov, like Vladimir Konstantinov, was among the quietest of Detroit's players. While Konstantinov was known as more of a prankster with a sharp sense of humor, Kozlov was known as a grump among his North American teammates. He didn't go out of his way to learn English because he figured he didn't have to. Growing up in the Soviet Union, he said, students were told they didn't need to learn another language because soon everyone in the world would be speaking Russian. When he got to Detroit, he still didn't bother.

"At first I didn't learn any English because my theory was that if people wanted to talk to me, they would learn Russian," he said. "But after two years, nobody started learning Russian, so after that the team hired a teacher for me. But English was very difficult for me. I am not good at other languages."

When Kozlov spent more than two hours on camera for a documentary film on Detroit's Russian Five, he preferred to conduct his interview in Russian. By then, in December 2015, he had been back in Russia for five years. Asked why people in Detroit described him as perhaps the most Russian of the Russian Five, Kozlov paused to give it some thought.

Then, in perfect English, he responded: "I think it was because I speak the worst English of the Russian Five."

With Kozlov's departure, Red Army had lost three of its best young players to the Red Wings in less than three years. The last vestiges of the Iron Curtain were gone. Eventually, the Russians did little to stem the exodus of its best and brightest players to North America – but they learned to negotiate stiff transfer fees that would enable them to keep developing world-class players. Within a few more years – when the players were locked out in the fall of 1994 – there were 84 former

Soviets playing in the National Hockey League. And when many of them returned for that homecoming series that fall of 1994, it was clear they were returning to something different from what they had left.

"We are glad to welcome them all back into Russia," said Oleg Soskevets, the First Deputy Chairman of the Government of the Russian Federation. "The past is forgotten. They came to an absolutely new country, to an absolutely new society. This is very important to understand."

Certainly the Red Army Club rolled out the red carpet for Kozlov, then 22, when he returned that fall. Team officials met him at the airport with a car and driver and whisked him off to a plush military hotel where he was free to stay during the five weeks he planned to be in Russia. The once-powerful club, then struggling at the bottom of the league standings, even paid all Kozlov's expenses, including the insurance premium to protect him against injury.

Red Army was thrilled to have him in the lineup. "If we had a couple more guys like Slava, we would win the league championships, for sure," said Vladimir Popov, an assistant to Soviet coach Viktor Tikhonov. "Also, it's important for our young guys to see him come back and play hard like he does. He's in great condition, and our guys are practicing more seriously since he arrived."

Gushin had misplayed his hand on all three players who wound up in Detroit. But he harbored no resentment toward them, either. In fact, it was clear how partial he was to Kozlov by the framed Upper Deck hockey card of Kozlov sitting on his desk. Gushin was still angry with the Wings, and during a wide-ranging interview accused them of trying to steal even more of his players. But the mere mention of Kozlov's name brought a warm smile to his face.

"He is a good boy," Gushin said.

CHAPTER 7

Lost in Translation

By the fall of 1994, the Russians were willing to forgive – and even forget. Barely five years after two of their most prominent young stars, Sergei Fedorov and Alexander Mogilny, defected, they were welcomed home with open arms. But they were nervous. Fedorov worried about repercussions, that somehow he might never be able to leave the country after walking away from his Soviet team in 1990. Mogilny faced potentially more serious punishment. He was a soldier in the Soviet Red Army, when he defected to Buffalo. Technically, he was a traitor; he could have been shot. But the Soviet Union didn't exist anymore. In the new Russia both young men were embraced as favorite sons – now that they were bringing fame and honor to the motherland as star players in North America.

They owed their warm homecoming to former Soviet national team captain Slava Fetisov and his considerable political influence. Fetisov and Red Army teammate Igor Larionov assembled a team of Soviet players who had left to play in the NHL. The group played a series of games to exuberant, sold-out crowds throughout Russia during the NHL's first player lockout. During their three-week series, Fedorov and Mogilny received their Russian passports in a ceremony at the Kremlin. They were no longer men without a country.

Relations between Red Army and the Detroit Red Wings, however, were worse than ever.

"I've tried to connect with the Red Wings many times, but they don't want to discuss it," Valery Gushin, Red Army general manager, said during a rant in his office when I visited the CSKA headquarters in November 1994. A bear of a man with blanket of silver hair over a face that was never difficult to read, the man who oversaw one of the most powerful and prolific hockey programs in the world was in a sour mood. He blamed Red Wings billionaire owner Mike Ilitch for raiding his program of its young talent.

After the Wings spirited away Sergei Fedorov, Vladimir Konstantinov and Slava Kozlov without the Russian Ice Hockey Federation receiving a dime and, more importantly, without the federation's permission, Detroit also signed and imported three other young Red Army players: defensemen Yan Golubovsky, Igor Malykhin and Dmitri Motkov. Again, the Wings didn't pay the Russians a cent in transfer fees.

"It really surprised me that such a rich person tells his employees to steal Russian players," Gushin said. "I don't understand that."

Jim Lites, the former Wings' executive vice president, orchestrated or oversaw every one of those clandestine deals. He scoffed at the notion that his club never tried to negotiate with the Russians. Lites and Gushin had been sparring since February 1990, when they first met over dinner and drinks at a Montreal hotel. A few months earlier, Lites had met with Fedorov in a Chicago hotel room and when they parted Lites had a strong feeling that Fedorov would be playing in Detroit soon.

"By then we had a good situation regarding contacting our Russian players," Lites said. "It had almost become kind of second nature, the feeling that the Russians would be coming. Exactly when was still unknown. So, I set up a meeting with the GM of the Red Army club and the head of the Russian Hockey Federation, Mr. Gushin. I was hedging my bets to see if I could just buy the player directly. So I had a very brusque, not-friendly meeting with this very severe Russian gentleman."

Gushin spoke as much English as Lites spoke Russian, so an interpreter translated their curt conversation.

"We are the Detroit Red Wings and we believe our Russian players are eventually going to play for us," Lites told Gushin. "So we are happy to pay you $35,000 for Sergei Fedorov to come out."

Gushin bristled. "No player is going to leave for that paltry sum," he responded. "It would have to be $300,000 for that player."

"Done," Lites said. "$300,000 it is."

"Oh, no, no," Gushin said. "You don't understand. Fedorov won't come out until he's 30. *Then* it will be $300,000."

"No, you don't understand," Lites said. "If you let Fedorov come out in the next few months, we will pay the federation $300,000."

"No. Never!" Gushin fumed. "This player will never play for you!"

In retrospect, Lites seemed amused by his attempts to bargain with the man.

"I had a relatively comic relationship with Mr. Gushin," Lites said. "It was repeated again and again. But at that time, he was very confident – downright cocky."

Russian players of significance would never leave, Gushin insisted. Alexander Mogilny's defection to Buffalo, he said, was an aberration that would not happen again. Lites gave up and turned on the charm.

"Well, we're going to always play by the rules," Lites said as politely as he could muster. "That's why I'm here."

Then he smiled like a fox leaving the henhouse.

"It was a head-fake," Lites said of that meeting, "because I had no intention of playing by the rules."

Lites left the meeting with Gushin more resolved than ever to bring Fedorov to Detroit – on Detroit's terms. And he did.

Fedorov left his Russian teammates at the Goodwill Games in the Pacific Northwest in August 1990, and a few months later he was playing for the Red Wings. When Fedorov's former Red Army team played a game in Detroit the following December, the Wings turned their attention to finding a way to get defenseman Vladimir Konstantinov in a Detroit uniform, meaning they were prepared to do whatever necessary to orchestrate another clandestine escape.

By then, of course, Lites had several balls in the air regarding Konstantinov. Valery Matveev, the agent and operative, had a plan to free Konstantinov from his military obligation, which would make it easier for him to leave the country without being labeled a deserter and a criminal. Michel Ponomarev, the Montreal photographer, was working another angle, trying to work with Gushin to negotiate a financial agreement.

While Red Army was in Detroit for a Super Series game against the Wings in December 1990, Gushin stopped by Lites' office at Joe Louis Arena. He demanded a $300,000 payment for Fedorov, who had defected four months earlier. Lites remained polite, but explained how that ship had sailed. The Wings had made that offer and the Russians passed. In the meantime, the Detroit club had paid a lot of money to Ponomarev, along with lawyers and other expenses, to free Fedorov. Gushin left the meeting angry, his face reddened and the veins on his nose flared. He needed a drink.

The following fall, Konstantinov had joined the Wings after faking cancer to win his freedom from his military contract. And Gushin – in Detroit to argue a federal lawsuit to settle a dispute with the Vancouver Canucks over Pavel Bure's contract – was back to see Lites again. By then the Wings were working to bring over Slava Kozlov, their third-round selection in 1990 who was recovering from serious injuries in the auto crash that killed his teammate.

"So Gushin shows up in my office and says, 'I want to get paid for Konstantinov,'" Lites told me. "He wanted $300,000 again. And again, I have another ridiculous conversation with him."

Now Lites was getting angry; he was done being polite. "Would you also like us to pay for Fedorov, too?" he asked Gushin, trying to stifle a sarcastic laugh. "That's not going to happen. We're only interested now in Kozlov. I will pay you for Kozlov right now, today, $300,000. If you don't take the money I'm never going to pay you – and he's going to be out. Those other two players are already out, playing in the National Hockey League. And this player (Kozlov) is going to play for us, too."

Gushin stiffened.

"Oh, he's injured. He will never come!" Gushin said as he rose to leave, storming out of Lites' office.

"Same conversation every time," Lites said. "Gushin was in Neverland."

Lites was right about Kozlov, who was in Detroit by the spring of 1991 without the Russians ever getting one American cent for his playing rights.

———※———

Emboldened by their success, the Red Wings kept drafting Russian players and bringing them over. Dimitri Motkov was selected in the fifth round (98th overall) in the 1991 draft. Igor Malykhin was taken in the seventh round (142nd overall) that year as well. Neither played a game in the NHL. The Wings took Yan Golubovsky in the first round (23rd overall) in 1994, and signed him to an NHL contract less than two months later.

That signing set Gushin into a rage. He instituted criminal charges against Golubovsky, who the Russians said was a private in the Red Army. During my visit to his office in 1994, Gushin slid a thick file across his desk toward me. In it were myriad official-looking papers showing copies of Golubovsky's military passport and his contract with the Red Army hockey club. They also included a warrant charging the player with desertion, a crime punishable by imprisonment up to five years. There was one document in English, the draft of a letter to the federal officials in the United States. Altogether, the documents appeared to suggest young Yan Golubovsky was in big trouble back home.

"Now it is bad situation for Golubovsky," Gushin said grimly. "Perhaps we can have him arrested in the United States. We're looking into that. Our minister of foreign affairs suggests to send this official letter to the U.S. government, asking them to send back Golubovsky as a deserter."

He also was threatening to sue the Red Wings in a U.S. court, but he was also willing "to help Golubovsky." If the player returned, Gushin said, "he will be welcomed back, friendly, with no problems."

Again, the Red Wings told a different story. Golubovsky, then 18, told Ken Holland, then the Red Army assistant general manager with the Wings, that the Red Army hockey club promised to waive Golubovsky's mandatory military service that all able-bodied young men in Russian were required to serve at the time. Gushin's file showed documents that Golubovsky's hitch began the previous April 4th.

The Wings signed Golubovsky to a contract a few minutes before midnight on August 14, a deal that included a $260,000 signing bonus. Then they took him to Detroit following the Four Nations junior tournament in Sweden in September, assigning the player to their top minor-league affiliate. Gushin produced a two-year contract Golubovsky signed it and initialed it in several places, on August 28. That contract would have paid the player between $700 and $1,000 a month, the higher amount when he competed with the national team or in tournaments abroad.

When Holland saw a copy of the Red Army contract signed two weeks after Golubovsky signed his deal with Detroit, he took the player aside demanding an explanation.

"You're signing contracts all over the place," Holland said. "What about the Red Army contract?"

Golubovsky, who spoke little English at the time, put a finger to his head as though it were a gun.

"He signed it under duress," Holland said. "As soon as they found out he had a contract with us, they put him in a room with Gushin and Tikhonov and made him sign the Red Army contract."

Viktor Tikhonov was the Red Army coach. He and Gushin also signed that contract.

Gushin dismissed the allegation that Golubovsky was coerced into signing the papers. The Soviets may have been guilty of that in another era, he acknowledged, but the times were different in the handful of years since *glasnost* and *perestroika*.

"There is a big difference now," Gushin said, leaning back in his chair in his sterile, cramped office at the Red Army sports complex headquarters. "We are a more open country. Detroit feels this is the same situation as before, when the Soviet Union was a closed country. But now we are not."

The Russians and the Red Wings appealed to the NHL to intervene, but nothing changed. Golubovsky spent the next six seasons in the Detroit organization, most of them in the minors. He played just 50 games in the NHL for the Wings, with one goal among six points, and six more games for Florida, contributing two assists, before his NHL career was finished.

Gushin argued that Golubovsky wasn't ready for professional hockey in North America, that he was too young and needed further development with the Red Army team. Perhaps he was right. There was a pride factor, too, Gushin stressed. The Russians wanted their players to perform at a certain level in the NHL. Anything less was a poor reflection on the Russian system. Absent the anger that surfaces when he spoke of NHL teams pirating his players, Gushin could be warm and affable. And what he said about developing players to perform at the highest level made sense.

"We are ready to send our players to the NHL – but when they are ready," Gushin said. "The important thing is that they show the traditional skills of Russian hockey in the NHL, like our best players there do now."

Spiriting Golubovsky away a few months after he was drafted, Gushin said, "makes no sense because he is not ready to play for the Detroit Red Wings. Detroit is a very good team right now, and it is not necessary to use him there immediately. He is not even ready for [the minors]. He is not strong enough. We had hoped to keep him here for one more season with Red Army and then he would be much more prepared for the NHL."

In the meantime, Gushin said, the Red Wings owed the Russians, by his count, nearly $2 million in developmental fees for all the players they drafted and imported from Red Army.

"They've stolen Sergei Fedorov, Vladimir Konstantinov, Slava Kozlov, Dmitri Motkov, Igor Malykhin and Yan Golubovsky, and they haven't paid us one dollar," Gushin fumed.

Jim Lites just shrugged it off. More than 25 years later, he repeated what he said then: "It's not like we didn't try."

CHAPTER 8

The Man with the Diamond Knuckles

From the moment Mike Ilitch hired him away from the New York Islanders at the peak of the club's dynasty in 1982, Jim Devellano was his most trusted adviser and confidant. But eleven years later, after five coaches, two front-office regimes and several colossal playoff disappointments, Ilitch was losing patience. He was intent on replacing Bryan Murray as coach and general manager with a guy of rather dubious reputation around the NHL. Devellano, knowing he was on thin ice as well after losing his general manager's job to Murray a few years earlier, was intent on stopping Ilitch from making a move he felt would be disastrous for the Detroit Red Wings. In an alliance with Jim Lites that would have far-reaching consequences for the organization and ultimately divide a close-knit family, the two men stood up to Ilitch trying to save the club from certain devastation if the owner followed through with a move he was orchestrating behind the backs of his team's senior management.

"Bryan got us close with some real good teams, but Mike Ilitch didn't think we could win with him," Devellano explained during a conversation in his office in the bowels of Joe Louis Arena, surrounded by 3½ decades worth of Wings photos and memorabilia. "That's when he started talking to Mike Keenan, and when we found out about it, Jimmy Lites and I just about had a fit. I mean, let's be honest, everywhere Keenan went he was out after three years at the most, and it was never very nice."

To Mike Ilitch in 1993, "Iron Mike" Keenan had that knack for turning teams around quickly and winning wherever he went, especially early in his career. But Keenan was also one of the most polarizing men in the NHL, which explains why his career resume includes assignments with eight NHL teams as either coach or general manager – and sometimes both portfolios at once. His teams in Philadelphia, Chicago and New York early in his career won a lot of games. But he was fired by Philadelphia in 1988 after taking the team to the Stanley Cup finals in 1987. He lost a power struggle in Chicago after leading the Blackhawks to the finals in 1992. He won a Stanley Cup in his only season with the New York Rangers, then abruptly resigned, citing a violation of his contract. It was a failed power-grab; he wanted general manager Neil Smith's job, too. After leaving New York, Keenan went to St. Louis as coach and GM for three seasons, ultimately alienating his biggest star, Brett Hull. Then it was on to Vancouver for two seasons, where he couldn't get along with his top player and captain Trevor Linden.

After a one-year coaching stint in Boston, Keenan moved to Florida as general manager (and sometimes coach) and eventually lost a power struggle with his good friend and coach, Jacques Martin, who succeeded Keenan as GM. Keenan lasted two years on the bench in Calgary, concluding his NHL work in 2009. He signed on in 2013 as coach in Russia's Kontinental Hockey League, leading Mettallurg Magnitogorsk to the league championship and the Gagarin Cup. He was the first North American coach to win the KHL championship and remains the only coach to win both the Gagarin Cup and the Stanley Cup. Magnitogorsk, however, fired Keenan in October 2015.

Despite Keenan's checkered history, Mike Ilitch was undeterred. Devellano and Lites, however, stood their ground and the confrontation turned ugly.

"Then who do you want to bring in as coach?" Ilitch snapped. "It's obvious Bryan Murray can't do it."

Put on the spot by his boss, Devellano felt grateful to have an immediate response.

"This team needs one of two guys, and both are available," he said. "We want Al Arbour or Scotty Bowman. Which one would you prefer?"

Arbour, then 60, played defense for the Red Wings in the mid-1950s, but not on any of the four Stanley Cup winners for Detroit. He did win Cups playing for Chicago and Toronto. Then he enjoyed a legendary coaching career with the New York Islanders. He was behind the bench for their four straight Stanley Cup titles that ended in 1983. Bowman never made it to the NHL as a player; a serious head injury sustained when he was playing in the minors ended those aspirations. But he went on to enjoy an unparalleled career as a coach, winning four straight Stanley Cup titles with Montreal from 1976-79, the first four of 14 Cup rings he would add to an incomparable jewelry collection.

Having a choice of two of the most successful coaches in the history of the league seemed to catch Ilitch off guard. He didn't offer a preference.

"Either one," he growled. "Just make sure you get one of them."

The only way he could save his job as senior vice president, Devellano was certain, was to hire one of those two men. But he had a delicate dilemma on his hands regarding Murray, who had been hearing the rumors about Keenan, too.

"Bryan had succeeded me as general manager, and now I'm charged with bringing in his replacement," Devellano said. "So, I went and had a talk with him in deep confidence. I said, 'Look, Bryan, the owner doesn't want you to coach anymore, but he's prepared to keep you as GM if we find another coach. Now it's up to me to go get either Al Arbour or Scotty Bowman, and I believe you can work with either one of them.' Well, as it turned out I was wrong about that."

Devellano knew he couldn't go wrong with either coach, but he approached Arbour first, figuring he was not only a perfect match for the Detroit roster but he'd fit in better with the management team. Arbour was tempted, but before the conversation got serious he politely declined and stayed as the Islanders' coach. So Devellano turned to Bowman, who had spent the previous two seasons as coach in Pittsburgh, leading the Penguins to a second straight Stanley Cup title the season before. Bowman was unquestionably the best coach in the history of the sport. He was available, and money wouldn't be an issue. It never was when Mike Ilitch was hiring coaches. The Wings were fully prepared to outbid the Penguins for Bowman's services, but they worried he would want some control over personnel decisions. They weren't prepared to meet that demand because they were keeping Murray on as GM. In the end, Bowman came to Detroit, as coach, for $1 million a season. Ilitch's courtship with Keenan was over.

Montreal-born William Scott (Scotty) Bowman was 59 years old and already very much a legend when he took the Red Wings' job in 1993. He had seven Stanley Cup rings in his collection by then, and two years earlier he had been inducted into the Hockey Hall of Fame. With his receding hairline, dark eyes, pronounced jaw and prominent chin, he looked like a man equally comfortable running a construction site or as foreman on an auto assembly line. He was all business all the time. When he walked, Bowman listed a little to the left, a condition caused by bad knees – a common affliction among former hockey players. But he skated every day with his team. By most accounts, despite a personality that made him the proverbial riddle wrapped in a mystery inside an enigma, Bowman was a coach's coach, and a man's man.

His first season in Detroit wasn't exactly a resounding success, however. His team finished first in its division, but ended the regular season with one fewer victory, two more losses and three points fewer than the club Murray coached the season before. Worse, Bowman's first trip to the playoffs ended in perhaps the worst in a series of horrible playoff failures. His top-seeded Wings lost in the first round to eighth-seeded San Jose, a team led by Igor Larionov. The ending was devastating for a franchise widely predicted to win its first Stanley Cup since 1955. But when the dust settled after another disheartening finish, it was the GM, Murray, who took the fall. He was fired, and Ilitch agreed to give Bowman power over the team's personnel, the authority to shape the lineup as he felt he needed to finally bring a championship to Detroit.

So Bowman became part of a unique management trinity; Devellano would remain as senior vice president, Bowman was now coach and director of player personnel and Ken Holland was elevated from chief scout to assistant general manager on a team without a designated general manager. While Bowman was moving around his chess pieces on the Detroit bench, Holland began a serious apprenticeship under Devellano, learning how to run a franchise, negotiate contracts, prepare for a draft, deal with the media, build relationships with other managers around the league and the multitude of responsibilities that went into running a professional hockey franchise.

Giving Bowman keys to the managerial kingdom was a dicey proposition, and Devellano knew it. While his coaching credentials were beyond doubt, Bowman had struggled in seven seasons as general manager in Buffalo, which included three different stints as coach. From 1979-80 until Bowman was fired twelve games into his eighth season, the Sabres trended downward in the standings. They won just two playoff rounds in his final six full seasons with Buffalo.

"When Scotty wanted manager powers, I told Mike [Ilitch], 'Give him some range, but be ready to veto him. Let's let him pick the pieces he needs,'" Devellano said. "Then I held my breath."

The three-headed managerial monster worked fine from the outset, largely because the NHL had locked its players out in a contract dispute for the first three months of the 1994-95 season. Many players used that time to stay in shape by holding a series of exhibition games around their cities.

But Igor Larionov and Slava Fetisov had grander plans, orchestrating that series of games in Russia during which Sergei Fedorov was welcomed home as a favorite son. Fedorov was rendered nearly speechless when he tried to discuss it. "Lots of feelings right now, so many things have happened," he said. "I'd like to just sit down and be able to think about it once or twice. It's impossible to say right now. It's just unbelievable."

Russian hockey fans are as passionate about their game as Canadians and Americans in certain NHL cities, and the games featuring their players who had left to play in the NHL were well-received. They raved about being able to witness something they thought they would never see again when the renowned Green Line was reunited. Igor Larionov at center between wingers Vladimir Krutov and Sergei Makarov with Slava Fetisov and Alexei Kasatonov on defense, universally proclaimed to be the best five-man unit in hockey history.

"It was excellent," Larionov said after inviting me into the NHL stars' dressing room after one game. "We had a chance to come together again for the Russian people to see all the best players on one team."

The series ended with a finale played between the Central Red Army club and the Russian NHL-ers at Moscow's Luzhniki Sports Arena in front of about 8,000 fans, including Yeltsin, sitting in a small, open box above the last row, where he was close enough to fans to be able to reach out and high-five them when someone scored a goal. The only NHL player competing for Red Army that night was Detroit's Slava Kozlov, who had felt snubbed by the organizers of the series. He badly wanted to be on the winning side that night, but he could not disagree with his friend, Larionov, about the quality of talent on the other team after the NHL Russians hung on for a thrilling 6-5 victory.

"If we stayed here, Russia would be the best in the world, no question," Kozlov said. "Nobody would beat us."

Vladimir Konstantinov did not take part in that Russian tour. He had a family to feed and wasn't on a huge NHL contract. Instead, he signed a short-term deal with Wedemark, in Germany, where he averaged two points a game until he returned to Detroit for the start of the NHL's abbreviated 48-game regular season. While his three young Russians were developing nicely, Bowman felt they could be even better with a little tinkering. And that tinkering started after the Russians returned. Fetisov, then 36, had not yet re-signed with the New Jersey Devils, and it seemed as though they were almost encouraging him to retire. The Devils were among the best teams in the Eastern Conference, thanks to some serious depth on their blue line. But Fetisov had no trouble keeping up with all the talent in the homecoming series in Russia, and I couldn't help mentioning it to Bowman on my return to Detroit.

"Scotty, if you still feel like your team needs some help on defense," I told him, "it looked to me from those games over in Russia that Slava Fetisov still has a lot left in those legs."

Bowman didn't say anything, but he gave me a look that suggested it was something worth thinking about it.

"Don't take my word for it," I added. "Talk to Sergei. He could certainly give you a more accurate scouting report than I could."

My thinking at the time was that if the Wings could get him at a decent price, Fetisov would be a good fit in Detroit, which throughout the previous decade had become a destination for prominent-but-aging defensemen to play a season or two before retiring. They included Brad Park, Dave Lewis, Borje Salming, Mark Howe, Mike Ramsey and Brad Marsh, among others.

Fetisov eventually re-signed with New Jersey. Then, as spring 1995 approached, he found himself watching more from the press box than playing. Bowman, meantime, had done his due diligence, including talking to Fedorov about Fetisov. So did Ken Holland.

"Would you, or would you not?" Holland asked Fedorov about making a trade for Fetisov.

"Absolutely. It would be great for our team," Fedorov responded.

"A five-second conversation," he recalled years later. "Simple as that."

As old as Fetisov was, though, and as limited as his playing time had become, he wouldn't come cheaply, and the debate over a potential trade caused some chafing in the front-office when Bowman first mentioned it.

"But, Scotty, he's on his last legs," Devellano said, "and they want way too much for him."

"Why did you bring me in here?" Bowman roared back. "Do you want to win, or don't you?"

Ilitch and Devellano acquiesced. Bowman got his way and made the deal.

"We gave up a pretty high draft pick for a guy who had been a healthy scratch in New Jersey," Devellano recalled. "It didn't make a lot of sense to me at the time. A third-round pick for Fetisov? I don't think so. But I was thinking more long-term, and of course Scotty was there doing what he thought he needed to do to win now."

For Bowman, it was an absurdly easy decision.

"It was tough to get good players, so I made the call," he said. "We were short on defense, and it made sense to do it."

Though Fetisov would turn 37 just 17 days after the April 3 trade, the deal helped immensely.

"It was certainly easy to play defense with him," Fedorov said. "He would not throw the puck around the glass. He would always find you. Slava brought to our team stability – and a lot of experience on the defensive end, where we had a little trouble."

With Fetisov logging crucial minutes and playing his best hockey in years, the Wings dominated the lockout-shortened season, finishing atop the league standings with 33 victories and 70 points in 48 games. Then they rolled through three best-of-seven rounds of the Stanley Cup playoffs with a 12-2 record by beating Dallas in the first round (4-1), sweeping San Jose in the second (4-0), and eliminating Chicago in the Western Conference finals (4-1) in a thrilling series that included three overtime victories, two of them in double overtime. Slava Kozlov's goal in the second overtime of Game 5 sent Detroit to the Stanley Cup Finals for the first time since 1966.

As fans were planning for the first Stanley Cup celebration in 40 years, the Wings were soundly and decisively swept by Fetisov's former New Jersey club. In a postgame news conference near the end of the series, Bowman said he was embarrassed by the way his team competed. As good as the Wings were, they weren't nearly good enough, obviously. Bowman knew he still had more work to do on his roster – and Fetisov had some ideas of his own. He wanted the Wings to acquire one more Soviet player, and he began planting some seeds.

"He was quite a guy," Bowman said of Fetisov. "He was a very friendly guy, and he was always talking about his buddy, Igor Larionov."

Bowman liked Larionov a lot, especially since the ill-fated 1994 playoffs, when Larionov centered a five-man unit that included four Europeans who helped the San Jose Sharks upset his Wings in the opening round. So he made the call to Sharks GM Dean Lombardi and learned that Larionov could be available, but again the price would be high. San Jose wanted Ray Sheppard, one of the leading goal-scorers in the NHL and a cornerstone of Detroit's high-scoring offense. When Bowman mentioned this to Devellano and Holland, there was more than a little friction again among the Wings' management team.

Sheppard was in the prime of his career at age 29 when Bowman decided he wanted to trade him for another aging Russian. After scoring 52 goals in the 1993-94 season, Sheppard scored 30 more in 43 games lockout-shortened season that followed. That's a 57-goal pace over a full NHL season. Now he was trade bait? For a Russian who had scored four goals in the lockout season and never more than 21 in his first four full NHL seasons?

"When Scotty first mentioned it, I thought he might have lost his marbles," Devellano said. "I mean, 50-goal-scorers don't grow on trees in this league. It's just hard to dismiss players who score goals like that, and when you look at how fucking old Larionov was at the time, you see his points. It just didn't make a lot of sense. We brought Scotty in to coach our team, and now he's trading away 50-goal scorers."

By then, however, Bowman had made up his mind – thanks in no small part to some gentle arm-twisting by Fetisov.

"Slava was a big supporter of the Russian system," Bowman said, "and when I mentioned it to him before we made the trade he said, 'You know, we would have five then, and if you ever want to, you could play them together.' He was really pushing to make the deal."

Devellano didn't acquiesce so easily this time. He met with Holland and Ilitch, and they discussed it at length.

"We didn't like it," Devellano said, "but eventually we knew we'd have to give our blessing."

On October 24, 1995, Bowman consummated the deal for the team's fifth, and arguably most important, Soviet-bred player, Igor Larionov. Fedorov was stunned when he heard the news. And overjoyed.

"Having already four guys, it was incredible. Now we're getting Igor, too?" Fedorov remembered thinking, "What's gonna happen now? Who's going to play with whom? I was like a kid in a candy store. You have mentors in your career, your friends who taught you, who show you the way for four years with Red Army – and now I am playing with them again on the same NHL team? It was unheard of, a mind-blowing thought."

Though Larionov would turn 35 in early December, the move proved to have resounding repercussions around the league. One of the NHL's most talented teams was suddenly trading assets to acquire old Russians. It seemed puzzling to many who wondered what Bowman and the Wings were up to with what seemed like a grand experiment.

"I didn't think about it much at the time of the trade," Bowman said of putting the finishing touches on what would be a game-changing five-man Russian unit. "I just more or less knew that he would be a better fit for our team. We had a surplus of right wingers at the time, and when we got Igor it just made sense to try them together."

"I've got to give the old bugger credit," Devellano said. "Scotty had been coaching so long, including those Team Canada clubs against the Soviets. He knew they were good players, and if there's one thing Scotty loved it was good players."

Typical of most coaches, Bowman also liked veteran players. He knew what to expect from them in critical moments of a game. More importantly, the right veterans could have a valuable influence on younger players. This is where Bowman saw the greatest value in Larionov.

"Fedorov and Kozlov were good young players," Devellano said. "Scotty knew Sergei was great, but he was a little frustrated by him. He was smart enough to know that Larionov was an older veteran who could come in and help bring those two young guys along. He knew the Russians were different. He couldn't always get the younger Russians to do what he needed them to do, so he brought in Fetisov and Larionov – to help coach them.

"He thought those guys would be good with the other Russians, and he was right. He wanted a motivator for Fedorov, who was at the top of his game. By doing that, it also pushed No. 19 [Steve Yzerman], who didn't want to be overshadowed by Sergei. That's the way Scotty was. He put it all together. We brought him in to close the deal and he made those trades, so hats off to him. We were all a little dubious at the time. But that's why he's the man with the diamond knuckles."

With the benefit of more than two decades' worth of hindsight, Yzerman speaks with a certain awe about how the culture of the organization changed – not so much because of the growing European influence on the bench, but because of the man behind it, a virtuoso puppet master, pulling all the right strings.

"We learned, myself included, all the players," Yzerman said. "We adjusted and we became different hockey players. . . He left us alone in the locker room. When he came in with his presentations, he prepared us for practice, prepared us for games. He'd sometimes talk to us between periods. But otherwise he left us alone. Everything, for him, was about winning. That was the culture he instilled in us. It was like he was saying, 'No hard feelings, guys. It's not personal. This is what you need to do to win, and that's the way it is.'

"And when Scotty tapped you on the shoulder, you went over the boards and you played to win."

His way. If you didn't, you weren't feeling that tap on the shoulder. Players want to play, and their ice time was the carrot in front of the big stick Bowman always carried. The mandate to win came through team management from the Ilitch family ownership, Yzerman said, but it was Bowman who carried it through.

"Scotty Bowman took a group of players from all over the world and molded them into a really close-knit team that was going to be successful in the playoffs," Yzerman said, "and everybody knew: 'If you're here for any reason other than winning, you're not going to enjoy it. You're not going to fit in.'

"That (culture) is hard to replicate, but we were able to do it. And it was, from my perspective, a really special time, a really enjoyable time because we had a really tremendous team. Those were the greatest years of my playing career, obviously because we won, but also because the process was a lot of fun."

The fun really began three nights after the Larionov trade, in Calgary, Alberta, when Bowman sent out all his Russians over the boards for a shift early in the game. It was the first five-man unit of its kind in NHL history. All Russians. All from the same Soviet Red Army Club.

"It was just beautiful to watch," Devellano said. "Every pass was tape-to-tape. They all knew where everybody else was. They showed us the pride of the Russians. I mean, they were Russians and here they were in America, playing in the NHL together on a top-notch team in Detroit. Who would have ever thought that?"

Scotty Bowman did. A legendary former Soviet star did, too.

Nearly 20 years after that night in Calgary, at Fedorov's induction into the Hockey Hall of Fame in Toronto, I ran into Vladislav Tretiak, the greatest goaltender in Soviet hockey history who played behind that famed Green Line that included Fetisov and Larionov. I mentioned how much we all enjoyed watching the Russian Five in Detroit, and Tretiak's eyes lit up.

"They show how Russians can play in the NHL! They win Stanley Cups!" he said. "It was because they had the best coach. Scotty Bowman, the very best. He knows how we play. He was the perfect coach for Russian players in Detroit."

Fedorov agreed. "When we were all united under Scotty's command, it was magic, unbelievable," he said. "Looking back, it was all Scotty Bowman. He created this idea, and thank God Kenny agreed. He asked us, and we said yes, yes! Scotty made the trades and we had a full throttle of Russian players."

But as good as they were, it wasn't always easy playing for Bowman, Fedorov admitted. The system the Russians grew up in under coach Viktor Tikhonov, the methods of the two coaches, were so disparate as to be incomparable.

"I could go on forever," Fedorov said of Tikhonov. "He was very hard on everyone. Scotty was a little more tricky, more mental games. He wants you to understand why, and not think about it. He's not going to treat you every day like a babysitter. No, he will actually make you understand: If you want this one thing, to win the Stanley Cup, then you gotta do this, plus double more, then you will be fine."

And if you didn't, you didn't play. The Wings were a team full of experienced players, and they all wanted ice time, which Bowman doled out like a miser.

"That's where he became Scotty, in our minds," Fedorov said. "All he wants from you is quality and the same level of intensity all the time. If you gave that, he would play you forever."

Only problem was, Fedorov said, he didn't really figure out Bowman's mysterious and demanding ways until he was out of the game for a decade.

"I think it still worked out for me and for the team," Fedorov said, "and for Scotty also."

It worked out for everybody – all the way to the end.

"I don't think the story of the Russian Five could have happened without Scotty Bowman, his vision, knowing those players and how they played in Russia," said Dave Lewis, an assistant to Bowman for all the years he spent behind the bench in Detroit. "I think it helped that it happened in Detroit. The fans know the game, and they really took a liking to all the Russian guys. But you've got to give it to Scotty for getting them all together."

Regardless of their nationality, Bowman could be tough on his players. He was an equal-opportunity tormentor.

"There were times when it wasn't easy," center Kris Draper remembered. "He'd always challenge you. He wanted to see how you'd respond, if you responded in a positive way. When you did, I really think he appreciated that. In fact, I know he did."

One of the most emotional moments of his career, Draper said, was at the end of the 2002 season. The Red Wings had just won their third Stanley Cup in six seasons under Bowman, who had decided to retire.

"I remember when he came over and shook my hand and said, 'I'm done. I'm going to retire.' And he thanked every one of us," Draper said. "We were able to, as players, let Scotty Bowman go out on top, something that any coach or athlete would love to do.

"You know, I had 10 years with Scotty. It was hard, and sometimes it was frustrating, but it was special. He made me a better hockey player, and he made me a better person."

Any of us who had spent significant time around Bowman could say that, including some of the players who remained bitter long after he traded them. Among that group was Dino Ciccarelli, who owes his induction into the Hockey Hall of Fame to Bowman. Some members of the selection committee wanted to deny Ciccarelli because of some unseemly off-ice incidents during his career. It was Bowman, a man with a high regard for moral and ethical standards, who went to bat for him. But Bowman has an even higher regard for the talent it takes to score 608 goals and 1,200 points in an NHL career, and he fought for Dino until he got him into the Hall of Fame.

Looking back on more than three decades in Detroit, Devellano needs all his fingers and a few toes to count the momentous decisions he made or approved of to help build the foundation of a team that would win those three Stanley Cup titles in six seasons under Bowman and another one in 2008 – amid 25 straight years of his team qualifying for the Stanley Cup playoffs. Among the most significant: drafting Yzerman with his first-ever pick as the Wings' general manager in 1983; turning to Europe, at the forceful urging of his scouting staff, to select Nicklas Lidstrom and Sergei Fedorov in consecutive rounds in 1989 (and Konstantinov in the 11th round that year); adding Kozlov with the team's history-making third-round pick in 1990; and hiring Scotty Bowman in 1993.

"It's been a hell of a ride," said Devellano, inducted into the Hockey Hall of Fame in 2010. "But it wouldn't have happened without the Russians."

And the Russians – the Russian Five – wouldn't have happened without Bowman, the man Devellano managed to hire when his boss wanted to bring in someone else in a move that would have changed the course of Detroit hockey history, and likely not in a good way.

Devellano paused a moment, and he appeared to be speaking mostly to himself when he added with a soft chuckle: "Stonewalling Mike Keenan. That may be the biggest thing I ever did for this franchise."

CHAPTER 9

Kicking Down the Curtain

"For nine years I was shackled in an Army I did not want to join, playing the game I loved for a man I despised. Now, at last, I am in the NHL. And most of all, I am free. . ."

~ Igor Larionov, in his self-titled book

Igor Larionov was enjoying a rare evening at home on a winter evening in early 1989 when his telephone rang. On the other end of the line he heard a familiar but angry and accusatory voice. It startled him. Aleksandr Maximovich Fetisov, the father of his longtime friend and Red Army teammate, was calling.

"So, why did you drop my Slava?" the elder Fetisov yelled. "How many years have you played together, played and seemingly were friends, and now the truth comes out? Slava is all by himself, taking the rap, and you keep on living the same way, and you do not care."

Larionov, who described the conversation in his 1990 autobiography, was stunned.

In the latest chapter in the ongoing struggle between Soviet Central Red Army hockey stars and their dictatorial coach, Viktor Tikhonov, Slava Fetisov, the team's longtime captain, had been exiled for a very public display of insubordination. Fetisov had learned, following in the footsteps of Larionov, that the pen could be mightier than the hockey stick. But wielding it, he knew, could have severe repercussions. He didn't care.

Fetisov had been promised for years that he would be allowed to finish his career with the NHL's New Jersey Devils, who had drafted him in 1983. In fact, six months earlier he had signed a contract with the Devils. But promises by Soviet officials regarding his "imminent" release were repeatedly broken, and he had had enough. So he consented to, and essentially co-authored, an interview that was published in a widely read Moscow newspaper headlined: "Viacheslav Fetisov: 'I do not want to play on Tikhonov's team!'"

Old Soviet power-mongers may have been losing their grip on the rest of the country in a dramatic new era of *perestroika* and *glasnost*, but they still ruled the country's renowned hockey program – and Tikhonov was its monarch. And he played his trump card. If Fetisov wasn't going to play hockey, then he was to serve the Red Army as a soldier. He would trim his hair, put on the military uniform and report to work daily, where he sat behind a desk. He held the rank of major.

"But I did nothing," Fetisov said. "Nothing. I just sat there behind a desk."

He sat, 30 years old and arguably the world's best defenseman, rusting while his teammates carried on, the World Championships in Sweden looming.

Larionov knew well from his own experience what Fetisov was going through. About three years earlier, Larionov had been left at home on several occasions when the Soviet national team went abroad to play. No explanation came from Soviet officials, other than something ambiguous about passport issues. Bureaucratic red tape. At first, Larionov wanted to believe that there was some misunderstanding, a mistake. But he knew better. The Soviet regime didn't make mistakes like that regarding its powerful hockey team that brought so much honor and glory to the motherland. When Western journalists would inquire about Larionov's absence, they were told he suffered from tonsillitis or some other health issues that prevented him from playing.

Igor Larionov did not sit quietly, however, and eventually learned that Soviet authorities deemed him a security risk. They worried that he would defect to the West.

"They suspected me of everything, accused me of everything," Larionov wrote.

They alleged he was involved in a close and continuous association with a foreign national, a Canadian woman who showed up unannounced on the doorstep of his parents' home in Voskresensk inquiring why Larionov had been left off the roster on a recent visit to her country for a series of games against NHL clubs. They accused his mother, a peasant who had labored honestly her entire life, of black market activities, profiting by selling items her son had brought home from his trips abroad. But mostly, and largely because he was open and honest in answering questions from the media during those trips, they worried that he would embarrass them by leaving the Soviet Union for a future in the NHL. The Vancouver Canucks had selected him with their 11th of 12 picks, and had been trying behind the scenes to secure his release from the Soviets since that day in 1985.

"Comrade Senior Lieutenant, you like the West very much. And in general everything from the West," a Soviet official told him at one of several unpleasant meetings when Larionov was striving to regain his place with the national team.

"I was at fault all around," Larionov wrote in his 1990 book. "That I gladly gave interviews to journalists. That I liked the NHL, and the organization of the hockey business there. That I like rock music. That the living standard there impressed me. All this was raked up into a pile. I was the enemy. Because, you see, if I liked the American way of life, then in general I was an American by heart. All of this they said about me.

"By nature, I am clearly a Russian. I do not like everything in America. It cannot be that somewhere everything is as in a fairytale, and somewhere else is total darkness and hopelessness. Particularly, it seemed, my sociability offended the preservers of government secrets and questioners of my reliability. I also knew a little English. Therefore, I had the possibility to rub elbows with whomever I might come in contact: hockey players, journalists and even immigrants. And, they assumed, to each of them I could give important information. . ."

Larionov eventually learned from a source he trusted that he would never be allowed to travel abroad, an edict he was told came from no less authority than the Central Committee of the Communist Party, or from the KGB. Either way, his road to the West appeared forbidden.

At 5-feet-9 and 170 pounds, Larionov appeared to be the least threatening of his teammates to stand up to the mighty Soviet hockey system. Until he started talking. Then, especially when he was wearing little round eyeglasses that reminded some people of John Lennon, he could easily be mistaken for the kind of revolutionary from a scene in the movie "Dr. Zhivago," plotting the overthrow of the Romanov Empire. When journalists asked him questions, Larionov answered them honestly and openly, a dangerous habit in Communist Russia.

"A human being has to live in such a way that he feels himself to be a human being – by one's own mind and conscience, no matter where he lives or what he does," Larionov wrote. "To me, that has always meant communication with people – not just Soviet people, but people everywhere. I have a need to do this, to relate to people. To isolate, to limit oneself only to hockey, that is not for me. Do it and you will soon regret that in your youth, in the best years of your life, you saw nothing but hockey on your horizon. I could not let this happen. Not to me, and not to my family."

By autumn of 1988, his battle with Tikhonov at an impasse, Larionov knew what he needed to do. He set aside his hockey stick and picked up his pen.

"I am a hockey player, and only a hockey player," Larionov said in an interview years later. "This is my profession, my favorite work, and I would not change it for anything. I had never given journalism a thought. . . In my wildest dreams, I never saw myself as an author of an article that would produce such commotion. So it is curious to churn over again the events which led up to the writing of my open letter. . ."

As he started writing, Larionov explained, emotions that had been roiling within him since 1981, when he was essentially conscripted into the Red Army program against his better judgment and will, began flowing onto the paper. In all, more than 7,000 words – all poison-tipped arrows aimed at Tikhonov, the domineering, untouchable autocrat. It appeared in the October 1988, Issue No. 42 of *Ogonyok*, a widely read and influential weekly magazine that reached its peak of popularity during *perestroika* under editor Vitaly Korotich, who advanced a pro-capitalist, pro-American editorial agenda. *Ogonyok* roughly translates to "small fire." In a literal sense, however, Larionov's letter was, in his words, a bombshell that set off a firestorm of controversy, the opening volley of a barrage from star players that would result, finally, in the kinds of dramatic changes in Soviet athletics that were happening throughout the rest of society.

"Dear respected Viktor Vasilevich!" the letter began. And with all those words on pages 18-19 of *Ogonyok*, Igor Larionov, then 27 and in the prime of his career, began to kick down what remained of the Iron Curtain.

His letter explained that while times were changing dramatically throughout the Soviet Union under Mikhail Gorbachev's *glasnost* since 1985, little had changed regarding the country's hockey team. The national team and the Central Red Army Club were coached by Tikhonov, who controlled his players with a whip like a lion-tamer. He sequestered them at a training facility for most of the year, allowing them precious little free time to spend with family and friends.

"So you, Viktor Vasilevich, have become transformed in the last years into this hockey monarch: you punish who you want, you pardon who you want!" Larionov wrote. "For 11 months of the year we were forced to be separated from home: endless trips, games, and if not games then training camps. A harsh regime. Listing what was allowed us was easy: There was a lot that we could do. They nursed us wonderfully well. We could play chess or cards, and we could sleep. All else that remained for us to do was to train. After the games, we were on the bus. Our wives and kids waved us 'goodbye.' They are going home. Thanks to you, Viktor Vasilevich, it's amazing how our wives could give birth to our children. These normal, mutual relationships between a hockey player and his wife do not have a part in your program."

Larionov closed his letter by calling for a unified revolt of the nation's elite athletes: "The country is learning to think in a new way. It is high time to take this upon yourself, sportsmen!"

Years later, he said he published the letter "to open the society's eyes to what really was being done in this system. I wasn't doing it for myself, I was doing it for the whole team." Naturally, it did little to improve Larionov's standing with his coach, and Tikhonov knew how to avenge his public embarrassment. The Red Army club and Dynamo Riga were set to play a series of games against NHL teams in December 1988 and

January 1989, and Larionov desperately wanted to be a part of it.

"For the hockey professional, playing a series of matches in Canada is always an event for which to yearn," he wrote in his autobiography. "There is no more severe test of one's mastery and character."

Larionov was not surprised when his name was not on the roster of players to make the trip. Nor was he done fighting, but he had only one move left to make. If it failed, he knew he was finished.

"All my hope was on my comrades, Fetisov, [Vladimir] Krutov, and [Sergei] Makarov. And they seemed to be standing on the sidelines, doing nothing," Larionov lamented. "If you repeated over and over again to me, after Ogonyok came out, your complete solidarity with my point of view and position, I would have said to prove it not with words, but with deeds."

He was bewildered by their passivity, exasperated, disappointed and spiritually tormented, he said. Nevertheless, he drove to the team's training camp in Novogorsk to confront his three linemates and make his plea.

"They had no doubt what was happening: The coach was having his revenge," Larionov wrote. "It was unfair, but. . . I drove home along the Leningrad Highway. I felt like shouting: 'Where are your friends in time of trouble?'"

Sitting demoralized at the breakfast table and trying to hide the feelings of despair from his wife, Elena, Larionov picked up the ringing telephone. It was Fetisov, calling from Novogorsk. He, Krutov and Makarov had signed a petition, telling their coach that Larionov was needed for the trip to Canada. Either he comes along, or the three of them would have to reconsider their roles with the team.

His friends had made their stand, issuing an ultimatum to their coach. The next morning, Larionov's phone rang once more. Assistant coach Boris Mikhailov was on the line. "Igor," he said, "quickly get ready to leave."

Now it was Fetisov's turn in the Tikhonov's barrel after another public humiliation of the coach. And here was his teammate's father at the other end of the line, accusing Larionov of the worst kind of betrayal.

Larionov pledged to Alexandr Maximovich that he in no way had forsaken his friend, and he shared the conversation in his book:

"I personally will go with him to the end. Together. Do you believe me?"

"I would like to."

"I give you my word. I swear on the health of my [daughter] Alyonka. I will not leave Slava!"

"May it be so; may it be so. But what is he supposed to do now? He is not playing, and he is no longer training. What will happen?"

"Do not worry, Maximovich. Just you wait. We will not give up that easily. We will think of something."

"Well, Igorek, keep your word. Good health to you."

"All the best, Maximovich. We will fight yet!"

By the end of the conversation, the elder Fetisov's mood had transformed from infuriated to near tears. The World Championships in Stockholm, Sweden, were fast-approaching, and despite a more vocal sports media in Russia calling for the return of the captain to the national team, nothing was happening. Tikhonov wasn't budging. Larionov could not imagine making this trip without his captain, but the pressure to act was building.

And so, he hatched a plan. Immediately after Red Army had played its final game of the regular season, its national team members were to head to Novogorsk for their training camp to prepare for the trip to Sweden. There was an 11 p.m. curfew. Igor Larionov, Sergei Makarov and Vladimir Krutov failed to make that curfew. Instead, they drove to Ostankino to appear on one of the nation's most popular television broadcasts, *"Vzglad"* – "Point of View."

There, in front of the cameras, the players explained their situation – Slava Fetisov's situation – and concluded the following harsh demand: "Either Fetisov be returned to the national team or we, all of us, would not go to Stockholm, but would remain in Moscow, and that the second line of the national team – [Andrei] Khomutov, [Slava] Bykov and [Valery] Kamensky – was also supporting our ultimatum."

Tikhonov was quoted the next day in the national newspaper *Pravda* that he would present a team featuring other players. The Soviet system, after all, produced many, many great players. But he quickly caved under a wave of public opinion against him – powered by that compelling TV interview.

Tikhonov nevertheless continued to undermine his players. As soon as they arrived in Sweden, Tikhonov called on the team to elect a new captain. Makarov had been acting captain in Fetisov's absence, and would win many of the votes of players on the team from outside the Red Army club. Larionov and Krutov, however, were in a vulnerable position. If they voted for Fetisov, it could be construed as an involuntary slap at Makarov. To vote for Makarov, however, would be a rejection of all the years of Fetisov's service and leadership.

In the end, Larionov and Krutov voted for Fetisov, who would wear the "K" as *kapitan* again – by one vote.

Fetisov, who hadn't played and only rarely skated in two months, led the Russians to the gold medal. He also was selected to the world all-star team and named the tournament's best defenseman.

A few days later, after a shopping spree with their well-earned bonus money, the Russian team gathered in the early morning for a flight back to Moscow. They were missing one player: Alexander Mogilny, the brilliant young left wing, was not among them. Two days later he emerged in Buffalo, New York. He had defected to the NHL's Sabres.

Nearly three weeks later, on May 23, 1989, Igor Larionov became a civilian. On July 1, he signed a contract to join the Vancouver Canucks, where Krutov would join him. Sergei Makarov would begin his NHL career that fall with the Calgary Flames. And Slava Fetisov finally got his chance to play for the New Jersey Devils. Ironically, Fetisov would eventually be joined in New Jersey by Alexei Kasatonov, Fetisov's defense partner on the Green Line and the one member of the team no one trusted. Like the good Communist that he was, Kasatonov always sided with Tikhonov.

But times were changing, and the Red Wings knew it. In June that summer of 1989, five months before the fall of the Berlin Wall, a monument to the power of Communism, the Red Wings went all in on Soviet-born players. They drafted Sergei Fedorov and Vladimir Konstantinov, igniting a new arms race an ocean away. Other clubs selected several other young Soviets even though there remained serious uncertainties about when they would be released from their system – if ever. Within a few years, as it turned out, most of them would be given the opportunity to play in North America. Tikhonov's reign of terror was over. The Central Red Army club was just another team in a crippled league. But hockey's Russian Revolution was under way, and the NHL would never be the same.

CHAPTER 10

Viacheslav Fetisov:
'A King of Man'

Brendan Shanahan doesn't remember precisely where his conversation with Slava Fetisov took place, but nearly 20 years later he could recite with vivid detail what was said when he finally got up the courage to ask: "Papa Bear, why are you so good again? How did this happen?"

Fetisov smiled. As proud as he was about his incomparable hockey resume, he knew these were valid questions.

"We were having a beer, I don't remember if we were sitting on the plane or out to dinner, but I just asked," Shanahan recalled. He was just 20 years old, a rising star with the New Jersey Devils, when Fetisov made his NHL debut with the club. Fetisov was 31 years old, and already a legend in hockey circles throughout the world. But even then he looked like a broken-down old man.

"We used to see you come in to the locker room in the mornings in New Jersey and we just. . . It looked like you needed some sleep," Shanahan recalled saying to Fetisov. "I just had so much respect for him, but he looked so tired when he first came over. I thought maybe they had worn him down too much over there. I know when he was trying to get out through the front door, they tried to embarrass him in many ways."

Fetisov nodded. He hadn't expected a hero's welcome when he arrived in New Jersey, but he certainly didn't anticipate the vitriol he encountered – not only from opponents, but even from some of his teammates.

"When I first came to play in the National Hockey League, there was more politics in the game," Fetisov said. "In the first place, it was still the Cold War. When I walk in the dressing room, I can feel there was still some guys that don't like you. Not because you're good or bad as a player, but because you came from Moscow, from the Soviet Union. You could feel it. Especially when you spend your whole life in the dressing room, and you have been a leader and captain of one of the best teams in history. You can feel it. Something's going on. It is too much pressure for me – and that is not an excuse."

By the time Fetisov arrived in Detroit, his English had improved to the point that he could have a conversation of some depth with a teammate who cared, like Shanahan.

"He was able to explain to me everything that had been done to him in Russia – the stuff that we're all learning about now – the struggles he went through to be able to come over here," Shanahan said more than a quarter-century later. "And when he finally got here, he thought, 'OK, I'm free. I've got my freedom to play in the NHL.' But he didn't anticipate the struggle he was about to face here from people taking cheap shots at him – even his own teammates – and not necessarily behind his back. He wasn't expecting [on-ice] officials to turn a blind eye when guys were doing certain things to him.

"When the Russians started coming over here, there was a lot of talk. The Commies, they were the enemy. And now they're over here taking the jobs from good old Canadian and American kids. It was a little bit more of an old-school view."

Fetisov told Shanahan about his years of fighting against the Soviet system, and he confessed that it would have been much easier to defect, like Sergei Fedorov and Alexander Mogilny.

"But for me it was impossible," Fetisov told me in an interview for the documentary film "The Russian Five." "I took the challenge and it took a lot out of me, mentally and physically. And when I finally came to New Jersey, I got no help. I was on my own. It's funny now, but I remember this: I had two choices in 1989. I could pack my stuff and go back, or I could fight through it."

Fetisov chose fight over flight, but he paid a brutal price for his right to compete in the NHL, with opponents taking cheap shots, referees looking the other way and teammates failing to come to his defense. He learned quickly, however, that he could retaliate in his own brutal way. Shanahan recalled one of Fetisov's first games in the NHL against Toronto, when Wendel Clark paired off with Fetisov during a scrum, dropped his gloves and pummeled the former Soviet national team captain. Fetisov wound up with a black eye.

"Now, if you know Slava, he's a very proud guy," Shanahan said. "Besides great offensive skills, he was a great checker. A really great hip checker. He could have done that in every game if he wanted. He did it a couple of times in training camp to our own players, and we had to tell him, and not in the most gentle way, that that doesn't fly here. If you hip check a guy, especially your own guy in practice, you're going to have four guys jumping on your back."

Fetisov got the message. The hip check may be part of the game, but there was an unwritten code, a gentlemen's agreement among NHL players, that such a tactic was forbidden.

"So he stopped doing it," Shanahan said. "But Wendel had embarrassed him, and I think he circled the date of the next time Toronto came to New Jersey. Slava was ready for him. I remember I was on the ice. We were in the Toronto zone and we turned the puck over. Their defenseman made a pass to Wendel coming out of the zone and I was close enough to him that I could feel the speed and see how low and how fast Slava Fetisov was coming, ass first, about three feet off the ice, so low. . . and he was going to take both of Wendel's knees out. It was fast and it was powerful and Wendel saw him at the last second and got about 90 percent out of the way.

"Of course, they wound up squaring off and I remember thinking, 'OK, I'm going to have to jump in there and fight.' But there was something about Slava's face that I could tell he wanted to fight Wendel, that he wanted to be a man about it. So we all stopped and backed off. Sure enough, Wendel grabbed him and hit him once. Slava wasn't used to fighting, so when he fell we all jumped in. But Slava got up from that fight just fine. Wendel Clark limped off the ice with a torn knee ligament. If he hadn't gotten almost out of the way, Slava might have ended his career right then and there. We could all see then that Slava was a pretty serious guy."

That game was on Jan. 26, 1990. Clark wound up missing more than two months, returning barely in time for the playoffs that spring.

But by the time the Wings traded for him, on April 3, 1995 for a third-round draft pick, Fetisov was hardly playing for the Devils. More often than not, he was scratched from a lineup that was deep with younger, faster and more physical defensemen. Coach Scotty Bowman said he made the trade because the Wings had just lost Mark Howe to injury just weeks from his 40th birthday. Fetisov would play, not watch from the press box, where players scratched from the lineup typically sat to watch the game.

Fetisov was thrilled with the change of scenery. Detroit, he knew by then, was a city with a rich hockey tradition. The Red Wings were an up-and-coming team with several talented players, three of them Russians trained in the same school where he grew up. He knew he had found his place when he returned from his first road trip with the Wings, and one of the most famous hockey players in the history of the game came into the locker room to greet him.

"Slava, welcome!" Gordie Howe said, extending his hand.

"He reminded me of an episode back in 1978, when we played a game against the Hartford Whalers and I hip-checked him," Fetisov said. "And then there was a big fight. He told me he was too old to be checked like that from a young kid. It was memories shared in a good way."

Steve Yzerman, the Wings' captain, wasn't sure what to make of the trade that brought Fetisov to Detroit. The 6-feet-1, 220-pound Fetisov was three weeks from his 37th birthday and had played in only four of the Devils' 24 games.

"I was intrigued by it," Yzerman said. "He was a pretty big name. I didn't know him, but I knew of him. We knew he came over here and there was a transition to North American hockey. Mostly I was just very curious.

"And when he came in and got on the ice with us, we could tell very quickly that this guy is pretty good. He could move the puck. He's really smart. He's a big, thick guy, and his personality was just awesome right off the bat. He was the guy right in the middle of all the conversations, the dinners, the card games. He was very outgoing, very funny, personable. And just a real gentleman as well, to everyone. He was a hit as soon as he joined our locker room."

On the ice, he was a revelation.

"All I know is that when Slava Fetisov came from New Jersey to the Detroit Red Wings, he was so much better than I thought he was," said associate coach Dave Lewis, a former NHL defenseman whose primary duty was to work with the team's defenders. Among them was Nicklas Lidstrom, a Swede who was just beginning to emerge as one of the best in the world at his position.

"When we first traded for Slava, I was just thrilled to be able to play with him because I had watched him growing up as a little kid," Lidstrom said. "I watched the Soviet Union dominate in the hockey world, and he was the captain of their team. He had so much character, and he helped us right off the bat when he came, with his presence in the room and on the ice as well.

"Slava Fetisov was probably the best defensemen outside of the NHL when I watched him throughout the '80s. He had a strong presence on the ice. You couldn't fight him off the puck. He was just the total package. But when he came over here, he was a little bit older and he had to adjust to a different kind of game where you're dumping the puck in a lot more. There were more physical players in a smaller rink. We're playing a little bit different game, so I think it was hard on him. Especially when opposing players took a run at him because he was from the Soviet Union. I'm sure it was very tough on him."

What inspired Lidstrom most about Fetisov, however, was the level of his professionalism. "Showing up for work every day and being real serious about everything," Lidstrom said. "It was like he was saying, 'This is my job. This is what I do for a living.' You know, we all did that, but he really showed it. He didn't take anything for granted. He was getting up there in age, but he was still being a professional about it. When you see a player of his caliber, at his age, and he's still bringing it every night and every day at practice, too, I think that helped us all just being around that."

That's what Bowman was trading for when he made the deal with New Jersey.

"Scotty knew what he would bring, especially for the young

Russian players we had, and he was exactly right," Lewis said. "Once Slava walked into the room, besides getting the respect of all the great players we already had who had played against him in the international tournaments – the Yzermans, the Lidstroms and the Shanahans, guys like that – he had the attention of the other Russians. They didn't actually bow to him, but you could tell they really respected him for who he was and the things that he could help them with. That was probably one of the biggest reasons Scotty brought him, knowing the effect he would have on our young Russian players."

The transformation from the broken-down player Fetisov was when he arrived in New Jersey to the efficient, stabilizing influence he brought to the ice when he got to Detroit six years later was remarkable. But Brendan Shanahan, acquired in October 1996, eighteen months after Fetisov, immediately understood how and why that could happen.

"We just played a style that was more conducive to the game he knew," Shanahan said. "It helped that he had the other Russians to play with, but he didn't just have success because of them. He had success because of the way Scotty Bowman coached the team."

Fetisov resoundingly concurred. "Scotty Bowman is the greatest man ever to coach a hockey team in the world," he said. "It's not the style, it's the players you have, and he was a coach who let the players play up to their potential. All his teams were like that. He built on the talent of the players. Psychologically, he feels his players better than anybody. That's why he had so much success. He can feel. He knows what he needs to do to help anybody be better, and he made for me the best years of my life, my hockey life."

For Sergei Fedorov and the rest of Detroit's forwards, Fetisov slowed the game down and made it easier to play. Unlike the typical North American-bred defenseman, Fetisov refused to just rim the puck around the glass, hoping one of his teammates might corral it and continue the attack. Instead, Fetisov would hold onto the puck, often drawing two and three defenders toward him in an attempt to take it away. Then, with a flick of his powerful wrists, he would send the puck ahead 20, 40, 60 feet away right onto the tape of a streaking teammate's stick.

"He would find you," Sergei Fedorov said of the trait that separated Fetisov from most other defensemen in the world. "He would always find you. I would tell him, 'Slava, this dot and this dot. When you're in the corner with the puck, I will be there.' We would always talk about those little kinds of plays. Slava brought to our team stability – a *lot* of experience at the defensive end, where we had a little trouble. He settled down every shift."

That stabilizing force enabled another Russian defenseman, Vladimir Konstantinov, to emerge and to help amplify Detroit's offensive arsenal when the two were paired, as they often were.

"Slava was at one time one of the best defensemen in the world, and he was always right there," said Russian center Igor Larionov. "If Vladimir goes up to join the offense, Slava was there to back him up. It helped him improve his game offensively. Defensively, Vladdie was very hard to play against, but on offense he gave us another weapon. Three forwards can do a lot, but when you have four guys attacking, it's going to be hard to stop. Slava was always there taking care of the defensive responsibilities.

"But he also never lost the touch to go and help to score, because Slava liked to score goals, too. He always tried to be involved, but when you get older you also become wiser. He only joined the rush when he knew the puck was going to be coming to him. Otherwise, Slava's responsibility was to cover for Vladdie."

Among Lewis's favorite memories from his time coaching the Russians was when they would return to the bench together, all five of them, for a time-out or a break in the action to fix the ice or mend a sheet of glass along the boards. Inevitably, Fetisov would start barking in the direction of the three younger Russians. Often, Larionov would follow up with his own comments, always in support of Fetisov.

Then, typically, Fedorov would turn and yell at Slava Kozlov.

And Kozlov would turn and shout at Vladimir Konstantinov.

Konstantinov would yell back, take a gulp of water and turn away. But invariably, it trickled down to him.

"It always trickled down from Slava and Igor to the other guys, and it seemed to me that Vladdie was always getting dumped on," Lewis said. "And they would be speaking in Russian, so we didn't know what they were talking about. But it was almost comical. No one ever yelled at Fetisov, though. Ever. And I don't remember anyone yelling at Larionov, either. The three younger guys got most of the abuse."

That kind of authority and management was not lost on the rest of the team.

"Slava is a leader for sure, and no nonsense," Yzerman said. "Igor as well. They were strong leaders, they were very smart guys, and they weren't afraid to speak their minds, especially to the younger guys like Kozzie, Vladdie or even Sergei, for that matter. They were like, 'Guys, this is the way it is. This is what we're doing.' They set a great example for them."

The Wings saw that clearly and forcefully at a critical moment in their quest to break their long Stanley Cup drought. Fedorov had suffered a shoulder injury earlier in the Western Conference Finals series against Chicago in 1995, and he felt he was unable to continue playing. Hockey players traditionally embrace a warped sense of pride about playing through injuries. If they get nicked in the face with a stick, a puck or an elbow, they hurry to the trainer's room to get stitched up and ask the medic to hurry so they can get back onto the ice without missing their next shift. That goes for players who have left their teeth on the ice, finishing the game with mangled smiles. Some have played on knees that forced them to limp when they were walking because of ligament or cartilage damage. Others have refused to come out of a game, playing with broken feet and even broken legs.

Fedorov was not among them, at least that was his reputation among his own teammates. Like all athletes, he was at his best when he was at his healthiest. But as an elite player – one of the best in the world during most of his NHL career – Fedorov worried that certain injuries would limit his effectiveness. If he couldn't play up to his own standards and the expectations of his team and its fans, he preferred not to play. It shouldn't matter what anyone else thought, he's the one who had to perform. But Fedorov didn't appreciate what his coaches and teammates knew: Even at 50 percent effectiveness, he was better than just about everybody else in the league. But it was nearly impossible to convince him.

"Sergei, at times, could be a hard person to talk to, to influence," Lewis said. "Slava Fetisov had no problem influencing Sergei. There was a mutual respect, for sure, but Slava was still the boss. His word was written in stone, almost."

But Fetisov needed a big assist from athletic therapist John Wharton to get Fedorov back into what was a fierce, punishing series against division rival Chicago.

"You work on his head and I'll work on his body," Wharton told Fetisov, who dialed Fedorov's phone number.

"Sergei, let's go to dinner."

"I don't know if I feel like it," Fedorov said. "I don't think I'm going to play tomorrow. It's too painful."

"Let's go."

Fedorov finally agreed. Fetisov then called Wharton, and the two met Sergei for dinner that went well into the night. After their meal, the two escorted Fedorov to Joe Louis Arena. While Fetisov and a reluctant Fedorov laced up their skates, Wharton turned on the arena lights. Fedorov still balked. He had suffered a Grade 2 separation where the shoulder blade attaches to the collarbone. It's a serious injury and extremely painful. Rather than shoot his shoulder up with painkillers, Fedorov wanted to rest it and allow it to heal. Fetisov had other plans.

Fedorov's best argument was that he didn't feel he had the proper equipment to protect the injured area.

"I probably tried out seven different types of shoulder pads with him," Wharton recalled, "and Sergei still wasn't happy."

Finally, Fetisov went to his locker and brought out his shoulder pads. Defensemen tend to play a more physical game and frequently opt for bigger protective equipment. Fedorov, still reluctant, agreed to give them a try.

"Let's just get this over with," he said. Then he went for a skate, a puck dangling at the end of his stick. "Hey, these feel pretty good."

He jumped into the air, twisting and turning, then he skated toward the boards, colliding with the Plexiglas.

"These are fucking awesome," Fedorov said, breaking into a wide grin. "I'm playing."

It was 2:15 a.m., the night before a critical Stanley Cup playoff game.

Fetisov had to round up another set of shoulder pads for himself the next day. But that was the least of his worries.

"Somehow I found the right words, and I put him in a situation where he figured out in his own mind he can play," Fetisov said.

Fedorov's teammates were surprised at his change of heart.

"Slava convinced Sergei that it was so important for him to play," Lewis said. "Not just for Sergei and not just for Slava and not just for the Russian Five, but for everybody in the locker room and everybody in the city and everybody in the whole state who were Red Wings fans. If he did, Slava told him, he would be a contributing factor in the game. And he was."

Game 3 against the Blackhawks was a rout because of one man. Fedorov, playing hurt but feeling safe and comfortable enough, scored two goals and assisted on two others. Fetisov had one assist in that game, but his biggest assist had been earned the previous night. After their 6-1 victory, the Detroit Red Wings needed just one more win. But it wouldn't be easy. Fedorov again was a hero, recording the primary assist on Slava Kozlov's game-winning goal at 2:25 of the second overtime to dispatch the Blackhawks and send Detroit to the Stanley Cup finals for the first time since 1966.

"I don't know if this game would have a different result if Sergei did not play," Fetisov said. "We will never know. But he was the best player on the team that night, and he showed it."

The Wings were swept by New Jersey in the Stanley Cup finals, but they eventually would have another chance. And by the time his Hall of Fame career was over, Fetisov had plenty of opportunity to showcase his immense leadership skills. But for him it ended in on a bittersweet moment. In June of 1998, the Wings held a comfortable lead midway through what they hoped would be a Stanley Cup-clinching game when the Washington Capitals scored a goal. Wings coach Scotty Bowman was livid as he approached Lewis at the end of the bench.

"It was you! You did this!" Bowman screamed.

"Me?" Lewis asked, surprised by the tenacity of his boss's reaction. As the assistant who rotated defense pairings, it was his fault. At least that's how Bowman saw it.

"I don't want Fetisov on the ice anymore," the coach screamed. "That's it!"

Slava Fetisov played sparingly the rest of the game. He took a penalty at 13:08 of the third period, with his team leading by three goals. Bowman was angry again, glaring at Lewis, who took the hint.

"He never got on the ice again," Lewis said.

Fetisov watched the final five-plus minutes of is redoubtable career from the bench.

"So in essence, I benched Slava Fetisov in the last game he ever played," Lewis said. "I think he still remembers that, but I blame Scotty. It wasn't me, Slava! It was Scotty!"

Two decades later, though, Shanahan was still counting his blessings at being able to call Slava Fetisov a teammate and a friend.

"I was so honored to meet him and play with him – early in my career and when I was reunited with him in Detroit," Shanahan said. "Even now, whenever I think of Slava Fetisov, I see him as just a king of a man – on and off the ice."

CHAPTER 11

Igor Larionov:
A Tale of Two Anthems

Communists ruled the Soviet Union with unforgiving power and might, and you can hear it in the captivating lyrics to their national anthem.

We fought for the future, destroyed the invaders,
and brought to our homeland the laurels of fame.
Our glory will live in the memory of the nations,
and all generations will honor her name.

When the celebrated Red Army Choir sings a song, it stays sung. And the group was in full throat, decked in military regalia and singing its epic ode to the motherland to open festivities prior to the first of two memorable games between the Soviet national team and NHL stars at Rendez-vous '87 in Quebec City. It was hailed as a five-day international celebration of the sport of ice hockey. The event was held in lieu of the league's annual All-Star Game, at a moment in the sport's history when political intrigue competed for center stage. Igor Larionov, the first-line center on the Soviet national team, was rather uncomfortably right in the middle of it.

The week's festivities in Canada's Quebec City opened on Monday, Feb. 9, with a 10-course, $350-a-plate banquet for 1,500 people, including players from both teams and the media, prepared by renowned chefs from Canada, the Soviet Union and the United States. But even before dessert was served, there were whispers circulating among reporters of a clandestine meeting of the star centers on both squads – NHL scoring leader Wayne Gretzky and Larionov, then 26 and the second-leading scorer in the Soviet league. Larionov was already well-known and highly regarded in NHL circles. His rights were owned by the Vancouver Canucks.

There were even rumors that Larionov might – with Gretzky's influence – choose this opportunity to defect, to play in the NHL. This, of course, would have been humiliating for the Soviets and, frankly, bad for hockey at a critical moment when the Russians and Canada were enjoying a kind of détente after their decades-long Cold War on the ice. Moreover, anyone who knew Larionov – and because he was such a private and complex young man, those numbers were few – would understand that if and when he left the Soviet Union, it would be out the front door, with the blessing, however grudgingly, of Soviet authorities.

Because he was under relentless suspicion by his Communist superiors, Larionov knew all too well that nothing good could come of any rumors meeting up with Gretzky again. Larionov had been embarrassed when a Montreal newspaper reported that he and Gretzky, along with Gretzky's Edmonton teammate Paul Coffey, partied until dawn in September 1984, during the Canada Cup tournament. It led to a kind of house-arrest for Larionov; he had been excluded from international tournaments outside the Soviet Union for nearly 18 months. In an interview with a wire service reporter at Rendez-vous '87, Larionov called the newspaper's allegations "a lie," and said that while he met with Gretzky, whom he befriended at the 1981 Canada Cup, he had returned to his hotel immediately after the game in question.

"I didn't party with Wayne," Larionov said. "Wayne went out, but I went to sleep. There was no party for me."

But it was a party for hockey that week in Quebec City that coincided with *Carnaval de Quebec*, the region's annual Winter Carnival. In an unparalleled salute to the sport, events included a variety show featuring not only local acts but the Red Army Choir and a troupe from the famed Bolshoi Ballet; a business lunch with flamboyant Chrysler

President Lee Iacocca, whose company was at the time one of the NHL's most important sponsors; brunch in a museum decorated by Pierre Cardin to resemble Maxim's of Paris; a fashion show and, heralding a future of world events that would forever change the sport of ice hockey, video messages of peace from U.S. President Ronald Reagan and Andrei Gromyko, chairman of the Presidium of the Supreme Soviet.

Fast forward nearly 14 years. After celebrating his 40th birthday six days earlier, Igor Larionov was the oldest player in the National Hockey League (not exactly a point of pride; he abhorred any discussion of his age). He was playing for the Florida Panthers against the visiting Colorado Avalanche. He was standing for the American anthem, beaming with pride, though on this Saturday night in December 2000, the source of his emotion had little to do with his membership in the world's best professional hockey league. Rather, it had everything to do with the spotlight shining on the performers. The man who once stood against the tyranny of the Communist system, often with harsh public criticism that threatened his permanent exile from the game, was now listening to his daughters, Alyonka and Diana, singing America's national anthem in a place called Sunrise, Florida, in the United States of America. His feelings nearly overwhelmed him.

"If you can imagine, this was my dream: My kids growing up in America, singing the U.S. national anthem," Larionov told me after the game. His daughters had begun their singing careers years earlier at a hospital bedside in suburban Detroit. Now, while his career was far from over, Larionov knew he was experiencing the happiest of endings to his story of struggle. "I am from the old school, the Communist system. I was never the enemy, but that is how people believed. Two different countries. Two different systems."

Eventually, he won his right to emigrate to North America, arriving in Vancouver, British Columbia, to begin his NHL career less than three years after he and his Soviet teammates split a pair of games against an all-star team of NHL players that week in Quebec City. Daughter Alyonka was barely three years old. Diana was born in Vancouver. His son, Igor II, was born in Detroit.

"An international family," Larionov said proudly. "It shows how the world has come together."

Igor Larionov's struggles didn't end when he entered his new world in Vancouver. For a player with long-proven proven world-class skills, he struggled in his first season with the Canucks, scoring just 17 goals among 44 points in 74 games – modest totals considering all the hype, not to mention expenses incurred by the Canucks in advance of his arrival.

"But he was in a strange land playing what to him was a strange NHL system of random changes of lines and linemates after a decade of playing on one line and one five-man unit," the late Pat Quinn, then general manager in Vancouver, wrote in his forward for Larionov's book. "A change of that magnitude takes time. Hopefully. . . the best is yet to come."

Off the ice, the changes in lifestyle were even more dramatic. Larionov, his wife – the former Elena Batanova, a two-time world junior champion ice dancer, and their daughter, Alyonka, arrived to too much house. As Larionov described it: four bedrooms, a playroom, living room, family room, kitchen, two-car garage and not one, not two, but three bathrooms in a lovely neighborhood of about six homes nestled amid the woods. All that for three people – and one of them would be gone much of the time, playing a busy NHL schedule.

In Moscow, Igor and his family had lived in a cramped two-room apartment – and they were among the lucky ones. Only because Larionov was a successful hockey player did he get an extra room for his family. Their first home in Vancouver was simply too big. Within three months, Larionov moved his wife and daughter to a much more modest – and still luxurious compared to what they had in the Soviet Union – two-bedroom flat (with just two bathrooms) in a residential building near downtown Vancouver.

The Russian experiment was disappointing in that 1989-90 season, at least in Vancouver. While Larionov had mixed success and at least at times flashed the kind of mastery on the ice that made him so successful in the Soviet Union, his countryman Vladimir Krutov was an utter failure. One of the most dominant wingers in Soviet hockey history, Krutov – who had played on Larionov's wing for most of his career – managed just 11 goals in 61 games with the Canucks. Unable to adapt to the more restrictive and physically punishing North American style of play, Krutov left the NHL after one season.

Larionov's numbers regressed in his second NHL season, when he scored just 13 goals among 34 points in 64 games. But in his third season, rejuvenated perhaps by the emergence of dazzling Russian rookie Pavel Bure, Larionov found his game. While taking Bure under his wing, Larionov enjoyed one the most productive of his 14 NHL seasons, at least statistically. In 72 games, he scored 21 goals and 65 points. Bure was voted the Calder Trophy winner as the league's rookie of the year.

But then Larionov quit. When the first wave of Soviet players was released to play in the NHL, part of their contractual agreement, endorsed by the league, was that a portion of their salaries went back to *Soveintersport* – then the cash-strapped governing body for sports in the former Soviet Union. To end that arrangement, Larionov spent a season in Switzerland, playing for HC Lugano.

He returned to the NHL in 1993, signing as a free agent with the San Jose Sharks in a deal that enabled him to keep all his earnings. There, he was reunited with Sergei Makarov, his friend and the other winger on the Red Army's celebrated Green Line. Makarov had spent the previous four very productive years in Calgary. In his first season in 1989-90, he scored 24 goals among 86 points in 80 games to win rookie of the year honors – which didn't sit well with a lot of Canadian fans. Makarov was 31 years old at the time and he had spent 11 seasons playing professional hockey in the Soviet Union. Not exactly a rookie by NHL tradition.

But he won the award fairly in a vote by members of the Professional Hockey Writers Association. Minnesota's Mike Modano, 19, finished second after scoring 29 goals and 75 points in 80 games for the North Stars in his first NHL season. That forced the NHL to change the parameters of the award. Starting in 1990-91, to be eligible for the Calder Trophy a player must not have reached his 26th birthday by September 15th of the season in which he was eligible. (Makarov, incidentally, was the first of six Russian-born players in a 17-year span to win rookie of the year honors.)

In San Jose, Larionov and Makarov reprised the starring roles they had played in the Soviet Union. Together, they helped orchestrate a 58-point improvement in the standings from the Sharks' previous season. And then, in their first Stanley Cup playoff experience, the Sharks defeated the top-seeded and heavily favored Detroit Red Wings in the first round – one of the more memorable upsets in NHL history. That's where Larionov caught the eyes of the Detroit coaching staff.

When Wings coach Scotty Bowman heard that the Sharks were shopping Larionov in 1995, he jumped. It was a bold move, trading a 50-goal-scorer to acquire him, and even some players in the Detroit dressing room were wondering what Bowman was doing. They learned quickly; Larionov's impact in Detroit was immediate.

"Once Igor got there, everything kind of fell into place, and the hockey that we started playing, the North Americans didn't understand," said Slava Kozlov, who grew up just a few blocks from Larionov in their hometown of Voskresensk. "Igor could give a pass under any condition. He had eyes in the back of his head. . . They didn't know how to play against us."

Captain Steve Yzerman could vouch for that. At any level of international competition, he found the Russians challenging to play against, and it was no different when they were his teammates.

"When Scotty put them all together, the five Russians, there was instant chemistry," he said. "It was unique. It had never been done in the NHL, and for us it was enjoyable, really enjoyable to watch, and obviously it helped us win hockey games."

Training against the Russians was another matter.

"We had to practice against those guys as well," Yzerman said. "and that's when you really appreciated their unique style of play and how cohesive they were. It was actually frustrating to play against them. We'd do these controlled scrimmage drills and when you had to go against them you'd never touch the puck. You'd just chase it around, and they just kind of toyed with you a little bit, with their style of play. It was about possession and patience with the puck. You'd chase them around, and all of a sudden somebody would slip in the back door and the next thing you know they had a breakaway. It was very frustrating."

As a gifted center-ice man himself and a lifelong student of the game, Yzerman spent a lot of time watching Larionov.

"Igor is a very, very intelligent guy, very well-thought-out in everything he does. It was like he just thought his way around the ice. He didn't waste any excess energy. He was very efficient in his management of the puck. And tremendous hockey sense – probably one of the smartest, and the best vision, of any player that I've played with or against."

To watch Larionov on the ice was to see a master at work, like watching Picasso at his canvas, and there was no lack of appreciation from those watching on the Red Wings' bench. Instead of rushing hell-bent into the opponents' zone, he'd slow the game down. If he didn't see a play, he would circle back, sometimes well into his own zone, and renew a more organized attack.

"With Igor, as he was going through the neutral zone and into the offensive zone, instead of looking at the net he was always looking behind him, waiting for people to come from the defensive side," Yzerman said. "He just waited for everybody to come to him. He drew people to him, and that created an open space. It was up to the other players to jump into that space.

"I use the analogy of European football – soccer – which is played on a surface much larger (than an ice rink). Igor played the game like a midfielder. Slava played somewhat the same way, although he was a defender. You didn't really see Igor, or any of the players other than Sergei (Fedorov), who had exceptional ability, try to beat guys one-on-one. The other four just let the puck do the work; they were all about drawing people to them, finding an open space and putting the puck there for a teammate."

The strategy was foreign, figuratively and literally, to players groomed in Canada and the United States, where hockey is a north-south game in which wingers are coached to stay in their lanes and look for body contact as much as play with the puck.

"We grew up in North America and we were taught to always keep going ahead," Yzerman said. "You gain zones. You gain lines. You get it in, and if you can carry it in, great; if not, you make sure you get it in and go chase it. Their philosophy was totally different."

Eventually, Larionov would create an open space or find a

teammate flying through the neutral zone and deftly flick the puck onto the blade of that teammate's stick.

"A different mindset, different logic, to the way they played the game," Yzerman said, his words oozing praise and admiration.

That's how it was in the Wings' locker room, too. Though Igor was not a very vocal guy, he had the respect of everyone in the room – including his coaches. Everyone marveled at the depth with which he could talk about not just hockey, but global politics, the theater, international cinema, fine wine, soccer and chess, among myriad other topics.

"He was called The Professor for a reason," said defenseman Nicklas Lidstrom, an alternate captain. "He was very smart, and we all knew how skilled he was on the ice. Not only the younger Russian guys, but all the rest of the guys in the room looked up to him, respected him, because we knew what he went through to come over here."

Listen to Larionov describe his game, and his role seems incredibly difficult, remarkably easy and impossible all at once.

"My job was to keep everybody happy, because everybody wants to be in the spotlight. Everybody wants to read their name in the newspaper the next day," Larionov said. "Who scored the goals? Who made the highlights? So my job was to help take care of the defense, pick them up, and when we go offensively to feed my wingers. It was like that with the KLM line in Russia, and the same in Detroit.

"I knew the ability of each player, and I had to choose: Who is in a better position? In my mind, I can see Kozzie going wide, and maybe taking a couple of guys with him. Then I see Sergei coming from behind full speed. Slava Fetisov finds me in the middle and gets me the puck. Now I have to choose, quickly, what's the next direction the puck should go? Vladdie (Konstantinov) is going too, so that's, you know, a lot of options. But you've got to decide quick because the game is so fast – and you have to keep your head up.

"My job was to direct the offense – to the right or left, or in the middle. So for me it was always a pleasure to have those guys with me because they're always hungry, and they're always in the right spots. I have to get it to the right guy. That was my game, to keep everybody happy. But it was also a big responsibility."

Off the ice, Larionov was an equally compelling and intriguing personality, bringing a level of sophistication rarely seen in a locker room of professional athletes.

"Very refined, his mannerisms, playing chess on our airplane, introducing his teammates to fine wines," said Dave Lewis said, Bowman's assistant coach. "That's how he got his nickname. He looked like a professor. He thought like a professor. He talked politics. He brought a worldly vision and experience to the rink every day, an awareness about what was going on in the world that the other guys certainly didn't bring."

Denise Harris, a flight attendant on the team plane, noticed a dramatic change, a cultural shift, as soon as Larionov arrived and brought a chess set on board their team flights.

"He was always calm, always thinking and always strategizing," she said. "Chess is a game of strategies, moves and counter moves. I think it sort of took some players by surprise. They were used to playing cards, spitting tobacco into a cup and having a Molson's. Now suddenly we have some classical music playing on another part of the plane, where they're having some fine wine, playing chess and reading literature. But Igor never said anything. He never put it in anybody's face. He just put it out there for the guys. It was his quiet type of leadership."

Soon, there were as many chess boards as card games, and Harris was challenged to find enough space on the plane for the wine along with the beer. But she did notice a certain rise in the level of refinement.

"Hockey players, they're not dumb," Yzerman said. "Some are very, very smart guys. But our interests are simple, and focused. Igor, just the way he goes about things. He's very bright. He's very well read. He's very current, up-to-date on what's going on around the world. He's a really interesting man, a great guy to have dinner with, to talk and to hear about his life, about the things he's done, his viewpoints on things.

"He was very unique as an athlete. Interesting in the way he played: He used his mind. He was a great athlete, in very, very good shape, who took really good care of himself. He instinctively just thought his way through the game."

Yzerman and his teammates were enraptured by Larionov and Fetisov when they could get the elder statesmen to share details of their lives before the NHL.

"We enjoyed listening to them telling their stories, of growing up and playing in the Russian system and how they were finally able to come over to North America," Yzerman said. "It was fascinating for us, what they had to go through and the things they had to do. We had an appreciation, a real appreciation, for what they went through, and how proud these guys were to come over here.

"They enjoyed winning. That's all they did in Russia was win. And they wanted to come over here and prove to everybody: 'Hey, we can play in this league. We can be good players. And we can win.' I have great appreciation for what they all went through, the adjustments they had to make, their willingness to change, too. And to become an important part of a Stanley Cup Championship team."

CHAPTER 12

Game-Changers:
On and Off the Ice

Detroit Red Wings television broadcaster Dave Strader knew he was witness to history in the National Hockey League on October 27, 1995, at Calgary's Olympic Saddledome, and he had the presence of mind to do something about it. When the game ended in a lopsided 3-0 Detroit victory, Strader carefully tucked away two copies of the final score sheet when he left the arena, intent on preserving a piece of that history.

Four months earlier, the Wings had advanced to the Stanley Cup Finals, only to be humiliated in a four-game sweep by the New Jersey Devils. Nevertheless, expectations among fans and the media were sky-high once again. But the new season began with a bit of a hangover. Detroit had won just four games, lost three and tied two in its first nine games that fall. Playing win-some-lose-some-tie-some hockey wasn't quite what fans – or team management – had in mind. But change came swiftly and dramatically on that night in Calgary, when anyone on either bench or among the near sellout crowd of 19,001 could sense that a seismic shift had taken place in the NHL. It happened in the early minutes of the game, when Detroit coach Scotty Bowman sent the first all-Russian five-man unit over the boards.

Newly acquired Igor Larionov was at center, flanked by Sergei Fedorov on one wing and Slava Kozlov on the other. On the blue line were two former Soviet national team captains, Slava Fetisov and Vladimir Konstantinov. International hockey was crashing the NHL party, and this would prove to be kryptonite against the long-held view – predominantly throughout Canada – that the more Europeans on a team the less likely it would succeed. Wings executive Jim Devellano said he heard it in his own dressing room from one of his most reliable veterans, who was blunt in his warning about relying too much on imports: "You keep drafting them Europeans, Jimmy, and they're soft," the unidentified player said. "We'll never win a Stanley Cup here with those guys."

Larionov, one of the more analytical minds the game has seen, understood the significance of the moment in Calgary and what it meant for his country and the pride Soviet players and fans had in their game. The "Us vs. Them" rivalry between the Soviet Union and Canada was celebrated in both nations for its fury, always passionate and often brutal. Like when a Canadian player used his stick as pole-ax to chop at the ankle of the best Russian player, sending him off the ice with broken bones. Throughout history, this was a battle of nations among worthy adversaries. Now the Red Wings were planning to deploy five Russians in a single unit on an NHL roster, melding two distinctly different systems. So, yes, Larionov acknowledged in a conversation with reporters hours before that game in Calgary, those five Soviet players carried no small burden into this historic moment.

"It's a lot of pressure because it's the first time in NHL history five Russian guys play on the same unit," he said. "And, of course, it's bigger pressure because it's the Detroit Red Wings, one of the best teams in the National Hockey League."

Fedorov, who moved from center to right wing when the Russians were united, was far less apprehensive. The best of a younger generation of Soviet players was coming off a season in which he was voted the league's most valuable player, cementing his status as one of the game's most prominent figures.

"Why not?" he asked, responding to a question about whether an all-Russian unit could be successful in the NHL. "We definitely understand each other because we went to the same school, Red Army school. We know how to play with each other. And it seems to me we know what the coach wants from us. We stick with the team game plan, and hopefully we go from there."

As it turned out, those five Russian players would revolutionize the brand of one of the oldest franchises in the NHL. Seemingly overnight, the Red Wings elevated their play to a level rarely witnessed in the league, breaking records and raising expectations sky-high. To say this new five-man unit dominated that night in Calgary is a colossal understatement. And they did it with typical Soviet-style flair and elegance. On the game's first goal at 10:06 of the opening period, the Russian Five transitioned from defense into offense so quickly that some Calgary players were still on the attack when the red light was flashing behind their goaltender.

Just seconds before, the Flames were moving the puck forward in the neutral zone beyond the center red line when Konstantinov pounced on a turnover in the Detroit zone and instinctively flipped a backhand pass to Fedorov at center ice. In one fluid motion and without the slightest hesitation, Fedorov dished a no-look backhand pass to Kozlov, who already had done an about-face, turning toward the Calgary net at the far blue line. Fedorov's pass hit Kozlov in stride, the puck landing on the blade of his stick, and there was nothing but enemy ice for 60 feet between him and helpless Flames goaltender Trevor Kidd. Kozlov sprinted in unmolested, and when his initial shot rebounded off Kidd's pads he backhanded the puck into a yawning net for what stood as the game-winning goal. With that single play, in a handful of seconds when the Wings looked like hockey's version of the Harlem Globetrotters against a team of pylons, the National Hockey League was forever changed.

Led by the Russian Five in their "Soviet Re-Union" that night in Calgary, the Wings won, 3-0. Larionov also scored a goal. Fedorov earned his second assist. Bowman's Russian unit recorded an astounding 15 of Detroit's 25 shots on goal, while Calgary spent the night chasing the puck around the ice. The Flames managed just eight shots on goal, a record low in the franchise's history. Then again, it's impossible to shoot the puck when the other team controlled it all night. That became the hallmark of Detroit Red Wings hockey that opponents have been trying to emulate ever since.

From the vantage of the press box high above the ice surface, where Strader was calling the game with partner Mickey Redmond, it was a virtuoso performance by five men who looked like they were playing a different game. It often looked like men competing against boys. After one particularly dominating shift by the Russians, the opposing skaters went to their bench clearly disheartened – and maybe even a little disoriented.

Up in the TV booth, Redmond turned to Strader, his broadcast partner, and said of the Flames, "They're going to need some Dramamine to cure their motion sickness after that one."

The day after the Russian Five's debut, Strader tracked down the five Russians and asked them to sign both copies of the game summary. This wasn't a 12-year-old autograph-seeker but a seasoned professional who, like most members of the media, wouldn't dream of asking a player for his signature. What Strader did that day underscored, and helped to preserve, what has become a significant moment in hockey history.

Strader gave one of the sheets to Red Wings public relations director Bill Jamieson for the team's archives. The other? Strader had it 20 years later when he was broadcasting Dallas Stars games. He called it one of his most cherished mementos of a distinguished career that includes the 2017 Foster Hewitt Memorial Award and a place in the Hockey Hall of Fame.

Red Wings great Gordie Howe, widely acknowledged to be the finest player the sport has produced, played a decidedly different brand of hockey than the Russian Five, but he agreed with them about one thing: the dump-and-chase strategy popularized in the National Hockey League was dreadful.

"Why the hell would you give the puck away by throwing it into the opponents' zone all the time?" Howe would say. "It's too damned hard to get back again."

That was the first thing people noticed when coach Scotty Bowman put the Russian Five together.

"When they were on the ice together as a unit – depending on the situation in the game – we'd sometimes be sitting there on the bench and just laugh," Hall of Fame left wing Brendan Shanahan said. "We'd see what they were doing, and it didn't always work either, but we laughed at the freeness in which they tried things."

In other words, the creativity that was the hallmark of Soviet ice hockey developed by the legendary Anatoly Tarasov was mind-blowing even to some of the finest practitioners of the game, like Shanahan and his Detroit teammates.

"You'd run into guys on other teams, and they'd always say, 'It's no fun playing against the Red Wings because you guys don't let us play with the puck,'" Shanahan said. "That always stuck with me."

That "it's our puck" mentality started with the Russian Five, spread throughout the team and eventually throughout the National Hockey League. Until then, it had been common to describe Russian hockey as "a possession game," meaning that they liked to control the puck while advancing it down the ice. NHL teams typically deployed a different strategy commonly known as "dump and chase" or "chip and chase." This required a more physical edge. Forwards would shoot the puck into the opponent's end and chase it down, often tangling with a defenseman to retrieve it and set up an offensive play as teammates arrived in the attacking zone.

Soviet-style hockey decreed custody of the puck. Russians liked to attack as a group of five players, the most important of whom were the four without the puck. They found open ice and soon one of them would get the puck and pass it to another teammate before defenders had a chance to recover. If they couldn't advance, they would circle back, often all the way back to their own zone, regroup and start over. This kind of play would drive most North American players and coaches crazy, but the Soviets did it with spectacular efficiency and success.

Hall of Fame Montreal goaltender and Cornell-educated Ken Dryden, in his best-selling 1983 book, "The Game," argued that it was hyperbole to described Soviet hockey as merely a possession game. Few paid more detailed attention to the nuances of the sport on or off the ice than Dryden. He noted that in a typical NHL game the puck changes hands between teams an average of more than six times a minute. That's about 130 times a period, nearly 400 times a game. The transition, the speed at which a team can flick a switch and go from defense to offense, is critical. No one did it better than the Soviets.

The goal by Kozlov on that historic night in Calgary showcased the chasm between North American hockey and Russian hockey. It illustrated flawlessly how a five-man unit working together can transition from defense to offense: How fast they set up; the patterns they created instinctively to take advantage of a team that, just an instant before, was on the attack; how they turned what seemed like a simple advantage into a critical, game-turning goal. That was what separated Russian hockey from the rest of the world. That is what made the Soviets so dominant in international competition – even against the best players in the National Hockey League.

"We had been the best. So however we played it was the best way," Dryden wrote, adding that the difference between the two styles of play were strikingly evident in the 1972 Summit Series between Canada and the Soviet Union, billed in both nations as a showdown of Armageddon proportions. The Canadians excelled in those parts of the game that featured physical domination –in the corners, along the boards and the front of both nets, body checking, stick play, face-offs, intimidation, shooting from a distance and emotion. But the Soviets were better, far better, in the game's fundamental skills – passing, team play, quickness, finishing around the net. These were the traditional skills the Canadians had developed and then forsaken as incompatible with the modern game.

"The Soviets showed us otherwise," Dryden wrote, noting that the Russians had perfected those traditional skills in ways that shocked all of Canada. "It is an all-ice commitment, but always under control. It was *our* game played *their* way."

As more and more Russians came to the NHL among the flood of Europeans starting in the early 1990s, a watershed change was under way. Suddenly, and rather dramatically, it wasn't the physically dominating, punishing teams that were winning. Nor were the teams so adept at clogging the neutral zone with an impenetrable defense designed to win a 2-1 hockey game. The European invasion showed North Americans in no uncertain terms that their game was inferior to what was being played in the Soviet Union, in Sweden, in the former Czechoslovakia, and in Finland.

The reason: Simply put, the game was taught differently abroad than it was in Canada and the United States, said Bryan Murray, the former Detroit coach and general manager.

"The Europeans, the Russians especially, were way ahead of us," he said. "We'd put our kids on the ice with one puck most of the time. You see the Russian kids practice and they had a hundred pucks. All of them were skating, and they had a puck on their sticks the entire time. In our practices, there was always lots of shooting, but the drills would usually consist of one pass, get the puck, shoot it, get the drill over with and move on, either score a goal or hit somebody.

"In Russia, and wherever they play hockey in Europe, they learn to pass, learn how to do things in the tight little areas with the puck. And you saw that with the Russian Five. When they were playing together, they weren't afraid to go back and regroup – because of their puck skills. They knew there weren't going to be many miscues. The Russians in particular, when they came over they had such great puck-possession skills, it literally changed our game."

Europeans also play on a larger ice surface, 200 feet long and 100 feet wide, compared to the NHL rink, which is 200 feet by 85 feet. That allows more room for gifted players to showcase their skills. In North America, hockey is very much a contact sport; physical intimidation and brute force are big parts of the game.

In the former Soviet Union, ice hockey evolved without influence from the North American game. After World War II, dictator Josef Stalin wanted to showcase Communism's dominance through sports, and he delegated the job of creating a world-class hockey program in a country with no history with the game to Anatoly Tarasov.

Tarasov built something special, integrating elements from chess, ballet and the traditional Russian sport of bandy, a game played on ice, using a single round ball, between two teams of eleven players on skates each using sticks to try to move the ball forward and into a net past a goalkeeper. Played on a rectangle of ice the size of a soccer field, bandy remains a popular sport in Russia as well as Scandinavian countries and in some parts of the United Kingdom.

When the Soviets began competing in international ice hockey events in the 1950s, their first players came from the sport of bandy.

In other words, as Igor Larionov doesn't mind saying, Russian hockey came from Russia, not Canada. And until he and other Soviets started to come to North America, Soviet and Canadian ice hockey were like different sports in the way they were played. The Soviet game was wide open, free-flowing, creative and offensive, with all five players deployed as a unit. North Americans played a simpler game – hit, shoot, score – deploying their five skaters in two units – a forward line of three players and a defensive pair, which were mixed and matched throughout the game, according to a coach's whim and intuition.

Europeans who came to compete in the NHL were widely looked on as timid compared to the average Canadian – at least until Vladimir Konstantinov arrived in Detroit and disabused the entire hockey-loving world of that notion.

But the Russian game, conceived by Tarasov and handed down to this day, embraced imagination and resourcefulness – ingenuity with the puck that was virtually instinctive. How could five men work together in a way to advance the puck from one end of the rink to the other through five other men and create a scoring opportunity – without the opposing team even touching the puck? Larionov explained.

"When our line hit the ice, the puck is always on our sticks and everybody is moving to open areas so you've always got like two or three options to make a play," he said. "Why give the puck away? There's no reason to do that. No reason. Their goalie is just going to stop it behind the net, and then you're going to waste like 30 seconds to chase after it and try to get it back."

Better, as the Russians have said since they invented their own brand of ice hockey, to try to make a play, which is much simpler when all five guys on the ice are of the same mind. And as each of Detroit's Russian Five has said repeatedly, it's almost second nature when they are all from the same school – the Central Red Army Club of the Soviet Union. That program produced some of the best players ever to hold a hockey stick, including Larionov and Slava Fetisov.

"Igor and Slava, they were always together," Sergei Fedorov recalled. "Remembering those guys, how they played defense and offense. They just communicated so well. Nothing really presented any danger to them. It was amazing chemistry. I've said many times, and I'm going to keep saying it: I was one of the luckiest hockey players ever to be a young guy on that (Red Army) team and see what those guys did day in and day out, two hours in practice, sometimes four hours in a row, day in and day out. That's probably why I had a chance to become that hockey player I was throughout my career."

Fedorov was among the next generation of great Soviet players with Vladimir Konstantinov and Slava Kozlov, who also counted his blessings at being able to play with two legendary countrymen in Detroit.

"When I was young I used to watch them on TV, how they played, The Five," Kozlov said of the celebrated Green Line of the CSKA. "They made Russian and Soviet hockey famous, and to be with such partners on the same line in Detroit, I got really, really lucky."

Kozlov was referring to the unit that included Larionov at center with wingers Sergei Makarov and Vladimir Krutov, and defensemen Fetisov and Alex Kasatonov. But Kozlov knew, too, that Detroit's Russians enjoyed some rather unique treatment by Bowman and his coaching staff.

"Our biggest privilege was that the coaches didn't touch us or try to teach us how to play hockey," Kozlov said. "We were amongst ourselves and would talk to each other. I was actually coached by the other guys. I adjusted not to what the coaches were saying but to what the guys were saying. I would do everything that my older partners told me.

"We were allowed to do more than the others, but everybody in our five, we were the masters of the craft, so we could do those things."

Kozlov spoke without an ounce of bravado. Conceit, arrogance, self-aggrandizement – whatever you care to call it – just isn't in his DNA. Like the others in the Russian Five unit, he was a "Master of Sport" in the Soviet Union – and he had the medal to prove it. When he said the coaches just let them play their game without getting in the way, he was merely confirming the same truth that Scotty Bowman spoke.

Larionov was the last of the five former Soviets to join the Red Wings, and arguably the most important. He was the switch – the one who really made the Russian Five go. He played the ice surface as though it were a giant chess board and he was always thinking three, four, five moves ahead – like the greatest players always did.

"It's all about breaking down the pieces, you know creativity and improvisation," he said. "You start five against five, so you have to beat one guy to make it five against four, you kind of break down any defense – and it's fun because everything is clicking. Then you try to make it four against three, three against two – always with the advantage. To do that, you have to be constantly moving. That's how we play. Sometimes make five, six passes, short passes, give-and-go, to make a big difference. Everything is clicking. We got chemistry going, and for us, we just enjoy every minute."

Inevitably, there is a defensive breakdown. Maybe two. Chaos ensues and the Russians have a serious advantage. That's when the fun really begins.

"All of a sudden, somebody – and it can be anybody from our line – maybe has a breakaway," Larionov said. "How many breakaways did Konstantinov have? And he was a defenseman, you know? And he had maybe one or two a game. That was unheard of in those years."

It was also cause for the occasional belly laugh for players on the bench – given the right moment, as Shanahan recalled.

"Suddenly, inexplicably, it was Konstantinov on a breakaway going forehand-backhand to score," Shanahan said. "And we'd be thinking, 'What is he doing up there?' Or we'd see Konstantinov and Fetisov going in together, and we'd sit there laughing. 'Yep, there's our two defenseman having a two-on-one break.' The Russians didn't always score, but they always had the puck."

If there was even a slightest frustration – for the Russians as well as for fans and media who loved watching them play together – it was that they didn't play together enough. Larionov often centered a line with Shanahan and Martin Lapointe, two big wingers. Fedorov would more frequently center a line with Kozlov on his left and Doug Brown, the only American player on the Wings' roster at the time. In fact, Brown played so frequently with the four Russians before Larionov's arrival that he was often referred to as Doug "Brownov."

"We always want to play more, but I guess the coach sees more than we do," Kozlov said. "I was the youngest one at the time, so I didn't analyze or think about those things."

Bowman said it was by design that he didn't play the Russian Five regularly. To do so would risk overexposure, giving opposing coaches more opportunity to design effective defenses against them.

"When they first started playing together, I said, 'Wow. Whatever they're doing, they're not doing it like we do, you know?'" Bowman said. "They were like an offensive machine. The way they played, it's like all great offensive players: If the other team can figure it out, there's a risk they could capitalize.

"So we tried to use them at the right time, when things were not going according to what we wanted. They were game-changers as a unit."

The Russians were Detroit's nuclear option.

"That was the genius of Scotty," Shanahan said. "The other teams had to prepare for it, but Scotty had a lot of other line combinations he could use. But I can think back to all those games from that one playoff year that the Russian Five were together. . . If you look at a lot of our big goals and overtime goals, the game-winning goals in each series, you can see one or two of those guys were directly involved."

Beyond the goals and the glory, though, was the impression the Russian Five made on their Detroit teammates. The North Americans learned by watching, and occasionally giggling, from the bench, as well as practicing against the Russians daily.

"It wasn't like we had a team meeting where we said, 'Let's adopt this style of play,'" Shanahan said. "We just started to realize that if you scrimmaged against these guys it was very, very frustrating. It wasn't fun. You'd skate around for 30-40 seconds and not come anywhere near the puck, so it just sort of became the way our whole team played.

"We used to say before games, 'It's our puck. Don't let the other team play with it. And even if we don't have anywhere to go with it, let's still hang on to it. Let's keep it.'"

As every hockey player knows, playing with the puck is a lot more fun than chasing it around, but the Russian Five took it to an entirely new level.

"All of a sudden, you throw those five guys out there and it was magical, what they were doing, how they were playing," said Kris Draper, the center on the checking unit called the Grind Line. "Sometimes you just had to sit there and laugh. They were throwing pucks into space, regrouping. But to me, probably the greatest thing is they were having so much fun out there, that's the amazing thing."

———⟫✦⟪———

Off the ice, the Russians were as integral to the team as they were on it. Card games were a favorite pastime among players throughout the league, especially those fortunate enough to have their own planes, like the Red Wings. For Slava Fetisov, a deck of cards amounted to a cottage industry of sorts.

"Never play cards with Papa Bear," Shanahan warned. "He somehow stays out of all the small pots, but whenever there's a big pot, Papa Bear's in, and he usually wins. Slava's the kind of guy that if you shake his hand you'd better count your fingers when you're done because he might have one of them without you ever knowing.

"I'm not saying he cheats. I'm just saying he's a very smart guy."

After Larionov arrived, however, the card games became fewer. Larionov introduced the team to chess, "and pretty soon the whole plane was playing it," Shanahan recalled. "Igor was the grandmaster. The rest of us were all sort of fighting for second place."

Shanahan and Larionov were common opponents. Sometimes players paired up, two-man teams against one another, often with a crowd of teammates overlooking their shoulders, trying to figure out the best move. Competition was fierce.

"It was like war," Darren McCarty told Mitch Albom of the Detroit Free Press. Larionov, who has played chess since he was six, recalled losing once to his Detroit teammates, but he shrugged it off.

"Consider the competition?" Albom asked.

"Exactly," Larionov said.

But winning and losing a board game, even a serious one like chess, was not as important as how it not only brought players together, but how it got them to use their brains in a different way, a way that might help them sort out the chaos in a fast-moving game like ice hockey. Larionov knew this, of course. So did some of his more cerebral teammates.

"It just shows how Igor always played the thinking game," teammate Nick Lidstrom said. "Instead of playing cards, he played chess – the perfect way of using your mind. And he got a lot more players hooked on the game on the plane."

Larionov also introduced a unique way to warm up before games by bringing a soccer ball to the rink – something he had initiated at previous NHL stopovers in Vancouver and San Jose.

"One of the traditions in Russia – in Sweden, too, for that matter – was a game called two-touch with a soccer ball," Lidstrom said. "We actually did it in the locker room."

Two-touch is a common soccer passing drill, stopping the ball with a foot and kicking it – touching it twice.

"I wasn't much of a soccer player but it looked like they were getting a good little sweat," Draper said, "and so one day I asked if I could join in and kick it around and get a warm up going. Next thing you know, we probably had three-quarters of the team warming up playing soccer and truly having fun with it."

The game quickly got so big they had to take it into the corridors outside their dressing room. And of course, the drill took on a bit of an edge among spirited athletes.

"It could get a little competitive," Lidstrom said. "You want to win, but you're playing against your teammates. I think that brings the team even closer together, because you're doing something as a team before the game even starts."

Shanahan could see how that early Russian influence changed the entire league off the ice, as well.

"I never got into it much, but you look around now and every team plays some kind of kickball before games," he said. "Off the ice, those guys were just as important. They mixed with everybody. They didn't just go around as the Russian Five. They were good teammates. They were real good teammates."

Not all hockey players are created equal. NHL teams typically are built under a modern-day caste system. Teams typically have four three-man forward lines, three pairs of defensemen and two goaltenders. Forwards strive to be among the top six, earning the right to play on one of the two lines designed to provide scoring, lines that tend to get more ice time in the game's most important moments. The so-called fourth line is typically designed to play defense, often against the opposing team's top players, or provide energy by playing with a physical edge. The third line frequently is a hybrid of offense and defense.

While scoring is important, the most successful teams in the end are typically those with four efficient lines, with the fourth unit contributing important minutes in every game. When Scotty Bowman put his Russian Five together, Detroit's fourth line of Kris Draper, Kirk Maltby and Darren McCarty (or Joe Kocur), gained the kind of stature typically reserved for some of the franchise's biggest stars. In fact, that Grind Line, as the Draper unit came to be known, may be the most renowned trio in Detroit Red Wings history behind the famed Production Line of Ted Lindsay, Sid Abel and Gordie Howe, which led the team to a Stanley Cup dynasty in the 1950s.

Merely practicing against the Russians each day helped them all to improve, Draper said. But sometimes a defining moment presented itself amid the tranquility of the dressing room, when Larionov would quietly hold court.

"I was so lucky," Draper said. "I sat beside Igor Larionov. He was a quiet guy. Very quiet. Nicknamed 'The Professor' for a reason. I remember times when he'd talk to me, Malts and Mac and tell us: 'You're better than what you think you are. You guys aren't just a chip-and-chase line. You can make plays. You can score goals. You can skate.'

"And all of a sudden, you have a guy like Igor instilling a lot of confidence in you like that. It helped to evolve our game. Obviously, when you're practicing with and against the best players day in and day out, you're only going to get better. That goes for any sport. But when you're surrounded by great people and great hockey players and you see the way they play and how they compete. They make everybody better. That's what elite hockey players like the Russian Five did. They made us all better players."

CHAPTER 13

Unexpected Turbulence

Detroit's flight to the hockey stratosphere was not without turbulence. There would be several painful, mind-numbing setbacks as the Red Wings tried to gain altitude. Denise Harris, the lead flight attendant on the private plane that shuttled the Wings around, remembered a moment so heartbreaking she thought about making other travel plans.

In June 1995, the city was delirious with anticipation. The Wings had dominated three playoff opponents, winning twelve games and losing just two, to advance to the Stanley Cup Finals for the first time since 1966. They were the overwhelming favorites to finally win it all. Optimism remained unbridled even after Detroit lost the first two games on home ice to the New Jersey Devils. Not to worry, everyone said, the Wings were too good. They would rebound. Losing this series was inconceivable.

"I remember when we were down, 2-0, I felt very comfortable that we could turn it around and win it," Sergei Fedorov said.

But Detroit's hockey season lasted just two more games. The Devils won both, by identical 5-2 scores; the Wings were swept in four games. Another opportunity squandered.

"That was ugly," said Harris, who for the first time in her career felt like taking a commercial flight home. "I didn't want to go, because I knew what that plane was going to be like."

She was wrong. It was worse.

The Wings' team plane, as Harris describes it, was like "a flying locker room," with all the typical banter. Leaving Detroit for road games, players broke out the cards or boards for cribbage or chess, and honed their already sharp competitive edges. Returning to Detroit after a game, the plane often resembled a flying medevac unit with players in various stages of disrepair. The most valuable commodity, after a healthy supply of cold Molson's, was ice. Plenty of ice to wrap around sprained ankles, swollen knees, discolored bruises and mouths or faces mutilated by errant sticks, flying pucks or skate blades.

Several players who had been nursing injuries needed routine medical treatment on the way home from New Jersey in that quiet airplane. But there was no immediate cure for the pain Slava Fetisov was feeling as he sat huddled by himself, a broken man. He was 37 years old with a lot of miles on those golden legs of his, and he wasn't sure how much longer he could stay in the game.

He had felt as though the Red Wings had rescued him in a trade just 2½ months earlier. He had found new life, his career rejuvenated. He had proved to all his doubters he still could play at a high level, scoring 14 points in 14 games to help the Wings roll into the playoffs as a heavy Stanley Cup favorite.

Now this. The ultimate insult. The team that had traded him was now parading around with the trophy.

"Slava broke down on the plane after that sweep, and it was hard to watch," Harris told documentary filmmaker Joshua Riehl. "Here's this incredible hockey player and he's crushed. He's embarrassed. For himself, for his team.

"It was a long quiet ride back to Detroit. The energy was so low. Nobody wanted anything. I didn't want to come out of the galley. I didn't even want to go down the aisle because there's nothing you can say, nothing that can make things better."

If anyone might have been able to offer Fetisov some words of solace, it was one of his countrymen. Sergei Fedorov, Vladimir Konstantinov or Slava Kozlov might have found the right words to console him in a language they all had in common. None tried.

"The younger Russians, I think, were in shock to see Slava emote so much over this loss," Harris said. "And I think that maybe it was a lightning-rod moment for them, to see how much he wanted to win the Stanley Cup."

Losses like these are always the most painful for the oldest players who know they're running out of chances, but this one was especially cruel for Fetisov because of the circumstances.

"I remember Slava being very down after losing to the Devils, the team that he had played for, and then they were the winning team," defenseman Nicklas Lidstrom said. "He took that very hard, but I think it kind of gave him more fuel to the fire to come back and try to win a Stanley Cup."

Years later, Steve Yzerman, the captain of that Red Wings team who, after retirement, found success at the general manager of the Tampa Bay Lightning, was more forgiving of his team that lost to New Jersey.

"When I look back on it, we were very banged up when we got to the Finals," he said. "We had a lot of guys who were limping around out there. And we need to give the Devils credit. They were playing playoff hockey. They were big and strong. They defended extremely well. They played hard and had a good power play and an awesome goaltender.

"They were a really good team and a deserving champion."

Truth be told, that New Jersey Devils team broke the Red Wings' spirit. Fedorov could feel it by the time the Wings arrived at the Meadowlands.

"I don't know why, but we were not excited that we can win. That's the feeling I got after a few games," he said. "We lost two games, and we have a great team. But I remember thinking: 'Why are we not excited?' We've been trying already 3-4 years now, and we lose again. It was very frustrating, and it crushed us. It really crushed us."

In his heart of hearts, though, Fedorov had more than an inkling that this was not a championship Red Wings team. Not yet, anyway.

"Some guys played their own game," he said. "It was not possible for me to think that way, but they were a little more inside themselves instead of giving to the team. It happens in sports. It happened to us. That's why we got swept."

The Detroit Red Wings were an elite NHL club. But they weren't good enough.

"We didn't have the right players," Slava Kozlov said. "So some of them had to leave."

And others would take their place.

In the front of that quiet, flying locker room that night, in that emergency ward that had no cure for a broken heart, coach Scotty Bowman already was contemplating the changes that had to be made. He was convinced he'd already seen the template – just the year before when his heavily favored team had experienced one of the greatest upsets in Stanley Cup playoff history – and arguably the best thing that could have happened to them in their rise to prominence.

With the best record in the NHL's Western Conference, the Red Wings earned the No. 1 seed in the opening round of the 1994 Stanley Cup playoffs. Their opponent: the upstart San Jose Sharks, a three-year-old franchise that made it into the playoffs with a sub-.500 record and just 82 points as the conference's No. 8 seed.

The Sharks were led by center Igor Larionov and right wing Sergei Makarov, two members of the famed Soviet Green Line. Johan Garpenlov, a Swede who began his career with the Red Wings, was on the other wing. On defense was Sandis Ozolinsh, groomed in Soviet-controlled Latvia, and Jeff Norton, an American from Massachusetts who played at the University of Michigan. Both were offensively gifted defensemen, and they melded well with the style of hockey Larionov insisted on playing – even if it defied his boss.

Kevin Constantine was a rookie coach with the Sharks in 1993-94, and just 34 when he took the job. Though born in Minnesota, he advanced quickly up the coaching ranks by embracing the hallmarks of the North American game: Physical and uncompromising. Get the puck to center ice, shoot it into the opponent's zone and then charge in after it, which typically involved battling along the boards, in the corners or behind the goaltender's cage.

This was the antithesis of the way Larionov learned to play the game, and over dinner he told his young coach in no uncertain terms how he planned with his linemates. "Look, I am not a big man," he told

Constantine. "I'm not going to give the puck away only to have to go in and fight to get it back. Not when I don't have to."

That 1993-94 team was never Constantine's as much as it was Larionov's. And the Sharks responded by making the playoffs with an astounding 58-point improvement from the season before when they won just 11 games. Now, in their first-ever Stanley Cup playoff appearance, they were up against the vaunted Detroit Red Wings, and the way the series unfolded to its shocking conclusion made a powerful impression on Bowman.

"That five-man unit of theirs with Larionov, they played a pretty different style than anybody in the NHL at the time – and they beat us in the playoffs," Bowman said.

Against unimaginable odds, the Sharks defeated Detroit in seven games, winning the clincher at Joe Louis Arena, 3-2. A defensive breakdown – the kind that leads to changes after disappointing seasons – resulted in the clinching goal that stunned the crowd of nearly 20,000 Red Wings fans – and everyone else.

"Game 7, oh my God!" Fedorov said with a wince more than two decades later. "It was pretty upsetting. . . I just remember my ice time went down. That's all I'm going to say."

Players always remember when their time on ice doesn't measure up to their needs or desires. They seldom remember why – and with Bowman there was always a good reason, at least in his mind. But in this series, it was obvious: Igor Larionov outplayed Sergei Fedorov in nearly every game.

"We were better. We should have won," Fedorov said. "Seriously, things were not going our way. Now I'm thinking there was not a good enough team effort. But Igor's team had like a 'Russian Five' already – and they played really, really well."

It's worth noting that the Sharks also featured a hot goaltender, Latvian Arturs Irbe, another product of the Soviet system.

A year later, with a slew of stars and other marquee names on his roster, Bowman's team still was manhandled by New Jersey in the 1995 Stanley Cup Finals. That Detroit club, with the addition of Fetisov in April, featured four Russians. One of Bowman's first moves after the start of a new season in the fall of 1995 was a big one, and it brought the fifth former Soviet Red Army player, Igor Larionov, to Detroit. Would he be the final piece to the perplexing puzzle in the Motor City? It sure seemed like it.

After a short and unpleasant off-season, the Red Wings began the 1995-96 season again as heavy favorites to win the Stanley Cup. Yet they played like a team still fighting a hangover. After eight games, they were a pedestrian 3-3-2. That's when Bowman decided he'd seen enough lackadaisical defensive play and traded one of the NHL's most prolific goal-scorers, right wing Ray Sheppard, to San Jose for Igor Larionov, six weeks shy of his 36th birthday.

On October 26, two days after Larionov learned he had been traded to the Detroit Red Wings, he flew to Calgary to meet his new team, which was just starting a swing through far Western Conference opponents. In the hotel lobby, he was greeted by assistant coaches Dave Lewis and Barry Smith, who invited the player to meet and talk about the system – the type of hockey the Wings played. They explained about their "left-wing lock" defensive scheme, a system popularized in Sweden that Smith brought to Detroit. "Everything is understandable," Larionov responded. And then the coaches delivered the kicker: He would be playing at times, though not exclusively, on a unit that included Detroit's other four former Soviet players, and when he was on the ice with his other former Soviet teammates everything they had just told him about their system did not apply.

"You guys figure out for yourselves how you want to play," they said.

And that is yet another example of the genius of coach Scotty Bowman. He knew enough about the Soviets to understand that they were well-schooled in a certain style of play – and he knew better than to tinker with it. He just sent them over the boards and let them do what they do.

"I didn't do any strategizing with those players," Bowman said. "It was a little tricky at the beginning, because Igor and Sergei were both centers. We played Sergei at center most of the time because he was good on face-offs, very strong. But Igor was a smart player. I think as the game evolved, Sergei and he kind of worked it out."

The Russians, of course, were thrilled.

"The greatest moment, for me, was when Scotty put us together," Slava Fetisov said. "It's like a fish brought back in the water, you know? To play the game with lots of excitement and fun again. But this was a historical moment for us. It was a big challenge. How are we going to look? Are we gonna play our game?"

On game day in Calgary, though, the Russians were confused again. At the traditional morning skate, Bowman had them playing on separate lines. This was a common ploy by the devious coach. While most teams practice with the lines they're going to play in the game later that evening, Bowman knew opposing coaches and scouts were in the building, too, and he didn't like tipping his hand.

"Coming to the rink before the game, we learned we are going to play together," Fedorov said. "We say, 'OK, fine.' And so the five of us, we come together and say, 'So, how we gonna play, guys?' Pretty basic question, right?'"

Kozlov was a natural left winger, but Fedorov and Larionov had to figure out who is playing where and when. Fedorov would start at center on face-offs, but he'd move to right wing so that Larionov could do what he does best: direct traffic in all three zones, organize the attack, distribute the puck and fall back on defense when the opponent had the puck.

"Oh my God, it was 10 minutes of intense exchanging information," Fedorov remembered. "And when it ended, everybody said, 'OK, let's go warm up.' And in the warm-up, we're not together again!"

But a few minutes into the game, the Detroit Red Wings made hockey history when Bowman sent all his former Soviets over the boards, and the Russian Five was born. Fedorov will never forget that moment. He stood in the face-off circle and looked around at his teammates on the ice with him. All countrymen. Comrades.

"Slava (Fetisov) comes to me, and I say, 'I'm gonna win it to you,'" Fedorov said. "And that's how we started."

Jim Devellano, who as general manager drafted three of those players and as senior vice president questioned Bowman when he traded for the other two in the twilight of their careers, remembered watching the game at home.

"What we saw is what Scotty sort of suspected would happen – though maybe not to the degree that it did," Devellano said. "The Soviets played an entirely different game, passing back and forth. It was possession, possession, possession and boy, was it pretty exciting to watch!"

The poor Calgary Flames, used to taking advantage of visitors who frequently struggled when they played at a higher altitude, didn't know what hit them.

"We were playing on a plateau. Dry air," Fedorov said, adding that those conditions, combined with the excitement they were feeling, robbed them of power. "You want to do more, more, more every shift. It was exciting, but also nerve-wracking for 60 minutes. We were feeling each other. We were comfortable from the start, but honestly we didn't show near our potential."

It was extraordinary, nevertheless, and defenseman Nicklas Lidstrom knew he'd seen this impressive act before.

"I grew up watching the Soviet Union beating up on Sweden back in the mid-'80s. They had tremendous teams back then," Lidstrom said. "And I saw similarities, the way they were hanging onto the puck, not throwing it away, never dumping it in unless there was a good purpose for it. If they couldn't enter the (offensive) zone, they would circle back and regroup, then come up the middle at full speed. I could see something special was happening to our hockey team."

Even Larionov, the unmitigated perfectionist, was astonished by how the group played – and how well it was received in the hockey-loving community around Detroit.

"We didn't have much time to practice, and I was the last who joined that unit," he said. "But right from the opening face-off, we started moving the puck. We clicked right away and had a great time.

And the rest of the story: When we started to play more games, we started winning more, we started to make some noise in Hockeytown. The fans started to understand this is a brand new style of hockey."

Kozlov described it as "true Soviet hockey. The kind that brings results, like when the fruit ripens." The credit, he said, belonged to one man, Scotty Bowman, for having the foresight to bring them together. "He saw that the Russian Five can do something very original. We turn hockey upside down."

In the process, the Red Wings bull-dozed their way to their second straight Presidents' Trophy as the team with the best regular-season record in the NHL. After Larionov joined the team, the Wings went 58-10-5, finishing with a league record 62 victories. Their 131 points was second in league history only to the 60-win, 132-point Montreal Canadiens in 1976-77, also coached by Bowman.

Goaltender Patrick Roy threw his arms up in disgust toward the home crowd in the Montreal Forum after the mock cheer when he stopped a long shot from Sergei Fedorov. Roy was having an off night, as even the greatest players do. By then, still in the second period, his team was behind 7-1. While giving up five first-period goals, he began looking toward the bench, the goaltender's plea to his coach: Get me out of here before I get killed.

But his coach, Mario Tremblay, ignored him. To the Forum fans, among the most knowledgeable in the world, it seemed cruel and unusual, almost sadistic.

Eventually, Roy had had enough. The Avalanche continued in the second period, when he gave up two more goals. After the second one, he was skating toward his bench even before he was finally, mercifully summoned. When he arrived, he was glaring at Tremblay. The coach, arms folded, was glaring back. Roy was seething at being embarrassed in the same building where he had twice led the Canadiens to Stanley Cup crowns. Before taking his seat, he approached team president Ronald Corey, sitting in his usual seat behind the Canadiens' bench. Roy leaned into Corey and spat: "This is my last game in Montreal."

Four days later, on December 6, 1995, Patrick Roy was traded to the Colorado Avalanche in one of the most lopsided deals in NHL history. Lewis remembered his phone ringing that day and on the other end of the line Bowman sounding distressed. "This is not good news, that trade," Bowman said. "This is not good news for us." The Avs were already one of the most talented teams in the league, and now it had the goaltender needed to make some noise when it mattered.

Blame the Russian Five.

"The great Patrick Roy was really upset," Larionov recalled. "But I don't think it's anybody's fault. Any goalie could play that night and it didn't matter. We could do anything. We were in sync, and everything was going like poetry in motion."

Larionov had a goal and three assists in that game. Fedorov had a goal and four assists. Slava Kozlov had four goals. Slava Fetisov and Vladimir Konstantinov each contributed an assist. Of the thirty points awarded to Detroit players in the game summary, the Russian Five had fifteen.

"Our unit was really on fire, I remember that," Fedorov said. "It was fun to play, and the Montreal crowd was fair. They were a little bit clapping to our game. They knew something big was going on. When the opposition coach finally decided to remove Patrick from the net, we all knew something was going to happen."

"It was unbelievable," Bowman said, referring to events that transpired that night in Montreal – the game still referred to by Canadiens fans as the "Saturday Night Massacre" – that led Roy to quit his team and demand a trade. "The Russians were good in that game. But we kind of created the monster."

That was the genesis of what, for much of the next decade, was the best rivalry in North American sports: the Detroit Red Wings vs. the Colorado Avalanche.

Roy managed to stop just seventeen of twenty-six shots he faced in thirty-two minutes that December night when he shed his *bleu blanc et rouge* Montreal jersey for the final time. But he would have the last laugh.

"They didn't get a lot of value for Patrick, but he was the last piece for Colorado," Bowman said. "They were similar to us. They had Joe Sakic and Peter Forsberg in their prime. They had good depth. They were good offensively, good defensively. They were hard to beat."

And with Roy they finally had the goaltending, which meant for the foreseeable future the road to the Stanley Cup ran through Colorado as well as Detroit.

"We understood that Colorado would be our rival now, and that was such a big part of the game," Fedorov said. "That happened for quite a few years. Those games against Colorado and Patrick were the hardest games I played – regular season or playoffs. Everybody knows our battles."

After their record-breaking season, the Wings began the playoffs in 1996 again as the overwhelming favorite to roll to a Stanley Cup title. Then they ran into Roy and the Avalanche.

Despite how they dominated the opposition through eighty-two games of the six-month regular season, the Wings found it difficult to dispatch the Winnipeg Jets in the opening round. It took six games, primarily because Winnipeg goaltender Nikolai Khabibulin, another former Soviet player, was outstanding. His 51-save performance in Game 5 in Detroit forced the Wings to make another trip two time zones away to get their fourth victory that turned out to be the last game the Jets played in Winnipeg. The following season they would be known as the Phoenix Coyotes.

The second round, against a St. Louis Blues team led by Wayne Gretzky and Brett Hull, was even more difficult. The Blues were poised to upset the Wings, taking a 3-2 lead in the best-of-seven series home to St. Louis for Game 6. But the Wings prevailed, 4-2, to force a Game 7 that remains a classic in Detroit hockey history. The teams were tied, 0-0, after three periods before an overwrought Joe Louis Arena crowd. The game remained scoreless after the first twenty-minute overtime. With the intensity ratcheted up to a fever pitch, the game finally ended when captain Steve Yzerman rifled a 60-foot slapshot off the crossbar in the second minute of the second overtime – one of the most iconic goals in Red Wings' history. The Wings were euphoric to be going to the Western Conference finals for the second straight season.

They were also more mentally and physically fatigued. Now a big, strong Colorado Avalanche club with one of the greatest goaltenders in NHL history was coming to Detroit for a series that would start just three nights later. It didn't go well.

"We bombed," Slava Kozlov said.

The Avalanche began the series by winning the first two games in Detroit – 3-2 in overtime in the first game and 3-0 in the second. The Wings split the next two in Colorado, winning, 6-4, in Game 3 and losing, 4-2, in Game 4. In the Game 3 victory, Detroit's Russians played a leading role. Sergei Fedorov had four assists; Vladimir Konstantinov and Igor Larionov each had a goal; Kozlov had an assist and took a penalty when he and hulking Avs defenseman Adam Foote went into the boards together. Somehow, the much-smaller Kozlov eluded the check enough to slip away, wrap his left arm around Foote and push his face into the glass. The result was shocking to everybody in the building. By the time Foote skated to the bench, blood was pouring from a nasty gash in his head.

In the must-win Game 5 back in Detroit, the Russians again came up big. Fedorov, Kozlov and Larionov each scored goals in a 5-2 victory. Fedorov and Kozlov had assists. But perhaps the biggest play of the night for the Wings was a big hit by Konstantinov on Avalanche agitator Claude Lemieux. The series shifted to Colorado for Game 6 – and a brutal moment that ignited one of the most vicious and ruthless rivalries in all of sports.

It started at 14:07 of the first period as Kris Draper turned toward his bench for a shift change. His back was to the action. He had stopped competing. For Lemeiux, he was an easy, defenseless target. Lemieux skated up and cross-checked Draper in the back of head. Draper fell forward, his face hitting the edge of the boards in front of his bench before crumpling to the ice.

Lemieux was assessed a five-minute major penalty and a game misconduct penalty for the hit, resulting in an automatic ejection. Draper didn't return, either. In fact, he didn't play hockey again until the middle of the following season. He needed the time to heal, and spent much of his off-season on a liquid diet, his jaw wired shut. He had suffered a broken jaw, a shattered cheek and a fractured orbital bone that required surgery, many, many stitches, and a lot of dental work.

The Wings lost that game, 4-1, yet despite the ugliness of the series they honored one of the game's longstanding traditions by lining up to congratulate the Avs, who were on their way to the Stanley Cup Finals.

Draper returned from the hospital to McNichols Arena in time to board the bus for departure. His face looked like something out of a horror film, swollen and discolored with a jagged line of stitches. His teammates were shaken. One of them, Dino Ciccarelli, was infuriated – mostly with himself. "I can't believe I shook his fucking hand," he kept mumbling to himself and to anyone else within earshot. To a man, the Wings were outraged by the Lemieux hit on their vulnerable teammate. Already there was talk of what would happen when the teams met again.

The season was over, however, and any revenge the Wings might have in mind would have to wait several months. Larionov wasn't thinking about revenge. Like Fetisov the year before, he was overcome by disappointment of an opportunity gone adrift. At 35, he wondered how many more chances he would get. Adding insult to the heartbreak, people began wagging fingers in certain directions in their attempt to explain why such an enormously talented team like the Detroit Red Wings couldn't close the deal when hockey's greatest prize was at stake.

"We had a lot of negative press, and a lot of it went toward the Russian Five," Kozlov recalled. Most of that criticism came from outside Detroit. Much of it from the Canadian media clinging to the misguided belief that no team with so many Europeans – especially Russians – could ever win the Stanley Cup.

As proud as they were of their accomplishments, their history and their place in the game, the Russian Five didn't particularly care for the criticism. Nor did they shrug it off.

"It just spurred us on. We continued to push forward," Kozlov said. "We became angrier. And hungrier."

CHAPTER 14

Sweet Revenge

As might be expected with a franchise relying on so many European imports, the Detroit Red Wings never bought into the "myth" about how teams that relied on players from across the Atlantic – especially Russians – could never win hockey's top prize.

"People often said with Russians that the Stanley Cup really wasn't their focus, but I always doubted that," coach Scotty Bowman said. "Our Russian players were like North American players or other European players. The dream of winning the Stanley Cup is the biggest thing in hockey. What you did in the regular season is not what you're measured by; it's the Stanley Cup. And the Russian players caught on pretty quickly how much the Stanley Cup meant."

Swedish-born defenseman Nicklas Lidstrom, who succeeded Steve Yzerman as captain and in 2008 was the first European captain to lead his team to a Stanley Cup title, spent most of his career playing with teammates developed in the Soviet system. He saw enough to know the whispering campaign about Detroit's Russians was categorically unfounded.

"I didn't believe in that rumor about Russians not caring about the Stanley Cup," Lidstrom said. "The Russians are just as competitive as anyone else. They want to win, whether they're representing their country or playing in their hometowns. They want to win as much as anyone else, and playing for the Stanley Cup makes it all the more special. In today's hockey world, everyone knows about the NHL, about the Stanley Cup. Most people know about the history of the Stanley Cup, too, so I think the myth is no longer there."

To be sure, Detroit's Russians helped destroy it in the 1996-97 season – when the Red Wings launched their ubiquitous "Hockeytown" marketing campaign, which in Detroit's 71st season in the NHL forever wedded the city and the sport.

Like the season before, it began as if the Wings were suffering from the after-effects from the way the previous season ended. They lost four of their first six games before righting the ship with six straight victories. After setting a record with 62 victories, it was clear that the Wings were approaching this season with a different mindset: Pace yourselves, save something for the end, when it's needed most.

But every signature moment that season seemed to have the Russians' fingerprints all over it. The first came on December 26, against Washington at Joe Louis Arena.

When it ended, so suddenly and spectacularly at 2:39 of overtime, Scotty Bowman stood behind the bench shaking his head as he spread all the fingers and his thumb on his right hand while he turned to his assistants.

"Five," the lip readers could see him saying on the TV screen. "All five!"

The next day, a newspaper said with the headline: "Final score, Sergei Fedorov 5, Washington Capitals 4."

"I remember that one, for sure," Fedorov said, that beaming smile spreading across his face as he reminisced.

The game-winner was a thing of beauty. Fedorov split the defense, and he was between the face-off circles when he took a pass from defenseman Vladimir Konstantinov and beat Washington goaltender Jim Carey on the glove side.

Five. A career best for Fedorov, who had previously scored all his team's goals in a 4-4 tie against the Los Angeles Kings in February 1995 – but missed a penalty shot in overtime.

One player scoring three goals in a hockey game is an uncommon occurrence and typically celebrated by fans throwing their caps onto the ice. Hence the term "hat trick." Five goals by a single player is rare. After Fedorov did it, it wouldn't happen again for nearly twelve years, when

Marian Gaborik, a winger from Slovakia, scored five for Minnesota.

"It was just an unusual night," Fedorov said the next day. "I scored two goals, and then all of a sudden I was in a mood to score more. I'm just a happy kid. I'm still shaking. I am so excited. This is wonderful. The puck was just going in for me. I think all of my shots went in."

Vladimir Konstantinov established a career high with four assists. Igor Larionov assisted on three of the goals. Slava Fetisov assisted on one.

Just another night at the office for the Russian Five, but Fedorov didn't allow himself to get carried away. He was schooled better than that.

"In Russia, my coach would always say, 'What you did tonight is part of history. Now let's go out and practice tomorrow morning,'" he said. "I don't want to spoil it by talking all about it."

Fedorov's big night was a memorable moment in a season punctuated by a couple of important underlying themes. One had everything to do with the Colorado Avalanche. Red Wings fans were smart enough to know that their road to the Stanley Cup now went through Denver, and that was unsettling. Though the Red Wings remained one of the NHL's preeminent teams, no one was taking for granted that this was finally their year to win it all. They had experienced too many disappointments for that. And they knew that until the Wings found a way to beat Colorado, it wasn't going to happen.

The other major theme, far more internal and understated publicly, was how committed the team's Russians were to help Detroit overcome a Stanley Cup drought of more than four decades. To dispel even the slightest bit of uncertainty, the two older Russians, Larionov and Fetisov, arranged a memorable team gathering that remains for the players one of the many enduring highlights of that season.

Scotty Bowman blew his whistle and gathered his team around him, as he typically did at the start of every practice.

"So, I hear the Russians took everybody out for dinner last night," the Red Wings coach began. The players looked around at one another nervously, not sure where this was going. The Red Wings were on an extended West Coast swing, starting in Vancouver, with a stop for games against Los Angeles and Anaheim and continuing to San Jose. Bowman enjoyed Southern California and so did most players – especially as the calendar approached mid-March and everyone was tired of the Midwest winter.

The team had two off days between games at Anaheim on March 12 and San Jose on March 15, and the Russians had an evening planned for the first off-night.

"We set up a nice Russian restaurant in the Los Angeles area, with a band to play music for us and everything," Larionov said. "We got the whole crew, all the players, the trainers, everybody. But not the coaches. And we had a nice dinner, kind of a get-together before the playoffs.

"We were getting to the final stretch of the season, and we just said, 'Let's go have a nice little meal together. All of us.' So we got the music going. We got the Russian food. We got the vodka on the table. It was nice to have all the brothers in arms together to talk about hockey, about life and thinking about moving forward in the playoffs and winning the Stanley Cup. We had a great night."

Nicklas Lidstrom called it a night to remember. If only they could. It was a long night.

"I do remember taking a team picture with all the restaurant staff and everyone," Lidstrom said. "I think there was a lot of vodka on the table, too. There's always a lot of vodka involved when you have those big Russian dinners."

Like most events involving Detroit's Russian players, this dinner was inspired by "our two elder statesmen," as Lidstrom described Igor Larionov and Slava Fetisov.

"They wanted to show the North Americans their traditions, their foods. I think they wanted to share how they were brought up, their culture," Lidstrom said. "And I think it kind of brought the team even closer."

Plenty of arm curls can do that for a group of guys.

"Oh, yeah, we had some toasts, obviously," Larionov said. "You know, in Russia you can't really have just a quiet dinner as North Americans do. Every time you got your glass full of wine or vodka, you gotta speak up, you know? You gotta have a speech, like a toast."

Many of the Wings, especially the Canadians and Swedes, were well-experienced in competing against Russians in international competitions. But playing together was still something new and unique. Having one another's back, especially with the Stanley Cup playoffs looming, was essential. And especially when doubts surface about the team's makeup after two straight playoff disappointments. In 1995, the Wings were swept in the Stanley Cup Finals by New Jersey. The following spring, they were beaten in the Western Conference finals by Colorado, which went on to win the Cup. Each year, Detroit was the heavy favorite. Why couldn't the Red Wings close the deal?

Nobody took it harder in 1996 than Larionov, who broke down on the way to the Denver airport following that brutal Game 6 loss to Colorado.

"Igor was in tears. He lost it on the bus," Slava Fetisov wrote in his memoir, "Overtime," published in Russia in 2016. "He kept asking, 'Do you really think we've got time to try to win again?'"

That's what players talked about on the quiet overnight flight from Colorado to Michigan.

"Well, when you get to that certain age – I was almost 36 at the time – you realize that time is running by," Larionov said. "And the only thing missing in your collection is the Stanley Cup. So when you're getting older – it's hard to get – and when you get that close, especially after having such a remarkable season and you end up short, not winning the Cup, it was tough."

It hurt even more when some in the media, predominantly from outside Detroit, pointed fingers at the Wings' many Europeans, particularly the Russian Five. Everyone knew that after the latest two post-season disappointments changes to the roster were coming. Would management consider dismantling the Russian Five, too?

"The media was saying, 'Oh, the Russians are good during the year, but in the playoffs, they aren't strong enough, and maybe mentally they are weak,'" Larionov said. "So that's when you start to realize the chances are getting thinner and smaller for us."

It's hardly a secret that the Soviets put extraordinary pressure on their hockey teams to be the best in Europe, the best at the World

Championships and, especially, the best in Olympic competition. On a visit to Red Army headquarters in 1994, I had an opportunity to ask coach Viktor Tikhonov where the Stanley Cup fit in the hierarchy of a Russian player's aspirations. He smiled at the question he'd been asked countless times and his response was so patronizing he might as well have reached over and patted me on the head.

"Our players dream of gold," he said, "not silver."

Detroit's Russian Five knew how important that silver trophy was to fans in Hockeytown, one of the NHL's Original Six teams that hadn't won the Cup since 1955.

"They knew it was going to be an exciting time, especially the veterans like Slava Fetisov and Igor Larionov," Bowman said. "They had it in their mind that it would be nice to be on a Stanley Cup team."

That dinner late in the season in Los Angeles was about bonding, a chance for the Russians to let their teammates know they understood the magnitude of the coming playoffs; winning the Stanley Cup was just as important to them as it was to the North American players and hockey fans around Detroit.

"All of us, we wore the red-and-white uniform with the wheel and the wing on the logo," Larionov said. "We represent the Detroit Red Wings. It's not the Russians and Red Army. We became Red Wings. We carried Russian passports, but we played for Detroit, and the only thing that matters to us is to be successful. So we have to prove to everybody that for us it was the ultimate goal to win the Stanley Cup, no matter what the media was saying. We have another chance. Let's go for it. We can get it done."

The last shot of vodka poured and the toasts finally proclaimed, players stumbled into taxicabs and headed back at their hotel. It was approaching 4 a.m. They had enjoyed a precious night out. They had done nothing wrong. They had broken no team rules. Most teams set curfews on nights before games at 11 p.m. But since there was no game the following night, the players were free to live their lives as they might, like most sociable adults. Their biggest challenge was to roll out of bed in a few hours to catch a flight to their next destination.

And face their coach. Bowman was legendary everywhere he went for how closely he monitored his players away from the rink. One day, he'd casually ask one of his players for a light, and the player would hand him a book of matches. A few days later, Bowman would be lecturing his players and close with an admonishment that went something like: "And one more thing, you guys are spending way too much time at. . ." Then he'd name the club and the players would all be wondering how their coach could possibly know about it. Turns out, he had read the club's name on a book of matches. And he didn't even smoke.

At other times, he would hurry down to the lobby with a hockey stick, a Sharpie pen and, offering up a nice tip, ask a bellman to do him a big favor. "Have the players as they come in sign this; it's for a sick kid. But don't let them know it's for me." The next morning, because he made his request of the bellman a few minutes before 11 p.m., Bowman would see all the players who had broken curfew the night before – by their own signatures.

On that mid-March morning in Los Angeles, the players rose for a short flight to San Jose. On arrival, the bus took them straight to a rink. Not a day off after all, apparently, the players were thinking. When Bowman mentioned the dinner the previous night, some of them had an inkling what this surprise practice was all about. Especially when he added, "and you guys didn't invite me. So now you're going to skate."

Then he blew the whistle, and around and around the ice they went. But that was just a warm-up. Then he lined them up at the blue line and the sprints blue line to blue line and back. A short pause, if the coach was so inclined to let his charges catch a breath. Then a sharp chirp from the whistle and they were off again on another sprint. Players call it "a bag skate" – forty-five minutes, no pucks. Just skate until the legs turn to rubber, until the aching lungs gasp for air, until the stomach no longer wants anything to do with its contents that begin rising to the throat.

"We had a really nice skate, kind of high tempo," Larionov recalled. "Kind of a little punishment for that great night we had in LA. But we took it. . . Scotty was so nice to us to give us that little workout."

But Bowman was hardly angry. He was just doing his part as a coach well-tuned-in to his team, putting a little bow on an important moment for his players.

"I could see Scotty trying to put his mind around it," Lidstrom recalled. "He knew what was going on, why they did it. I think Scotty liked it, especially that it was the Russians who did something for the rest of the players."

The next night, the Red Wings went out and demolished the San Jose Sharks, 7-4. They were a team in ways they hadn't been a few days before. But the issue with Colorado still loomed, and time was running out.

After three games between the two clubs that season, pessimism was beginning to grip everyone around the team. Three times the Wings played the Avalanche that season, and three times they lost. The first game was at Joe Louis Arena on November 13, and speculation was rampant in the media in both cities and around the NHL that this would be Detroit's chance for revenge. Nothing happened, and the Wings were relatively passive in a 4-1 loss. The next two games were in Colorado, the Avs winning, 4-3, by scoring the last three goals on December 17, and 4-2, with an empty-net goal, on March 16.

The Wings had one more chance to prove themselves a worthy contender for the Stanley Cup when their fiercest rival returned to The Joe in the first week of spring, and they did not disappoint. The man with the pivotal role in this story remembers it well.

As he always did before 7:30 p.m. starts at home, Kris Draper showed up at Joe Louis Arena at 5 p.m., but there was nothing routine about what was awaiting him as soon as he walked through the doors.

"Right away, there's about 4-5 cameras filming me," he said, "so I kind of knew something was up, that there was a lot of expectations of how this game was going to be. There was just an eerie feeling before the game, getting dressed, and you kind of knew. There might've been 20,000 fans at the warm-up, so I think they kind of knew, too."

Draper was right. The Joe Louis Arena stands were full an hour ahead of the opening face-off, and everybody in the building felt the buzz. Everybody around the National Hockey League did as well. That's why all those cameras were in Draper's face.

"Yeah, there was a bit of an elephant in the room, for sure," Brendan Shanahan said. "Three games had gone by already. This was the last time that we were facing Colorado, and nothing had been done yet."

Three games and 301 days, to be precise.

Hockey players have long memories. They take their work seriously, with an eye-for-an-eye mentality. It was now or never for the Detroit Red Wings. Would they finally demand retribution for that cheap and disgusting play in that season-ending game the previous May 29th? All the Red Wings knew for sure was that a one-game suspension was far too mild compared to the justice they had in mind for Claude Lemieux. Even Igor Larionov, a pacifist among pugilists, understood that. Which is why everybody in hockey had circled the date of that final matchup.

"By that time, we knew we lost to them three times so far in the course of the year, and we knew this was going to be the last game we play them in the regular season before we go into the playoffs and meet them down the road," Larionov said. "At some point, we have to send them a message, let them know that we are not that team who is going to give up easily.

"We have unfinished business, and we have to show that in this game."

Every self-respecting Red Wings fan – and most Avalanche fans, too – knows well what happened that night on March 26, 1997, in what is irrefutably the most memorable game in Detroit's 91-year NHL history. But not many can recall with any precision how, exactly, the drama began. Even those involved can't help but mention the irony – and smile at it – when they reminisce about that game.

Larionov was carrying the puck up the ice late in the first period, still in the neutral zone when he felt a whack, then another one, then one more on the back of his helmet. They were more than love taps, too, from Colorado's feisty star center Peter Forsberg – who played the game like a Swedish Vladimir Konstantinov. Larionov expected to hear a whistle, with the referee calling a penalty for Forsberg's liberal stick work.

"I'm controlling the puck. It's on the blade of my stick and the referee didn't see that?" Larionov said. "That's when I decided, 'Well, how many times can he hit me?' You have to be patient. You can't take penalties in games like that, but at the same time – one, two, three, four, five times you get hit? And it's not being noticed by the referee? So I decided to turn around and at least do something."

And he did. Letting the puck go, Larionov turned and, with his glove still on his left hand, he landed the first and only punch he had ever thrown in his Hall of Fame career. He didn't back off, either, putting Forsberg in a headlock before both fell to the ice.

"And then all hell broke loose," said Lidstrom, who was trailing the play on defense. Players paired off quickly, Lidstrom grabbing onto Colorado forward Valery Kamensky. Detroit's Darren McCarty started tangling with Avalanche defenseman Adam Foote, but immediately called for teammate Brendan Shanahan to intervene. McCarty wanted to fish in deeper waters. When Shanahan arrived and grabbed Foote, McCarty turned to hunt down Lemieux. By now, 20,000 rabid fans were on their feet, screaming deliriously in anticipation.

Rather than fight, however, Lemieux went to his knees, turtling beneath his helmet. McCarty ripped the helmet off Lemieux and rained punches down on him with haymakers from his left fist, then his right. But before he was finished, McCarty dragged Lemieux to the Wings' bench to give Draper a ringside view. It was gruesome, as blood poured from Lemieux's face onto the ice.

Twenty thousand strong at the Joe roared their approval, and it got better. With all ten skaters grappling, Colorado goaltender Patrick Roy began to wonder what he was doing standing idly in his crease. Instinctively, Roy sprinted toward the scrum, meeting Shanahan, who turned and met the leaping goaltender. Both players went airborne before falling to the ice. By then, Detroit goalie Mike Vernon was there, only too happy to pair off against his counterpart and even the pugilism. Shanahan quickly turned to exchange punches with Foote. Everyone now had a partner.

The goalies squared off near center ice. Vernon's catch glove and blocker went airborne and the fists started flying. Vernon was shorter by five inches, but he was the better fighter. Roy ended up with a bloodied face. So did Forsberg and Lemieux, who needed assistance getting off the ice. A pool of Avalanche blood, all from Lemieux, puddled right in front of the Detroit bench. Linesmen tried to scrape it off with their skates so the final minute and a half or so of the period could be played.

Four seconds into the second period, however, the fighting started again. This time, Foote was bloodied in a rematch with Shanahan. That was the first of five fights in the period.

"We had twenty soldiers dressed for this game, and every one was important," Larionov said. "You gotta win the battle. You gotta win the war. We lost three battles before that and this was our final one before the playoffs. We have to establish ourselves. Everybody on the team knows this."

Between all the fights, there was a pretty good hockey game, too. The Wings found themselves down, 5-3, but managed to score two late goals midway through the third period to force overtime. Larionov started the winning sequence, too.

"Igor made a great play at the blue line, sent Darren and I in on a little bit of a break," Shanahan said, reciting the choreography as though it happened minutes before, not nearly two decades. "Darren was the star of the show. Amazingly, he was able to score the winning goal."

What McCarty did to Lemieux that night was historic in terms of Detroit's ascendency in that era, but it wasn't as important as that goal, Shanahan surmised.

"Winning that game was even more important than winning the fights," he said. "I don't know if that game brings our team together as much if we don't also get the victory."

Larionov agreed. "Every guy did their job to help the team win that game, and it kind of turned things around mentally and physically for us," he said. "It gave us the proof that we can beat anybody."

That said, Larionov confessed that he had some mixed feelings about his role in igniting the fireworks in that game.

"Never in my life did I have any fights, and I'm not proud about that situation," he said. "But there are certain times when you must stand up for yourself, you know? It was nice to get some relief, to get through that hump before the playoffs, to show everybody who was at that game, ESPN and the whole audience, that Detroit was not the easy team to break. We can bend, but we're not gonna break."

"It was a big moment for that 1997 team," Draper said. "You could just feel that coming into the locker room after the game."

The message had been sent – and received. "It just gave our team the momentum, knowing we could beat Colorado," Lidstrom said, adding that he and his teammates were pretty sure they would meet the Avalanche again in the playoffs that would begin in just a few weeks.

CHAPTER 15

To the Summit

The Red Wings had begun a new season in the autumn of 1996 with a cloak of despair draped over the team. The fans sensed it, gripped by a malaise that was starting to feel comfortable. No longer were they giddy with hope and expectations. They had grown disillusioned after four straight spring times wrought with profound disappointment. Beyond wary, they were building a barrier around their hearts to keep them from being broken yet again.

Players, too. Captain Steve Yzerman was beginning to doubt that it was in the cards to have his name engraved on the Stanley Cup.

"There are definitely times when you wonder," he said in a CBC interview. "My wife and I talked about it quite a bit over the last couple of years. She said, 'Well, if it doesn't work out now, then maybe you were meant to win as a coach or in some other capacity.' So yeah, there were times when I wasn't sure. But one thing I learned is that things change from year to year. Things don't always go according to plan, and the favorites don't always win. You never know what's going to happen."

Sports teams are skilled in the art of seduction, and just two days into the new season the Red Wings had their fans dreaming again when they made a blockbuster trade with Hartford to acquire Brendan Shanahan, one of the game's premier power forwards. At 6-feet-3 and a trim 215 pounds, with a mop of dark hair and chiseled handsomeness, he looked straight out of central casting when he skated onto the ice – after a mad dash from the airport – in time for the home opener on

October 9. At 27, Shanahan was at the top of his game and hailed as the final remnant of the delicate fabric needed for the Wings to polish the Stanley Cup. But Wings fans had heard that talk before, and they weren't buying it so quickly. Especially when their team lost three of its next four games after beating Edmonton, 2-0, in Shanahan's debut with the club.

The Wings played out their season like a luxury sedan going down the highway on cruise-control, finishing with a respectable 94 points – a whopping 37-point drop from the previous season in their forced march to the record 62 victories. But unlike the previous spring, they were in much better shape, physically and mentally, for a long playoff grind. Their fans remained skeptical. The only real consensus around town was that the Wings were on another collision course with a formidable opponent. The Colorado Avalanche, defending Stanley Cup champions after an easy four-game sweep of Florida in the finals the previous spring, finished with the best record in the Western Conference, 13 points better than Detroit, which owned the conference's third playoff seed.

Both clubs were tested early in the playoffs. Both were tied in the first round after four games. In Colorado's match against Chicago, both teams won their two home games before the Avalanche won the last two games to take the series, 4-2. Detroit got a scare against St. Louis. Their series was tied after four games as well, but the Blues' victories had come by shutout. The Wings rebounded to win Games 5 and 6 to clinch their series, 4-2, and move on. Igor Larionov was among the team scoring leaders in the series with five points, all assists.

In the second round, Colorado had an easier time with Edmonton, eliminating the Oilers in five games. The Wings had a much more difficult time with Anaheim. Though the record books say Detroit swept the Mighty Ducks, it might have been the most difficult sweep in playoff history. The Ducks took Detroit to overtime before losing, 2-1, in the series-opener. Game 2 went to triple overtime before the Wings won, 3-2, on a power-play goal by Slava Kozlov. The Wings won Game 3, 5-3, with the Russians accounting for 10 of Detroit's 13 points, including two goals from Kozlov, a goal and two assists from Sergei Fedorov and three assists from Konstantinov. The Wings then needed double overtime in Game 4 to finally dispatch the Ducks again, 3-2. Three Russians topped the team's scoring chart in the series: Fedorov had two goals, including the game-winner in the only game that didn't go into OT, among five points. Konstantinov and Kozlov had four points each.

Now all hockey-watching eyes were fixated on another epic Detroit-Colorado series. It did not disappoint, and once again the Russian Five answered the call resoundingly. The teams split the first two games in Colorado, the Avs taking Game 1, 2-1, and Detroit rebounding for a 4-2 victory, with help by goals from Igor Larionov and Fedorov. In Detroit, the Wings took the pivotal Game 3, 2-1, with Kozlov scoring early in the first period and midway through the third period. Then it looked like they delivered a knockout blow with a 6-0 victory in Game 4 to take a three-games-to-one series lead. But Colorado returned the favor in Game 5 back in Denver, winning 6-0, as Claude Lemieux scored twice in the game's opening 11 minutes.

Even though the Wings had two chances to clinch the series, they treated Game 6 like a must-win match. They had no interest in returning to Colorado for Game 7. Playing since Game 3 with shots to mask pain from a severe rib injury, Fedorov scored what proved to be the winning goal at 6:11 of the third period. The 3-1 victory ended Colorado's season and sent Detroit to the Stanley Cup Finals for the second time in three years. Larionov assisted on the first goal, by Martin Lapointe, and the empty-netter, by Shanahan. The five Russians, playing together or separately with other partners, were superb. Fedorov was the leading scorer in the series with three goals among seven points. Larionov and Kozlov each had two goals among five points, and each scored a game-winning goal.

But as well as the Wings played en route to the finals, their doubters emerged exponentially. This would be a replay of the finals two years earlier, when Detroit was swept by New Jersey, the cynics said. The Philadelphia Flyers – the Broad Street Bullies reincarnate, as they were frequently described, were even better than the Devils team that so easily handled the Wings in 1995.

Philadelphia's size and strength surely would overpower the smaller Wings, no matter how much speed they had and regardless of the creativity they showed with the puck. The Flyers were led by captain Eric Lindros, only 24 but already a Hart Trophy winner, as a league MVP.

How would the Wings avoid being subdued by Philadelphia? The consensus? They wouldn't. This would be another sweep, and the "Euro-Wings," with all their fancy Russians, would be disappointed again. That's how most of the media outside Detroit foresaw it, at any rate.

"Everyone was talking about the size, strength and speed of the Philadelphia Flyers and they were questioning Detroit, once again, with so many Europeans," Wings center Kris Draper said. "We're too small. Yeah, we're fast, and we're a puck-possession team, but we're not strong enough to get the puck from Philadelphia."

A reasonable scouting report, except for one thing: The Wings weren't buying it.

"Our guys had been through a lot – especially losing the year before, the 62-win season, so we had some battle scars on us. And I think that helped," Draper said. "We were quite resilient at that time. We didn't really care what the media was saying. We didn't appreciate it, in the locker room anyway, some of the comments about the Russian Five, that they were too weak physically, that their style of play was wrong. There was a lot of criticism, but we got to a point where it didn't faze our guys."

One of the dominant storylines going into the series was how the Wings' most notorious hitter, Vladimir Konstantinov, would measure up against Lindros, the 6-foot-4, 240-pound bully of a center who had his way with most opponents. Especially with the fervently anti-Russian Philadelphia crowd showing up and chanting, "USA! USA!" during the pregame warmup.

On a line known for good reason as The Legion of Doom, Lindros was flanked by John LeClair, at 6-3, 225 pounds, and Mikael Renberg, at 6-2, 235 pounds. That line was responsible for 104 goals and 235 points in the regular season. They helped lead the Flyers to a 12-3 record en route to the finals, dispatching each of three previous opponents in five games.

"They were a strong team led by a terrific line of really big guys," Wings coach Scotty Bowman recalled. "We'd never seen that before in the NHL."

Shanahan remembered watching replays of Game 1 of that Stanley Cup Finals, with "Hockey Night in Canada" broadcasters anointing the Flyers. In the featured clip, aging stars such as Mark Messier were saying things like, "it's your time now, Eric." As Shanahan described it, he sounded as if he wanted to gag. "They were just going on and on about how big and tough they were and how Philadelphia was going to run us around," Shanahan said. "People just assumed it was going to be another sweep."

Then the puck dropped and a funny thing happened. The Red Wings surprised everyone in the building with a critical change in tactics. Defending against the Lindros line was vital, and while no one doubted that Konstantinov would hold his own in any situation, Bowman and Dave Lewis, the assistant who worked with the defensemen, had another strategy in mind. The Wings started their two finesse defensemen, Nicklas Lidstrom and Larry Murphy, on the blue line, with the Grind Line of Draper flanked by Darren McCarty and Kirk Maltby.

"We just thought, why wouldn't we play Lidstrom and Murphy against Lindros?" Lewis said. "We weren't big enough or strong enough – that's what everybody kept saying. So why would we play Konstantinov and Slava Fetisov against Lindros when we could play Lidstrom, obviously our best defenseman, against them?"

Murphy and Lidstrom were skilled puck-handlers, and they were defensemen, but they were among the least physical players on the Detroit roster. But Bowman's surprise tactic worked beautifully.

"Scotty doesn't fit into the norm – like our team didn't fit into the norm," Lewis said. "I remember vividly how they would dump the puck into Larry Murphy's corner and he would go back, as slow as he was, to get it. And just as he absorbed the hit, he'd sort of bump the puck over to Lidstrom, and Nick would make the pass and out we'd go."

The Wings were suddenly on the attack while those big, lumbering Philadelphia forwards sauntered back to their defensive zone.

Shanahan, still describing the "Hockey Night in Canada" call of that series opener, remembered the commentators not saying much as the first few minutes unfolded, so he provided his own play-by-play of the series-opening seconds from his seat on the Detroit bench.

"As I recall, we throw the puck in and boom! Maltby hits somebody, and then the puck goes D-to-D (defenseman to defenseman) and boom! McCarty hits somebody," Shanahan says. He recalled how Detroit kept the Flyers pinned in their end for an entire shift while the Wings changed their defensive pair.

"The Flyers pass it up the wing and boom! Vladdie hits somebody," Shanahan continued. "So in the first minute and a half, we were quicker and heavier and meaner and hit harder and at a certain point in all of this, you're watching it and you're saying, 'What's happening here? I thought this was the soft, slick Russian Five team.' Suddenly, we were fast and hard and mean and skilled, and pretty soon one of the commentators said, 'Well, you can't, you know, underestimate how talented this Detroit team is as well. They have a chance here. . .'"

Though Konstantinov wasn't matched against the Lindros line, he still found plenty of memorable opportunities to put his signature on the series.

"Every time that Vladimir was on the ice it was a game within a game," Bowman said. "I don't know if he intentionally did it, but he always targeted one of the bigger, tougher players on the other team. He was not a guy that would fight a lot, but he would hit a lot and that bothered many of aggressive players because they weren't used to that. It was a surprise element of getting hit from an unexpected source, so it can change a lot. Vladimir Konstantinov was a game-changer."

"Vladdie certainly let the Flyers know that the Red Wings weren't going to be pushed around," said Jimmy Devellano, the club's senior vice president.

Konstantinov made his statement early in Game 1 when Flyers winger Trent Klatt carried the puck across the blue line. Konstantinov lowered his body and launched himself upward, timing the hit perfectly in Klatt's chest, upending him and separating him from the puck. Klatt lay on the ice, woozy from the collision, while Konstantinov slowly backed away, circling the ice like a shark looking for more prey.

He found it when Lindros, the biggest, baddest of all the Flyers who played the game like a schoolyard tyrant, went after Konstantinov and cross-checked him, drawing a two-minute penalty. Konstantinov didn't retaliate. He never did. Instead, he took great pride in knowing that not only did he get in a good lick against a bigger opponent, but he gave his team a power-play advantage because an opposing player took a dumb penalty.

"Vladdie didn't care who he played against or how hard he hit," Lidstrom said. "He just knew he was going to hit somebody, and that competitiveness really came out in tough games. Not many Russians played the way he played, with that physical presence, and I think it really helped our team to have that dimension. The guys on the other team were always talking about keeping their head up and watching out for that No. 16, because he's going to hit you."

Flyers center Dale Hawerchuk made that mistake – and he would never make another one like it again. After winning the first two games of the best-of-seven series in Philadelphia, by identical 4-2 scores, the Red Wings had no intention of giving the Flyers an opening if they tried to elevate their physical game in Detroit. The Wings were leading, 4-1, late in the second period of Game 3 when Hawerchuk – one of the most skilled players in the game – turned his head at the middle of the rink to look for the puck coming his way. Konstantinov was there waiting. He turned his shoulder into Hawerchuk's chest and sent him sprawling to the ice with a devastating body check.

"That was the epitome of his game, right there," Lewis said. "Dale Hawerchuk was one of the most respected players in the league, but Vladdie didn't care who you were or where it was, he played his game. Right there, at the biggest moment in hockey history – as far as a player goes, playing in the Stanley Cup Finals – and he just freight-trains this guy at center ice. Our guys were on the bench going, 'Wow!' And the game just went on."

More or less. For the Flyers, the wheels were coming off. They lost their composure, running around seeking retribution for the big hit while the Wings went back on the attack. Just 24 seconds after the ferocious mid-ice collision, Shanahan scored from behind the Philadelphia goal, banking the puck into the net off goalie Ron Hextall's pads to make it 5-1. The end was near. The adoring Joe Louis Arena crowd went wild. And the Flyers pretty much caught a cab. They had lost their interest in trying to compete against the Red Wings. They retreated from the fight.

"One of the hardest hits I'd ever seen," Draper said. "It was just a bit of a statement, like, 'You know what? We can play hard, too. You want to play physical? We can play physical, too.'"

Shanahan had a good view of it. "It was just a classic, feet-on-the-ice shoulder hit," he said. "But there was something extremely dense about Vladdie when he hit you. And that's one of the hardest hits I've ever seen him throw. And the timeliness of it, right at center ice against a superstar. No penalty, either. And now the other team is chasing him around and we're going up the ice on a three-on-one break to score a goal."

The Flyers ended up on the wrong end of a 6-1 score. Afterward, in a moment of astounding truth and clarity, their coach, Terry Murray, called his players a bunch of chokers. For all practical purposes, the series was over.

"When Vladimir Konstantinov hit Hawerchuk, it changed the game. It changed the series. It was over at that point," Lewis said. "They had no response to Vladimir Konstantinov. There was nothing, nothing they could do. Lindros couldn't do anything. None of their tough guys could do anything because it didn't affect Vladdie. His game was a game that nobody in the league played – and I don't know if anybody since has played the kind of game that he played."

"Vladimir Konstantinov just hit everything in sight," Devellano recalled. "I think he actually had Philly a little bit scared."

One thing is certain: Nobody called them the big, bad Flyers any longer. Not even in Philadelphia.

Dale Hawerchuk, meanwhile, was finished. He didn't play another game, ever. While the violent confrontation with Konstantinov was hardly the defining moment in a 16-year NHL career that earned Hawerchuk a place in the Hockey Hall of Fame, it was certainly his final moment. He was a spectator for Game 4, and a few months later he retired from the game at age 34.

With their team leading three games to none in the best-of-seven series, all those long-suffering Wings fans suddenly – finally – dared to dream again. The city of Detroit reverberated with anticipation. Every other car around town, it seemed, had red-and-white Wings flags clipped to the windows on either side. The Detroit Tigers, also owned by Mike Ilitch, were into the heart of their season, and the Detroit Lions were holding minicamps. But neither team could command many column inches in the local newspapers or get a word in edgewise on local sports-talk radio. It was Red Wings 24/7, with well-schooled listeners carrying the conversation. Their team was one victory from winning the Stanley Cup. A hockey-worshipping city, Hockeytown, had reached the transcendent state of nirvana.

Even though the Wings were playing at home in Games 3 and 4, they weren't sleeping in their own beds. To limit distractions for his players, Bowman sequestered his team at a downtown hotel – where they had a greater sense of the excitement that gripped the city.

"Going to the rink in the morning of that last game, you could feel the buzz in the air and see all the people wearing Red Wings jerseys on the streets," Lidstrom said. "I remember driving to the game that night with Steve Yzerman. We're sitting there in the car, and Stevie says, 'There's something special about to happen tonight.' Just going down to the arena for that last game, it was a tremendous feeling."

What a difference a year makes, a year full of self-doubt and second-guessing, of wonder and torment.

"This year, coming into the playoffs, we weren't even thinking about the Stanley Cup," Yzerman recalled. "We were just playing the games – and it went by relatively quickly. Before you knew it, we were in the Stanley Cup Finals."

Even then, there was no thought of winning. They had been there, done that just two years earlier, and it ended badly.

Players in any sport insist that the clinching game of any playoff series is the most difficult to win, and Game 4 between Philadelphia and Detroit on June 7, 1997, was no exception.

Philadelphia, to its credit, regrouped and delivered a spirited effort. But on that night, it was the Red Wings who were too big, too fast and too good to be denied. Darren McCarty, who made himself a star of mythic proportions only 73 days earlier when he pummeled Colorado's Claude Lemieux into submission, offered his best Sergei Fedorov impersonation with the Stanley Cup-clinching goal. His end-to-end rush in the second period gave Detroit a 2-0 lead, rendering harmless a late goal by Lindros.

LeClair had scored the Flyers' lone goal in Game 3. In other words, the overhyped Legion of Doom was a non-factor in the series. Detroit's Russians, conversely, were outstanding. Fedorov led all scorers in the four-game series with three goals, including the game-winner in the first game and third game, among six points. He finished with a team-leading 20 points in the 1997 playoffs.

But one man in the Detroit lineup was the difference in those Stanley Cup Finals, causing all that carnage against those big, bad Flyers. And as the final seconds faded off the clock on the big scoreboard above the Joe Louis Arena ice, one man was making sure the Flyers wouldn't get a chance for a dramatic tying goal.

"I was actually on the ice with Vladdie in those last seconds," Lidstrom said. "We were up, 2-0, and they scored with less than a minute to go. All of a sudden, it's a game again. If they get another one, it's going into overtime. I remember those last seconds winding down. . . You're just waiting and waiting for the buzzer to finally go off."

Those final seconds lasted an eternity, but they gave captain Steve Yzerman a moment to indulge himself. "Right near the end, you start to think, 'We've got it!'" he said. "It was a great feeling."

After a face-off with six seconds left, the puck is deep in the Detroit end, behind the Wings' net, just sitting there like a live grenade capable of mass destruction. Lidstrom feels a rare flash of panic.

"And then I see Vladdie, falling on the puck on purpose to keep it beneath him," Lidstrom said. "And finally, the buzzer goes off. Our goalie, Mike Vernon, is raising his hands. You can see the whole arena going crazy. The guys are starting to come off the bench to celebrate, and Vladdie is laying there by the boards behind the net with puck still beneath him."

Tall and slender with his blond hair always neatly trimmed, Lidstrom resembled the hero in an Ingmar Bergman film. The way he looked, the way he carried himself, the way he played every game in his Hall of Fame career contributed to perhaps the most accurate nickname in sports: "The Perfect Human." Though he grew up in Vasteras, Sweden, about 70 miles northwest of Stockholm, he spoke better English than most of his Canadian and American teammates. But as he recounted that scene unfolding on the ice in the waning seconds of a sweep in the Stanley Cup Finals, his speech lingered uncharacteristically as he described what it felt like to finally hear the final horn blaring.

"It's hard to, you know, talk about, to put words into it. It was such a tremendous feeling. Such a relief," Lidstrom said. "After losing in the

Finals in '95, then winning 62 games and losing like we did in '96, then in '97, it finally happened to us."

For the first time in 42 years, the Detroit Red Wings were Stanley Cup champions. But they were destined to make more history that night.

CHAPTER 16

Paying it Forward

When Steve Yzerman finished his long-anticipated victory lap around Joe Louis Arena and turned to his teammates, he had no idea that what he was about to do would have such historic significance and global implications for the sport of hockey. It just turned out that way.

The captain of a the newly crowned NHL champion skating around the ice with the Stanley Cup over his head – grinning in a way that shows he had sacrificed some teeth at the altar of the game he loves – is one of the most iconic images in sports. Coincidentally, this is a tradition that began in Detroit in 1952. That year, the Red Wings swept Montreal in four games in the finals. Until then, the presentation of the trophy to the new champions had been a rather formal event. Whoever ran the league would present the trophy to the captain of the winning team, who would carry it into the lockerroom for a private celebration – and the hockey season was over.

But Detroit Red Wings captain Ted Lindsay changed that forever when NHL President Clarence Campbell presented the Stanley Cup and Lindsay immediately raised it over his head and waltzed it across the Olympia Stadium ice. Lindsay explained later that he did it so that fans could get a better view of the trophy. He was sharing the moment with the most important people in the building. It's been that way ever since. But over the past generation or so, the tradition has taken on a level of intense speculation. It now involves a question whose answer can reveal much about a team: Which player gets the Stanley Cup when the captain finishes his victory lap? So after Yzerman took his lap and skated briefly over to the bench so owner Mike Ilitch could lift the trophy over his head to a thunderous roar, all eyes were on who got the Cup next.

On June 7, 1997, the Red Wings captain left no doubt about how he and his teammates felt about one man when he approached Slava Fetisov, the 39-year-old former captain of the Soviet Red Army club, and presented him the trophy. With that single, thoughtful gesture, Yzerman once and forever validated the presence of Russians in the NHL and extinguished the incessant and patently prejudicial whispering campaign that insisted teams led by Russians could never win the Stanley Cup. No more.

"None of us had spoken to Steve about it, and I think he just made the decision on his own," left wing Brendan Shanahan said, "but it was so fitting – and just. For me it was like going back to being a 19-year-old kid again and watching Slava Fetisov come over, looking up to him so much and seeing how he was mistreated in so many ways."

Fetisov is a man well aware of his place in hockey history, but that perfect moment nearly overwhelmed him.

"The captain – *my captain* – he gave it to me," Fetisov said. "It is not describable, this moment. It was very much special."

As Yzerman handed him the trophy, Fetisov knew what he had to do.

"I started thinking about Igor," Fetisov said. "I was thinking maybe we can share this moment together, instead of going around by myself. So I said, 'Igor, let's go.'"

And they did, two fabled Soviet teammates skated around the rink with the Stanley Cup, showered by as much love and adoration from Detroit hockey fans as Yzerman, Lindsay or Gordie Howe ever got before them.

"I've been playing professional hockey for 20 years," Igor Larionov said at the time, "and this is the happiest day in my life."

After Larionov had a chance to savor that moment for a couple of decades, he tried to put it into perspective. Sitting in a large room beneath his fashionable Bloomfield Hills home –a miniature rink with a regulation-size goal that he and his son used to sharpen their shooting skills – Larionov tried to put it in perspective.

"That was really special for us – and very, very good of Stevie for doing this for two old Russians," he said. "When everybody believes that the Russians aren't good enough, not tough enough to win the Cup. . . for us that was amazing. When you get the Cup and skate around the rink with 20,000 people are there cheering, that was a nice feeling."

For their Red Wings teammates, as well. "For Steve to give it to Slava and see him and Igor, how they were so excited to hold the Stanley Cup." Shanahan recalled. "I'd never seen two people holding the Cup up together like that and skating with it. It was just a perfect moment."

Associate coach Dave Lewis immediately felt the significance of that scene.

"I remember that vividly," he said. "It was Stevie showing respect for what Slava brought – not just during the short time he played with the Red Wings, but to hockey, to international hockey. The defiance he showed standing up to the Soviet regime. Slava Fetisov brought international hockey to Detroit and won the most coveted trophy in hockey, the Stanley Cup. Stevie knew that. He knew of his character. He knew that he was a special athlete, a special breed. And it was special for me to see that."

So it was for Nicklas Lidstrom, who as a Swede understood how Europeans were widely denigrated by North American players.

"By doing that, Stevie really showed respect for the Russians, for Slava," Lidstrom said. "And when they skated the Cup together, Slava and Igor, it showed that they kind of broke a barrier from where they came from."

Sergei Fedorov will never forget that moment and what it meant to him.

"Respect," he said. "Respect! It was the first Cup for the Red Wings in a long time, and it was the first Cup for a bunch of Russian players skating on an NHL team. I'm so glad Stevie did that. I would never have thought of that in a million years. And when Slava asked Igor to join him. . . They were friends forever."

"This was really important to Slava and Igor, and the most important thing was that Steve Yzerman showed the respect and the team showed the respect to them," Slava Kozlov added. "They deserved it. They deserved that recognition, and it was all so amazing. They worked very hard for the Stanley Cup to come back to Detroit."

The moment was awfully important 4,800 or so miles to the east, around the headquarters of the Central Red Army Club, and to its fans throughout Russia.

"Those years when all five of us played together in Detroit, there was a huge wave of interest in the National Hockey League," Larionov said. "When we were playing in Russia, we also wore the red uniform. We were the 'Big Red Machine.' In Detroit, we play for the Red Wings and when we were playing for the Cup the games were televised back home – at 3 o'clock in the morning, and many people were watching the games.

"It generated huge interest. So the Detroit Red Wings became like, the people's team back home."

Fedorov added: "Because of our team, many Russian fans realized they had somebody to cheer in North America, in such an exceptional and very intense league. They could see that their Russian players are not that bad. That's when they realized Detroit is their favorite team."

Several years later, Fedorov was continually reminded how closely those fans were watching. He had left Russia as a young man, known to very few outside the Red Army sports complex, to seek his fortunes in North America. But when he returned to Russia a decade later, people were stopping him on the streets. They recognized him as their star player – on the Detroit Red Wings.

"I'm thinking, 'Wow!'" Fedorov said. "But I know it was from that moment when Slava and Igor raised the Cup together. That was it – for fans in Russia and around the world."

In an interview with a TSN, the Canadian sports network, a few days after the Wings' sweep of the Flyers, Yzerman confessed he contemplated that moment of what he'd do with the Stanley Cup – if he ever got his hands on it.

"I had been thinking about it over the last few days – about who to give it to," he said. "There were a few people I kept kind of going back and forth on, but then I decided on Slava, most importantly because I wasn't sure if he was coming back or not the next year. I wanted him to have it because he's had a tremendous career. He's accomplished everything and he's been a real good guy, a super guy on our team. And if he's not coming back, then that's the way I wanted him to go out."

That Fetisov decided to call on Larionov so that they could skate with the trophy together just made it better, Yzerman said. "It worked out beautifully."

Years later, Yzerman said that while he understood and appreciated the symbolism that people attached to his handoff to Fetisov, it was more about the immense respect he had for a veteran teammate. And love.

"The logic of it, for myself, was to go to our veteran guys like Slava and Igor. Those guys were really admired and respected, not just by the other Russian players but by all our guys. They were really popular guys. They were unique personalities. They were very proud of their Russian heritage and really proud of what they had accomplished in their careers.

"But they also really wanted to win the Stanley Cup. There was no questioning that. These guys were teammates. Our friends, and we loved them."

At the post-game news conference, Fetisov was beaming when he raised a plastic cup of champagne and toasted the assembled flock of reporters.

"Cheers, guys," he said. "I wait 39 years for this moment. For me to find the Cup now, almost at the end of the career, was probably a gift from above."

He added that promenading the Stanley Cup around the ice with his Red Army and Red Wings partner, Igor Larionov, "is something I will be remembering for the rest of the life."

So will Grind Line center Kris Draper, who can replay the moment in his mind's eye with perfect clarity.

"Stevie skated the Cup over to Slava, and Slava motioned Igor to come. He wanted to do that lap together and, you know, that kind of gives me chills right now just talking about it, the excitement of it," Draper said. "You can only imagine everything that those two guys had been part of together, playing for the famed Red Army team and going through what they did to get over here.

"I would have to imagine that in the '70s and '80s, you knew these guys were going to win world championships. You knew they were going to win Olympic gold medals. You probably never would have thought they were going to be Stanley Cup champions one day. But, sure enough, they did. Here they were, in Detroit, ending a drought and being able to call themselves Stanley Cup champions."

CHAPTER 17

The Irony of Fate

Freddie Mercury's voice boomed over the loudspeakers around Joe Louis Arena as only Freddie Mercury's voice could, serenading the Detroit Red Wings as they held the Stanley Cup aloft and skated around the ice. Queen's "We Are the Champions" might be the most enduring cliché in sports. It can be endearing, too.

It echoed in the locker room after the game on that unforgettable Saturday night in June 1997, when the Wings ended their 42-year Stanley Cup drought. The team played it when season-ticket-holders gathered at The Joe two days later for an evening to honor the champions once more. And again the next day, when fans packed the downtown parade route along Woodward Avenue. Over and over, the Wings played that song. No one seemed to tire of it.

Soon, however, there was no need to play it at all, because Vladimir Konstantinov was singing it everywhere he went. Non-stop and loud. To the point of driving his teammates a little batty. They were seeing a new side to a rather serious guy who always had kept to himself, especially in public.

"Vladimir was starting to kind of loosen up a little bit. He was happy, very, very happy, and he was singing that song all the time," Igor Larionov recalled. "It was like he couldn't stop singing it."

Fans saw a transformation in Konstantinov, too. Not only did they admire and appreciate his emergence as one of the best players in the National Hockey League – he was a finalist for the Norris Trophy awarded to its best defenseman in that championship season – but they also saw a blossoming personality off the ice, as if they were witnessing an ordinary man transforming into a superhero. All he needed was a pair of dark glasses. He already had the accent. "I'll be back," The Vladinator (neé Terminator) would say.

"Vladdie was on his way to becoming maybe the most popular player on our team," said Steve Yzerman, the captain who basically had enjoyed that status since he joined the Wings 14 years earlier. He said it without an ounce of envy or animus.

The last time Larionov heard his friend sing "We Are the Champions" was on a Thursday night, five days after winning the Stanley Cup, when the team gathered with wives and plus-ones for the evening at Morton's The Steakhouse in suburban Troy. The Larionovs rode home with Konstantinov and his wife, Irina.

"It was 1 o'clock in the morning, maybe 1:30, and when he dropped us off he was yelling to the whole neighborhood, *'We are the champions. . .!'*" Larionov said. "We were going to the house, and he was in the car singing very loud."

Until then, nobody had heard Konstantinov sing. Turned out, he could carry a tune.

"We don't expect like a Freddie Mercury kind of voice, you know?" Larionov said. "But he was doing actually pretty good."

At Morton's, each player stood up, said a few words and offered a toast – a custom acquired from their Russian teammates. It was there in the restaurant, a long night of laughs and tears among this band of brothers, that they decided to congregate the next day for a golf outing at The Orchards, a club located in Washington Township in rural Macomb County north of Detroit. They craved one final day together before heading in various directions for the summer – the North Americans to their summer cottages, the Russians to Russia, the Swedes to Sweden.

The next morning, on June 13, after a long season and a short week of partying with his teammates, Vladimir Konstantinov woke up happy. He woke up singing: *"We are the champions, my fri-ends. . ."*

Mid-morning was approaching when Konstantinov and many of his teammates met in Birmingham at the home of goalie Chris Osgood. This "one more day" outing wasn't particularly well-received among some of their wives. But one of them, on seeing the line of limousines on the street, couldn't help but turn to her husband and say, "Well, at least you guys are doing this thing right."

Brendan Shanahan wasn't a golfer, so he ignored his morning wake-up call. Instead, he timed his arrival for when most of his teammates would be coming off the course.

"We were going to have dinner at the club, play some cards," he said, "and just spend one more night together with the Cup."

That surely would include something like a pub crawl, stopping at several favorite hangouts to spread the joy.

"We were being responsible," said Nicklas Lidstrom, one of the team's two alternate captains. "We decided we'd get a bunch of limos, so no one was going to have a few beers and drive away."

Vladimir Konstantinov, Slava Fetisov, the oldest player on the team, and Sergei Mnatsakanov, who doubled as the Wings' massage therapist and equipment handler, were among the first to leave in one of six limos the group had reserved. Mnatsanakov, 43 then, was the sixth member of the Russian Five. To their credit, Wings executives concluded that because the team had so many former Soviets it would be wise to have a Russian speaker on the training staff.

Mnatsakanov was a round, joyful man, rarely seen without a wide, natural smile. Whenever he and I met, we'd exchange greetings. I'd speak in Russian to him, and he'd respond in English, always with a gregarious grin and a genial handshake. He seemed grateful beyond words in any language for the new life he and his family, which included two young sons, had found after emigrating to America.

Detroit's Russians didn't golf much, either, but those three spent their day in carts, riding around with cold drinks to help keep their teammates hydrated. They also collected signatures on dozens of items for various charities.

"I remember everything, like it happened a couple minutes ago," Fetisov said in an interview in Moscow in December 2015. The Russians had planned a dinner with their wives, and perhaps a meet-up with their teammates later.

"We was all happy, happy, happy, going home to drink some beers, maybe have a glass of champagne," Fetisov said. Their limo was waiting in the parking lot. Fetisov entered first, sitting in the back. Konstantinov and Mnatsanakov followed, relaxing on the long bench to the side. Like many stretch limos, this one was equipped with a small bar, which served as the perfect ottoman on which Slava rested his feet. Just as the limo started to pull out, Shanahan arrived. The vehicle stopped quickly and Shanahan leaned in to greet his teammates.

"Where are you guys going?" Shanahan asked. "The night's just starting."

"Too tired. Too much. We've had it," came the chorus from inside the limo as Fetisov shoved several Red Wings jerseys toward him to sign. "You're the only one we don't have."

Disappointed that some of his teammates were leaving already, Shanahan signed the items while twisting their arms. "I kept saying, 'C'mon, can't I talk you into it?' And they keep saying, 'No, no, no. Too much partying all week. Too tired.' Then they drove off."

The last of the golfers had come off the course at about 8:30 p.m., including athletic therapist John Wharton, who with assistant trainer Tim Abbott had spent the day escorting the Stanley Cup around the course. Stanley was the hit of the party. At some holes, players poured cold beer into the bowl and quenched their thirst. At others, the trophy was laid gently on the green, giving putters a much-needed bigger target.

Inside the club, dinner dishes were being cleared and plans made for the rest of the evening. Darren McCarty made a phone call to a tattoo artist. He was leading a group that included teammate Aaron Ward, Wharton, Abbott and a few others. They were all going to get their flesh decorated with the Stanley Cup with the Red Wings logo. Some players were staying behind to play cards and catch up with the group later. For these newly minted Stanley Cup champions, the hours in one last memorable night together celebrating a lifelong brotherhood etched in silver were just beginning. They were relaxed, relieved, radiant.

Then Sergei Fedorov's cell phone rang. It was shortly before 10 p.m.

"All of a sudden, Sergei handed his phone to Steve (Yzerman),"

Shanahan said. "Sergei looked like a ghost."

The others grew quiet, their faces a mixture of confusion and anguish. Several teammates asked Fedorov at the same time: "What's going on?"

Depending on the route, it would have taken 30-40 minutes to drive from the golf club to Osgood's home, where the cars were parked. Nearing the end of their trip, the limo carrying the three Russians was headed southbound on Woodward, a wide boulevard that slices through some of the world's most exclusive suburbs north of Detroit. They headed toward Sixteen Mile Road, which meant they were about 16 miles north on the same artery where more than a million people had gathered just three days earlier to honor them as they rode in red Mustang convertibles in the Stanley Cup parade.

The lavish alabaster sedan was about a minute from downtown Birmingham when Fetisov felt it begin to drift across the other lanes in what seemed like a 45-degree angle. At the same time, it was picking up speed.

"What is he doing?" Fetisov wondered, his eyes on the driver.

He screamed. "Hey! Hey! HEY!"

The three passengers in the back, two of them world-class athletes of remarkable strength, stamina and eye-hand coordination, were helpless to do anything as the limo, at roughly 50 m.p.h., crossed three lanes, careened off the roadway and hurdled the curb, heading straight toward a healthy, old maple tree.

"This happens so fast," Fetisov recalled. "I see something coming, and now I see my life showing before me."

An eight-year-old boy standing in line for 10 hours just for the chance to spend a few minutes on the ice trying out for the Red Army Hockey School. . . Returning a year later and finally being accepted. . . Representing the Motherland at the Olympic Games as a young man, only to return home humiliated after losing that crazy "Miracle on Ice" game. . . World Championship gold, two Olympic gold medals. . . Becoming a husband, a father. . . Freedom. . . Detroit. . . Comrades. . . The Stanley Cup. . .!

"Then it was big hit. Like this," Fetisov said, snapping his fingers.

Glass around the vehicle, much of it darkened to lend the sense of privacy in the rear, shattered on impact, metal shuddered as it wrinkled like tissue paper, the limo's front end suddenly intruding into the luxury compartment. Bodies and debris catapulted forward as the driver's airbag exploded in his face. This symphony was a soundtrack to Fetisov's memory bank, scoring the highlight reel playing in his mind even as he was lurching forward.

BAM!

Then silence, save for the hissing, ticking and clicking of a dying engine, punctuated by the onerous groan of the tree as its roots tore from the earth and began to topple in front of the twisted wreck.

Just like that, the summer of celebration 42 years in the making was over. It had lasted six days when it faded to black.

Word of the crash spread quickly. Back at the golf course, Fedorov handed his phone to Yzerman and turned to his teammates.

"There's been an accident," he said, explaining that the caller was an officer from the Oakland County Sheriff's Department. No one said a word. Instead, they clustered around their captain, who stuck a finger in his ear to block the surrounding noise.

"We couldn't hear what was on the other end, but we heard Steve say, 'Slava? Vladdie? And Natsa?'" Shanahan said. "So we knew who he was talking about. Then he said, 'Natsa's dead?' And then we all looked like ghosts. 'Is Vladdie going to make it?'"

The Stanley Cup, until that moment the epicenter of their universe, was quickly forgotten. Ignored. Reduced to a gratuitous postscript.

"I couldn't even tell you where it was. I really have no idea," said Wharton, who had spent the entire day with it. The group was stunned.

"We didn't believe it was true," Lidstrom said. "We thought it was. . . we thought, this can't be happening now. We just won the Stanley Cup. We were doing everything right. We were being responsible. And then something like this happened?"

Yzerman ended the call and quickly briefed his teammates. The injured were being transported to William Beaumont Hospital in nearby Royal Oak, not far from the crash scene. That's where he was going right now. "And you should get there, too," he said, pointing toward Wharton. "You're the trainer. You need to be there."

The group dispersed quickly, all headed for the limos they had reserved for the evening. All the limos headed directly to the hospital. On the way, Yzerman phoned Larionov, hoping to get more details.

"Igor, something has happened to our Russian boys. Can you call try calling Slava or Vladdie or Sergei Mnatsakanov and see if you can find out anything?"

"What happened?" asked Larionov, who had remained home with his family after taking his daughters to a swimming pool earlier.

"Some kind of accident."

Larionov dialed each of his Russian teammates. No one answered their mobile phones. At the same time his wife, Elena, turned on the TV. The accident was breaking news on every local channel, and soon it would make global headlines worldwide.

Slava Fetisov is still haunted by the shock of the collision.

"It was big hit. It kind of shook everything up," he said. "Then it was kind of a dark moment."

In retrospect, he believed that minibar on which he had rested his feet probably saved him. On impact, it disrupted his momentum somewhat while the other two men were thrown forward violently. Nevertheless, Fetisov wound up near the front of the limo, on top of one of his teammates.

"I look and it's Sergei Mnatsakanov," he said. "His face was in pain. And then I lost them. . ."

Passersby who had witnessed the crash raced to the limo. Birmingham police were called at 9:13 p.m.

"The people came and helped us out of the car and put us on the ground, our guys," Fetisov said. He knew immediately that his teammates were seriously injured. They were unconscious. Mnatsakanov was a gruesome mess. One of the crystal bottles designed to hold liquor in the limo's bar area was propelled forward like a missile, splitting his head, parts of it embedded in his brain. Konstantinov looked as if he were asleep. Fetisov thought at first that both were dead. Then he started taking inventory of his own situation.

"I could move my hands. . . and I feel like I am going to be more or less OK. But there is blood all over me."

With each breath, pain shot through his chest. He had suffered broken ribs, a punctured lung and a bad gash on his leg. In the emergency room, three doctors tended to him. He soon learned that each doctor had served in the U.S. military, and he tried to joke about how ironic it was that they were back home in the United States, patching up a former major in the Soviet Red Army.

"It was a little bit funny, but I was always asking them where the boys were, you know? How they were doing?" Fetisov recalled. "But they give me no information, just try to kind of put me back together in one piece."

About the time the doctors were done with Fetisov, his wife, Ladlena, came bursting into his room, hysterical.

"It was a tough moment for her," Fetisov said, explaining that hospital personnel called all three wives and apparently mixed up the messages.

"My wife, she came running in the emergency room. She was crying," Fetisov said. "She said, 'They told me you were unconscious, that you are in a coma.'"

He knew then, for the first time, how fortunate he was and how bad things were for his teammates who were with him in that limo.

"That is what I remember," he said softly. "It stays with me all the time."

The limousine's driver, Richard Gnida, then 27, told police that he had "blanked out" at the wheel he had no business commanding – legally. His record was a mess. He had two drunken-driving convictions. He did not hold a valid driver's license at the time of the crash. It had been revoked twice, most recently on April 17, 1996. He was not eligible to have his license reinstated until January 22, 1998. The limo company never adequately explained, even in court later, why it had allowed this man from suburban Westland behind the wheel of one of its vehicles carrying some of Detroit's most revered athletes.

While doctors worked frantically to stabilize Konstantinov and Mnatsakanov, heartbroken fans gathered in a spontaneous vigil outside the hospital. Some took flowers, notes of prayer, balloons, stuffed animals and other tokens of love and sympathy to the crash site near the downed tree.

For several days, the Wings' contingent occupied three rooms in Beaumont's ICU. (Fetisov's wife soon occupied a fourth after a sudden attack of appendicitis required immediate surgery.) Fetisov needed dozens of stitches to patch up the gash in his leg, and his chest was dressed to immobilize his banged-up ribs. But as soon as he was able, Fetisov visited his teammates in their rooms. He felt helpless. Both were in critical condition. Both were in a coma, their conditions grave.

"The prognosis from the very beginning was terrifying," Irina Konstantinova, Vladimir's wife, said in an interview years later with ESPN. "His brain was getting more and more swollen, and at one point I remember we were given just a few hours, (doctors) saying that most likely he was going to die."

Physicians were more than guarded during their press briefings in the immediate aftermath, primarily because they didn't have much positive information to share.

"The long-term prognosis for this is impossible to tell," trauma surgeon James Robbins said of Konstantinov in his initial public statement. "The next few days are going to be very important to determine which way he is going to go. Can he recover? Absolutely. . . that's what we continue to hope and pray for."

But doctors were more forthcoming with John Wharton, the team's physical therapist and head of its training staff.

"The team kind of relied on me as the medical liaison between the players and the doctors," Wharton said in an interview with "The

Russian Five" documentary film director Joshua Riehl. Wharton had a tough assignment. Doctors had confided that there was less than a 10 percent chance of survival for Konstantinov and Mnatsakanov because their injuries were so severe.

"That kind of news was not only shocking, it just seemed mean, you know? Just cruel. Like how could this be?" Wharton said. "These were two of the healthiest people I know in my life, and one of them (Konstantinov) was one of the strongest, most courageous warrior-types I've ever seen in any sport. How could he possibly be in this condition? It didn't seem real."

Gnida was examined at Beaumont and released. He walked away unscathed but for a few minor scratches. Treated for those minor injuries and released. Doctors speculated that the limo's airbag saved him. Test results later showed he had marijuana in his system.

Jim Devellano, the Wings' senior vice president, was in the middle of an interview in his apartment overlooking the Detroit River when his phone rang. It interrupted his conversation with Jason La Canfora, the beat writer for the Detroit Free Press, who was there for an in-depth interview about the Wings' long path to the Stanley Cup. It was nearly 10 p.m. The caller was Cynthia Lambert, who covered the Wings for the Detroit News. She asked Devellano what he knew about the accident.

"What accident?" he replied. He hung up quickly and called his team's owners, Mike and Marian Ilitch.

"They had a few more details," Devellano recalled. "It wasn't good." He left for the hospital immediately.

Coach Scotty Bowman had been home in Buffalo, New York, barely two days when he learned of the crash. He drove back to Detroit early Saturday morning, arriving in time for the doctor's briefing at the hospital. Meantime, the vigil there continued to grow. That morning, more than a dozen people also had gathered quietly at the crash site, kneeling in the median to pray for the members of their beloved team. By afternoon, the crowd was much larger, and so was the shrine of mementoes. By Sunday, the crowd had grown so large that police surrounded the crash scene with barriers of yellow tape to keep mourners and motorists safe. Activity at the site had caused two minor accidents.

A similar scene was unfolding at the hospital.

"A lot of people lined up outside with flowers and signs," Igor Larionov said. "The support of the fans, you know, that was really emotional. You could see the whole city was trying to do as much as possible to get those boys out of the coma, to get them back to a normal life."

Fetisov recalled a thousand people holding vigil outside the hospital, though his memory might have multiplied the numbers a few times. There were dozens, to be sure. Maybe more than 100, not including a throng of media, in the earliest hours and days after the accident. One man had pitched a tent, vowing that he wasn't leaving until those comatose men walked out of the hospital.

That would never happen.

Vladimir Konstantinov had suffered a deceleration head injury, which is caused by a sudden, rapid stoppage when his body collided with the partition between the cab of the limo and its luxury compartment. That pushed his brain violently against the skull on one side and then the other, doctors explained, sometimes causing major, irreparable damage to the tissue. Sergei Mnatsakanov also sustained massive head injuries, his skull fractured above his right ear.

Five days after the accident, Slava Fetisov was discharged from the hospital, though he would return often in the days and weeks that followed to look in on his teammates.

"While I am happy to be going home," he said at a news conference upon his departure, "Vladimir and Sergei still need your thoughts and prayers."

The intensive care unit at Beaumont Hospital, like many others of its kind, aggressively restricts visitors to critical-care patients. Only family members can visit. But officials at Beaumont were about to learn something important about hockey players: Teammates *are* family, and those Red Wings were not to be denied their support of Vladimir and Sergei. Hospital officials acquiesced. Each injured teammate had a steady stream of visitors – including and especially their brothers with whom they shared a locker room.

On the day Fetisov was released, doctors finally were able to offer some welcomed good news about the two who remained in critical condition. Dr. Karol Zakalik said in a media briefing that Mnatsakanov was responding to simple commands, like squeezing his right hand.

Many weeks later, Konstantinov, too, showed signs of awareness. "He seemed to wiggle his toes to Russian instructions," Zakalik said. "He even opened his eyes."

Coming out of his coma was a long process for Konstantinov. Nothing like the movies, where the eyelids snap open like a window shade and the patient wonders why he's there and for how long – in perfect clarity. Nothing like that at all.

"It seemed like forever," Wharton said. When his eyes finally opened, it appeared to be a reaction to someone speaking Russian to him. There was no focus, however, and Vladdie was still largely comatose.

But doctors were encouraged. "He is definitely aware that people are speaking to him," Zakalik said. On the occasion when his eyes opened, they remained fixed. He seemed unable to follow a nurse moving around his bed.

Uncertainty lingered on separate floors where Vladimir and Sergei fought for their lives. Doctors still were unable to say with any certainty that either man would survive.

Walking into their rooms was unnerving, even for a medically trained therapist like Wharton. Both men were surrounded by what looked like more equipment than was needed for a moon landing. Tubes and wires connected bodies to machines, many of them emitting their own unique sounds of survival – the steady beeping of the heart monitor, the ominous sucking sound of a respirator providing life-sustaining oxygen to a body incapable of breathing on its own. The rooms reeked of stifling sterility, the sounds and smell of human tragedy. A sight that can make your knees buckle if you're not prepared.

Wharton visited the men every day. So did several others.

"We had a handful of teammates revolving every single day, as well as, obviously, family members," Wharton said. "A lot of the time, we'd just talk to him, but sometimes we'd play 'We Are the Champions,' because Vladdie really liked that song, and after we won he would sing it in broken English and make all of us laugh. You know, that's one of the last things the players who saw him heard before he left in that limo – he was singing that song. So we played it a lot for him."

On occasion, Larionov would bring his young daughters, Alyonka, 10, and Diana, 6, and they would sing that song for Vladimir. After several weeks with little measurable improvement, Wharton had another idea. He put in a call to Phil Pritchard, the NHL's "Keeper of the Cup."

"I just thought Vladdie needed to see it," Wharton said, "or at least be in the presence of it." Pritchard brought the big trophy up to Konstantinov's room, and he and Wharton placed it gently on the bed. Wharton explained to Vladimir what they were doing. He took Konstantinov's limp hand and placed it on the shining silver that soon would have his name engraved on it. The Stanley Cup tends to draw a crowd, so there was no shortage of medical personnel in the room as well. Some of the machines hooked up to Konstantinov began to record some heartening changes.

"His nurse said it was one of the first times that they got a real solid response in his vitals – and a hand squeeze," Wharton recalled. So he decided that the Stanley Cup should make periodic visits.

But routine visits to the hospital were difficult for some teammates, Wharton said. "It's really hard to see somebody that was so vital, so strong and so passionate about what he did, in that condition," he said. "That's never an excuse not to visit, but I think it kept some guys away. I think the reality of it struck them, it struck a chord in them."

Meanwhile, with the celebration stopped dead in its tracks, teammates moved solemnly forward with their summer plans. Nicklas Lidstrom took his family back to Sweden for a summer that would never be the same.

"I just remember all that fun we had a week earlier, everything that we had been through," Lidstrom said. "Suddenly, winning a Stanley Cup – it didn't matter anymore because your teammates were hurting. And you didn't know what the outcome was going to be. It was very tough."

———————————※※———————————

Nine days after the crash, the Red Wings sponsored a celebrity hockey game for charity. Fetisov had been out of the hospital only a few days when team officials approached him about attending the game and dropping the puck for the ceremonial face-off. The idea, clearly, was to bolster the fragile morale of a heartbroken city.

"They said, 'Slava, you know, there's so much uncertainty in the town,'" Fetisov recalled. "'People care so much about what's going on. They worry, and there's really no information to give right now. So we ask if you can come.'"

Of course, he would.

Fetisov arrived at the rink and, as they do for all such pre-game ceremonies, the Wings rolled out a red carpet onto the ice. Fetisov felt at home inside the familiar Joe Louis Arena, inspired, but also apprehensive because he didn't know what to expect. And just before he walked out onto the ice, he noticed the hitch in his gait.

"I was limping because my whole right side was beaten up pretty good," he said. "Then they announce my name and I realize, 'I cannot limp.' I should go straight out and try to smile a little bit, you know. So it's positive energy."

When he was introduced, the 15,501 fans rose to their feet, their applause thundering, sending chills down his spine. Finally, here was something – however small – to feel good about.

"I feel it, you know, through the skin. It was very special going out on that ice," Fetisov said. "People took this as a personal tragedy, and now. . . This is a moment I will never forget. It will stay with me. . ."

After the ceremony, Fetisov visited the Red Wings' locker room. That's where things began to unravel for him.

"When you go back to this situation again, to the dressing room," he said, his words coming slowly. "You see the stalls, the names of all the players. And one thing you think about is you are happy for yourself because you can still walk, at least, and be in this room.

"But at the same moment, you think about what has happened with Vladimir and Sergei, and you realize it's not ever going to be the same, from now on."

Fetisov paused and took a breath. His eyes began to water.

Vladimir Konstantinov's recovery, meantime, was slow and unsteady. After two months, there was little improvement.

"He seemed to go in surges where he'd make a lot of progress, then he'd plateau, then he'd make some progress and plateau again," Wharton said. "That was frustrating, because in the middle of a surge, the last thing you wanted was a plateau. And every time he'd hit one of those it was difficult. I'm talking about over a period of weeks and months, of course, and eventually over years."

As he slowly improved by ebbs and flows, Konstantinov seemed to have some awareness of some meaningful things in his life, based on interactions with family members and his Russian teammates. Wharton figured it was time for another visit with the Stanley Cup.

The trophy is made of silver and nickel alloy, standing 35¼ inches tall and weighing 34½ pounds. Its value varies based on the price of silver on the world's trading exchanges, but to those who compete for it, it's priceless. One of the most wonderful things about the Cup is that the names of every player on every championship team are engraved on it. Another special feature is that at its top sits the original bowl. Nearly 11½ inches in diameter and about 7¼ inches deep, it's a perfect vessel for champagne or beer – and quite often a quixotic mixture of both when the winning teams skate off the ice with it to celebrate in their locker rooms.

Drinking from the Stanley Cup is a rite of passage for every champion – and often for his family and friends. But it typically takes three people to sip from it without making a big mess. Wharton figured a sip out of the big trophy would be good therapy for Konstantinov, and it was. When Pritchard arrived with the Cup, Wharton asked the nurses to round up some of those little containers of apple juice hospitals always have on hand. He poured eight of them into the bowl at the top. Sitting slightly upright in his hospital bed, Vladdie's eyes followed every move. Assistant coach Dave Lewis was on the other side of the bed. Then Wharton and Lewis tilted the Stanley Cup toward Vladimir's mouth and he began to drink.

"Gulped every drop of it down," Wharton said. "Didn't spill a drop. And he had this big smile on his face."

Nearly two decades later, Sergei Fedorov still remembers taking that phone call from the police, still remembers the cold, business-like voice at the other end telling him about the crash, and still hasn't come to terms with it.

"I am not crazy about this subject at all, this question about the limo accident," he said when I interviewed him at the Central Red Army's headquarters in Moscow. "I knew you were going to ask me this, but I don't like to talk about it. A couple of close, dear friends got hurt in this accident. I don't want to go through not-happy emotions. Forgive me, but it's not going away. It's probably never going away."

Fedorov could not, however, avoid the scene of the crash. He passed by it at least twice a day on his way to or from his work at Joe Louis Arena. He saw how fans reacted so beautifully, gathering there with candles for weeks afterward.

"That's why I have a hard time talking about it even now," he said. "Yeah, nobody died, but a couple of guys were badly injured. We cannot share those days of happiness together, like normal people would do."

Considering his ever-present smile and the laughter that came easy to him, Sergei Mnatsakanov's injuries seemed especially cruel. The bottle that split his head open damaged the part of the brain that controlled emotions. Like Konstantinov, Mnatsakanov suffered severe brain-stem damage, but Sergei's head injuries were so dramatically different they were treated on separate floors of the ICU. When the two men had recovered enough to spend time together, Sergei was very happy. But because of the brain damage, he expressed his happiness in tears. He wept a lot, sometimes uncontrollably, Wharton said. Though he recovered with his mind fully engaged, Sergei would spend the rest of his life in a wheelchair, the left side of his body rendered largely immobile from paralysis.

Vladimir Konstantinov, doctors eventually determined, had suffered a traumatic closed-head injury. His brain had been torn in several places, disrupting his ability to communicate, to move with balance. It affected his cognitive skills, his ability to make sound judgements. And it destroyed his short-term memory.

About six months after the accident, Konstantinov, with his wife, Irina, and his daughter, Anastasia, moved to Florida, where he could focus on intense rehabilitation with around-the-clock therapists. Slowly, he learned to sit up in his chair, to stand for a few minutes and eventually to get from room to room with the aid of a walker. Speech returned more slowly. A word here and there, usually in Russian. His long-term memory, too, began to reemerge. He seemed to remember his early days in hockey. On visits to the Wings' dressing room years after the accident, Konstantinov recognized his old teammates, greeting them all with a firm handshake. He loved to play cards during his recovery, particularly Uno. And in the past several years he developed an interest in oil painting, work featured in several shows.

Richard Gnida, the limo driver, was sentenced to nine months in jail and two years of probation after pleading guilty to a misdemeanor second offense of driving with a suspended license. Investigators determined that the limousine did not crash because of a mechanical failure. They figured that Gnida had fallen asleep, based on Fetisov's description of events and Gnida's admission that he had "blanked out" behind the wheel. Investigators could not determine whether Gnida had smoked marijuana the day of the accident or whether the trace amounts that showed up in toxicological tests were the byproduct of frequent pot smoking. Without the former, prosecutors decided they could not pursue a felony charge.

Gnida was also ordered by Oakland District Judge Kimberly Small to undergo outpatient therapy and 200 hours of community service in a rehabilitation center for patients with closed-head injuries. "If you have to change bedpans for those individuals," the judge told Gnida, "that's what you'll be doing."

He was released from jail two months early for good behavior.

However, Small ordered Gnida back to jail within six months for violating his parole. He had quit attending court-ordered drug counseling and Alcoholics Anonymous meetings and never showed up for court hearings to schedule his community service. Gnida then served 75 additional days in jail, until March 1999, but he was no longer required to get counseling or perform community service because his jail sentence replaced his probation requirements.

Two years after he nearly killed three members of the Detroit Red Wings in that limousine he was driving illegally, Gnida was arrested on drunken-driving charges. On July 2, 1999, he ran a stop sign immediately after leaving a topless club, according to police. His blood-alcohol content was 0.12, above Michigan's legal threshold, at the time 0.10, for intoxicated driving. For his third drunken-driving conviction, Gnida was sentenced to one year in jail.

Numerous other legal proceedings followed the crash, the biggest of which was a $290 million lawsuit filed by the team members' wives in U.S. District Court. By a 6-1 vote, however, the jury found that Findlay (Ohio) Ford, which sold the vehicle to Gambino's Westside Limousine Service, in Belleville, Michigan, had used reasonable care in checking over the vehicle, ensuring it was safe for passengers before it left the dealership. During the 15-day trial, the families rejected offers of $4 million and $6 million to settle the case out of court. They received nothing.

Findlay Ford's lawyers argued in briefs filed with the court that Gnida and the limo company's owner, John Gambino, were to blame. "Gnida fell asleep at the wheel," the auto dealer's attorneys reasoned. "Mr. Gnida did not have a valid driver's license at the time and Gambino's owner, John Gambino, who knew he was unlicensed, allowed him to drive."

The three team members sued Gnida and the limo company, whose insurance policy had a $2 million limit. That ended with a three-person mediation panel's unanimous award in favor of the injured men. The insurers also agreed to provide for certain lifetime medical costs. Ford Motor Co. agreed in 2001 to pay about $163,000 to Konstantinov and $64,614 to Mnatsakanov.

The legal proceedings left the victims' families angry and bitter.

Igor Larionov had every intention of joining his teammates on the golf course that day. He really did. But when he woke up on that Friday morning in June to a beautiful 85-degree day – the best yet in an otherwise unseasonably cool spring, his daughters had other ideas. They were eager to enjoy the sun by poolside at a club to which his family belonged.

He was caught in a kind of no-man's land between team and family that many professional athletes feel at some point. You're no man if you can't join your teammates for something as special as a final hurrah with the Stanley Cup. And you're not much of a father if you turn your back on two little girls who have seen little of their dad in the past nine months because he's busy playing more than a one hundred hockey games from the start of training camp in mid-September until the conclusion of four best-of-seven playoff series in June.

"I told my daughters that I had already made a promise that I would be there. I have to go," Larionov recalled. "I thought maybe I could go to the golf club and play nine holes, then come back and go to the other club with the girls.

"And they kept saying, 'No, let's go to the pool. It's our time now. Spend some time with us.'"

The girls won. Larionov drove them to the pool. One thing led to another. Soon he got a call from his Russian teammates, letting him know that they were on their way to the golf club.

"It was too late for me to go with them," Larionov said. After several hours at the pool, he returned home to spend some time with his brother, who was visiting from Russia.

"Then, around 10 o'clock, I got a phone call."

They turned on the TV. Breaking news. A frantic dash to the hospital.

Igor Larionov's most enduring final memory of a healthy, vibrant, happy – and maybe a little tipsy – Vladimir Konstantinov is from that Thursday night before, when the Wings had gathered for dinner at Morton's. Walking toward his house with his wife, Larionov heard that song.

That song. What has it become now for Igor Larionov – an anthem of happiness or a requiem of regret? Does it make him happy, or sad? The question seemed to catch him by surprise. He bowed his head, pausing for a moment to give it some thought.

"Well, you know, it's happy when you win, but it's only like a couple of minutes, and after that you go back to your normal life," he said. "Then we played the music for Vladimir, and the girls would sing it to him. I think maybe it was stimulating him because it made him feel good, you know?

"But now, for me? I would say it's a sad song because all of that glory, all of that happiness – all of a sudden, it ended. It shows you that life is so unpredictable. . ."

Twenty years later, Larionov's words still echo. They may serve as the best possible explanation for those heartbroken, disillusioned, frustrated and angry fans who still wonder why something like this could happen to their team and to its adored players.

The Russians have a phrase for it: "the irony of fate." In fact, there is a film by that name from the Brezhnev-era 1970s. It is regarded as a classic piece of Russian popular culture, a love story that forces the viewer to examine all that is important in life. The film is widely shown throughout Russia and its former Soviet republics each New Year's Eve in much the same way Americans watch "It's a Wonderful Life" each Christmas.

In Detroit, we're left to wonder about beautiful lives destroyed inexplicably by a notoriously bad driver. After all those years of hoping, waiting, wanting. . . finally the Red Wings bring the Stanley Cup back to Detroit and this happens? Why? It's not fair. It's wrong. And it hurts like hell.

CHAPTER 18

A Cup of History

In the shadows of Lubyanka Square, an unambiguous reminder of the ominous power of the Soviet Union and the home of its ruthless security police force, the KGB, stood the former House of Culture, where ballerinas with the eminent Bolshoi Ballet once performed. But in the summer of 1997, that building was home to one of the hottest, most notorious – and, some said, dangerous – clubs on the planet. On entering, patrons walked through a metal detector, then were frisked by some of the beefiest, most terrifying men who stood sentry at each entryway. Word was they were former KGB grunts, the kind who would do anything – *anything* – for a buck. Or even a shrinking ruble.

These fierce-looking bouncers were especially busy on a Sunday night in August 1997, when The Hungry Duck, a club designed to accommodate perhaps 300 people, had three or four times that many crammed into it as rumor spread that something special was on tap. Vodka was flowing like beer in an American college town, and several young women were dancing atop the 50-foot horseshoe bar, a legendary Duck tradition. There were many, less-flattering traditions at the notorious club, like flying bullets – eight were fired inside the bar, five in the ceiling and three in the floor – and disappearing owners. Four of the Duck's original owners were dead within a few years after the doors opened. The last guy standing had his life threatened a half-dozen times and was once roughed up in an attempted kidnapping.

It should come as no surprise, then, that NHL officials were more than a little concerned when the Russian Wings informed them they would be visiting the club during their extraordinary Moscow homecoming – with the Stanley Cup in tow. This was precisely what NHL Commissioner Gary Bettman was worried about when Slava Fetisov first broached the idea of taking the Cup home to Russia just moments after the Wings had won the championship in June.

Bettman was still on the ice after Fetisov and Igor Larionov took their celebrated lap around the Joe Louis Arena rink with the Stanley Cup. And after they handed it off to teammates for their own special moments, Fetisov skated over to the commissioner and made a spur-of-the-moment appeal that he knew would not be well-received. It was delivered more as a statement than a request.

"Gary, you know I'm going to need the Cup in Moscow now," Fetisov said.

"No way. Absolutely not!" the commissioner responded.

"Yes, this is my right after we win."

Since 1989, a tradition had evolved regarding the Stanley Cup celebrations after the champion was crowned. Each player on the winning team could have the trophy for a day or two, depending on seniority, which produced some unprecedented good will throughout North America as the Cup made its rounds. Fetisov knew long before he ever won it exactly what he would do with his time.

"No, no, no!" Bettman said. "There's too much crime in Russia now. It's too dangerous."

"We can talk about it later," Fetisov said, "but I need to take this Cup to Moscow."

On a dreary Saturday afternoon of August 16, a plane landed at Moscow's Sheremetyevo International Airport carrying precious cargo. Fetisov was there with Igor Larionov and Slava Kozlov to receive the Stanley Cup on its arrival in Russia. It was accompanied by several NHL executives and a security team that included Phil Pritchard, curator and self-proclaimed Keeper of the Cup from the Hockey Hall of Fame in Toronto.

Pritchard opened a large trunk, lifted the burnished trophy out of its velvety cocoon and handed it to Fetisov, who turned and walked toward a chain-link fence. On the other side were several hundred of his countrymen who had come to celebrate this moment. They poked their fingers through the fence to touch the silver chalice and stamp their fingerprints on history. Later in the day, the Stanley Cup was given a place of honor at the Central Sport Club of the Army, CSKA headquarters of the Red Army hockey organization that produced all five players in Detroit's Russian unit.

Outside its home in Toronto, there may have been no safer place in the world for the Stanley Cup than this distinguished military institution. But Moscow, once among the safest cities in the world, was changing. The Communist KGB had lost its iron grip on society. Petty crime was prevalent, if not rampant, and serious crime was no longer uncommon. Worse, the entire country was on edge with the start of the first Chechen-Russian Conflict. Russia and Chechen nationalist and Islamist forces had engaged in armed conflict dating back more than 200 years. As the Soviet Union disintegrated, Chechen separatists declared their independence in 1991. War broke out in late 1994, and fighting continued on and off for five years until Russian security forces established tenuous control.

Adding to the country's woes, the Russian mafia – a term used to loosely describe a collective of various organized crime elements – was growing exponentially in the absence of a strong police force. In other words, the NHL couldn't depend on civic law enforcement agencies to help protect the Cup.

So league executives were skeptical for a very good reason.

"I've talked to some guys who would really like to steal that thing," said Hungry Duck owner Doug Steele, the city's most notorious saloonkeeper in the middle to late 1990s. "They think it would look great at their *dachas* (country homes)."

Steele, then 46, was a Canadian ex-pat. Born in Timmins, Ontario, he moved to Nova Scotia when he was 12, and somehow grew up a passionate fan of the Detroit Red Wings. I met Steele through our mutual friend, Alan Adams, a Toronto newsman who was in Moscow, like me, to cover the Cup's appearance in Russia for his newspaper. We were enjoying some Cuban cigars during a quiet moment just ahead of one of The Duck's signature happy hours that began at 8 p.m. Though it was barely 5 p.m., every seat in the place was occupied, but only a few patrons were drinking or eating. Most were just sitting at tables or booths, socializing and content to wait the three hours until happy hour began, when six-for-one shots – typically vodka, tequila or gin – would begin. Which meant that one round at a table for six would mean 36 shots would arrive. An hour later, at 9 p.m., the happy-hour deal was trimmed to five-for-one, and each hour that passed the deal narrowed similarly until midnight. But by then it was bedlam. The alcohol always had the desired effect; within a few hours, dozens of people, including young women peeling off clothing, were dancing on the bar.

During that quiet moment before the first rounds were being served, Steele broached the subject he knew would be sensitive.

"Do you think you could convince those guys to bring the Cup here?" he asked. "I promise it will be worth their time. I've got some big plans if they can make it happen."

I winced. I didn't like asking athletes or coaches for favors beyond a few minutes for an interview, or a special sitting for a photo to accompany a story. A notable exception: In the spring of 1997, when my good friend and Detroit Free Press colleague Corky Meinecke, one of the best NBA writers of his era and one of the finest newsmen I've ever worked with, died of cancer. He was 44. It was devastating for all who knew him, those he worked with and the thousands more who had read his work for years in Detroit. Corky left a beautiful wife, Valerie, and three amazing kids who were in college, or soon would be. My newspaper's sports department organized a bowling event/silent auction to raise money for their education, and I wasn't shy this time about asking the Red Wings' organization and the players for help. Their generosity overwhelmed me. I left with an SUV filled to the brim with game-used sticks, skates, sweaters, gloves, pucks, photos and more, much of it signed. Among the most generous of all were the Russians. They gave me armloads of stuff, all autographed. The silent auction raised thousands of dollars for Corky's kids. I left the bowling alley that day with three items I'd purchased with high bids – signed sticks from Slava Fetisov and Vladimir Konstantinov, and a home Konstantinov No. 16 jersey with the signatures of each member of the Russian Five. Those, along with a Louisville Slugger signed by Al Kaline and a box with hundreds of press passes, represent the sum of my sports memorabilia collection.

Most of the Russians I've known, from language school in California to virtually every NHL dressing room, are good people with big hearts. And among the kindest, most thoughtful and generous of them all was Slava Fetisov, who might be the most famous and recognizable athlete in all of Russia. It sure seemed that way on a Sunday morning in Red Square, the ancient and cobblestoned parade ground that many Americans recognized as the place the Soviets would march their soldiers and show off their military hardware each year on May Day (May 1), when their workers of their world united in a government-orchestrated show of might and supremacy.

On this morning, sunny but unusually cool and breezy for mid-August even in Moscow, the square was bustling. Tourists were there to visit the Kremlin behind the tall, red-brick wall, snap pictures of St. Basil's Cathedral, perhaps the most recognizable church in the world, where czars once read their edicts. People came to pay homage at the tomb of V.I. Lenin, the inspiration behind the Bolshevik Revolution and the first leader of the USSR. Many others were there because they had heard rumors that the famous hockey trophy from North America might be making an appearance.

"It's amazing to think of the Cup in Red Square," said Todd Carmichael, who was there with Monique Couture, both attorneys from Ottawa, Ontario, working for a firm in Moscow. They were armed with a camera, posing in the foreground while players held the Stanley Cup near *Lobnoye Mesto* – the "Place of Skulls," – where 16th century czar Ivan the Terrible was said to behead his rivals.

"I never thought we'd see the day," Carmichael said. "And the people of Moscow – the ones who know about it – are really pumped."

Among them was Andrei Chursakov, a sergeant of the Kremlin guards who held an autographed photo of Slava Fetisov, Igor Larionov and Slava Kozlov as they posed with the Cup. He was mesmerized by the star power in the photo and lamented the loss of most of Russia's best players to the NHL.

"I don't watch as much hockey as before," Chursakov said. "All the players have left. But I watch the NHL now so I can follow these guys. I'll put this picture up at home, and I will look at it all the time."

The players walked from place to place around the square as Kozlov, by far the youngest of the three, lugged the Cup. Each wore his Wings jersey. Fetisov also wore some of his other cherished hardware, including several gold medals. People would stop and stare. Not at the big trophy, but at the men accompanying it.

"Oh my God, is that Fetisov?" one would whisper to another. "Yes, yes! That's Fetisov. And there's Larionov, too!" And the crowd behind them would grow. The men who had brought so much joy to Russian hockey fans – the world championships, the Olympic gold medals and now even the Stanley Cup from North America – were right there among them in Red Square.

"It's very nice to see all these Russian people around us,'" Larionov said, noting they seemed curious about the trophy. As he spoke, he signed autographs on whatever people brought him to sign, including T-shirts, cigarette packages and even a 1,000-ruble note.

Fetisov saw the beauty of the moment in the eyes of the people he met in Red Square, and he knew he was right to insist to the leaders of the NHL that they consent to this tour with the Stanley Cup.

"When I see the smiles of the people, I know why we came here," Fetisov said that day.

Nearly two decades later, it was the smiles he remembered most about those days with the trophy in Russia.

"I'm telling you," Fetisov said, "from first moment when Cup arrived on the plane and we meet it on the field after an international flight, you can see the smiles on the people, on the Customs people, the policemen, the people who work in airports. You see the smiles and you realize we bring so much happiness to so many people."

And no one was more moved than Aleksandr Maximovich Fetisov, Slava's father, who was 65 when the Cup visited Moscow.

"I am so proud of Slava because now he has all the hockey trophies there are to have," the elder Fetisov said. "And now he's walking through Red Square with the Stanley Cup!"

Father and son posed for pictures with the other players and a few of us from the media at Lenin's tomb. Slava was in high spirits when I tentatively broached the subject of taking the Cup to The Hungry Duck.

"What do you think about bringing the Cup to this wild and crazy club we've discovered here in Moscow, Slava?" I asked. And then I explained that the owner was a Canadian ex-pat and passionate Red Wings fan who promised to turn his establishment into an homage to Detroit if he could entice an appearance of the Stanley Cup.

I told Fetisov that the owner, Steele, said he was prepared to spend upwards of $10,000 to recreate a slice of Detroit hockey in his bar – complete with all the Stanley Cup banners the Wings had won to that point in their history: 1936, 1937, 1943, 1950, 1952, 1954, 1955 and – after a 42-year drought – 1997. He also planned to honor the greatest players in Red Wings history, the ones whose numbers were retired to the rafters: Terry Sawchuk's No. 1, Ted Lindsay's No. 7, Gordie Howe's No. 9, Alex Delvecchio's No. 10 and Sid Abel's No. 12, by creating similar banners. Steele would have a replica of the Stanley Cup on hand, along with fire-brewed Stroh's beer on tap from the iconic Detroit brewery. Naturally, there would be plenty of extra security there as well. Fetisov seemed impressed.

"Yeah, sure, why not?" he said.

"Seriously?" I said, thinking of plenty of reasons why not.

"We will be there," he said. "I want to see this place. . . Sometime after 11 o'clock, OK?"

Steele had a crew of carpenters working around the clock to transform his bar, bringing a little bit of Motown to Moscow. After the visit to Red Square, the three Wings did a lap around the ice at Sokolniki Arena before joining a team of Russian-born NHL stars playing against Spartak, host of the Spartak Cup, a celebrated summertime hockey event. (The three Wings did not skate in that game.) There, Moscow Mayor Yuri Luzhkov addressed a standing-room-only crowd of 4,500.

"I am not a hockey expert, but I am sure that the Stanley Cup is one of the most prestigious awards in the world of sport," Luzhkov said, "and our hockey players have demonstrated the greatness of Russian hockey and sports abroad."

Kozlov spoke, too. "The Stanley Cup is here tonight for you," he told the crowd. "As you can see, it is a very beautiful trophy."

This triumphant and momentous trip was less-than-perfect, however, for two reasons: one heartbreaking and the other disheartening. Two of the five celebrated Russian players were missing – Vladimir Konstantinov, back in Detroit recovering from near-fatal injuries from that unfathomable limousine accident, and Sergei Fedorov, the playoff scoring leader who passed on the opportunity to make the trip with his comrades. He also didn't accompany his Russian teammates to New York earlier in the summer, where they were feted by that city's enormous Russian community. Instead, Fedorov was spotted from Wimbledon, England, to California with a famous young Russian tennis star, Anna Kournikova, who had sat next to him in a red Mustang convertible during the Wings' championship parade down Woodward Avenue. And his reputation took a hit from his closest teammates.

"That tells me a lot about a guy," said Fetisov, who expected more from the young star. He blamed the new generation of Russian-bred players who didn't have to fight for their freedom. "The young guys, they make huge money, but they do not help. Everything was too easy for them."

Never shy about speaking his mind, Fetisov took dead aim at those young guys – and one in particular.

"I understand why so many people want to come to America. It's a very special country," he said. "But if you forget your roots – you're not really an American, and you're not a Russian anymore. This is a very special moment for us. He (Fedorov) has to find a way to share it, even if it's just for a day."

Some speculated that Fedorov's absence was his way of showing disappointment, frustration or anger over his less-than-amicable contract talks with the Wings. Either way, he missed an extraordinary moment at home.

By early that Sunday evening, The Hungry Duck looked a lot more like Joe Louis Arena than a notorious Moscow night club. And it was beyond packed. "The interest in the NHL is huge here," Steele said, "because of the Russian players over there now. The (New York) Rangers were the most popular, but now it's Detroit. It's all about where the Russians are playing."

Steele had roped off a VIP area, where he joined reporters and a few of his friends as we waited for the Cup's arrival. And waited. And waited some more. When 11 p.m. passed, I shrugged it off; players are typically late for things like this. Midnight came and went, and now I was wondering whether something had gone wrong. The crowd was getting a little restless, too, but no one was leaving. Steele began to speculate that NHL officials had pulled the plug on this visit, and it probably wasn't going to happen. My head wanted to agree with him, but my heart wasn't so sure. Let's be patient. Slava Fetisov was nothing if not a man of his word, and if he said he'd be here with the Stanley Cup, then he would be.

Finally, well past 1 a.m., a murmur grew to a roar as Slava Kozlov approached from a back entrance holding the most recognizable sports trophy in the world. Steele gave me a quick look and a nod, his eyes reflecting surprise, relief and unmitigated joy. The Stanley Cup was in his bar, brought to him by three stars of the team he idolized as a boy. Close behind Kozlov were Fetisov and Larionov, waving to a wildly exuberant crowd. Immediately behind them were several NHL officials, nervously scanning the room for trouble.

They were uneasy, obviously, because they had done their due diligence and knew that The Duck had a rather checkered reputation. Since Steele took over the bar on March 15, 1996, a few months after its doors opened, until the day he closed it on March 15, 1999, police had opened 256 criminal cases involving The Hungry Duck. Network television filmed inside the bar on 43 occasions, and three motion pictures shot scenes there. The Duck was raided frequently, and one night 79 patrons were arrested on suspicion of narcotics, according to Steele. All were subsequently released without charge.

It was the only bar ever denounced in a national parliament, and there were allegedly 30 separate attempts by non-police agencies to close the bar. Its most popular regular event, besides iconic happy-hour drink specials, was Ladies Night, which invariably ended with women dancing hip-to-hip on the bar – an average of 15 of them bare-breasted at any given time. Eventually, The Duck had forged formidable enemies, not the least of which was the building's director – a famous ballerina in her 80s named Olga Lepeshinskaya – who bragged that she used to perform solo for Stalin. When she began to hear the salacious details of what was happening in that former House of Culture, she moved to have The Duck expelled.

"She was a trip," Steele wrote years later in a piece for the website exile.ru. "Not only did she boast openly of her closeness to Stalin, but she praised the glorious history of this building. . . Once she turned against us, no matter what the other members of the building's board said, we were through. In Russia, artists are elevated to a higher level than probably anywhere in the world. I'm not sure how this building was handed over to her after the collapse of the Soviet Union, but that's what happened, and no one, not even top officials, would dare upset her. Russia's top artists are untouchable, like ayatollahs."

But the night the Stanley Cup made its visit, Aug. 17, 1997, the massive crowd celebrated without an incident. The Free Press had supplied me with several hundred placards featuring its now familiar photo of the Russian Five in profile. It was used for promotional purposes in newsstands, and people were lined up at the VIP area getting them signed by three of those men in the picture. And the scene I'll never forget from that night is of those burly KGB thugs, those modern-day Cossacks hired to maintain order and protect the Cup and those who brought it. They were rendered speechless as their boyhood heroes Viacheslav Fetisov and Igor Larionov – the Gordie Howe and Wayne Gretzky of Soviet-era hockey – signed the placards. The biggest, scariest-looking one of them all was sobbing like a baby.

Two days later, the Stanley Cup continued its tour at the Podmoskovie Sports Palace in Voskresensk, otherwise known as "Hockeytown East," hometown of Igor Larionov and Slava Kozlov. They grew up a few blocks from one another in a community about a 90-minute drive from Red Square. The gleaming 4,500-seat arena with stained-glass windows also served as a veritable museum honoring the history of the local professional club, Khimik Voskresensk. It was directly across the street from the apartment where Larionov grew up, which was right next door to his school.

The arena was packed, and I was surprised to be welcomed as an honored guest with the offer of bread and salt, a greeting ceremony in many Eastern European cultures. But the crowd knew who the real honored guests were. The citizens of Voskresensk were all there to see Russia's hockey royalty and this magnificent trophy they called *Kubok Stenli*.

It was an emotional moment, for Larionov especially, after the events of a tumultuous summer.

"Because of the car accident, we were thinking how we could celebrate when our friends were suffering in the hospital," he said. "But at the same time, you must carry on, to promote the game. The Russian players were a big part of the success in Detroit. We got the trophy, and we decided this is the way. We were proud to bring the Stanley Cup to Russia and share the experience and history of the Cup with the fans who had been behind us for the past two seasons in Detroit."

Larionov's entire family was there. So was Kozlov's. Their former coaches and mentors were there, too, along with several hundred young hockey players among thousands of others who came to honor Detroit's Russian Five – and especially the two from Voskresensk – in what was in every respect a conqueror's homecoming.

"It was a great feeling for us," Larionov said, "to share this moment with them. And it was very nice of the NHL to let us take the Cup home to Moscow."

The Stanley Cup had made a glorious maiden tour around Russia's capital city. From various hockey rinks to a soccer stadium with 80,000 people that included President Boris Yeltsin and Prime Minister Viktor Chernomyrdin to a nightclub that symbolized a new kind of pop culture in a fast-changing Moscow society.

"We start a new life in the history of the Stanley Cup," Fetisov said. "We cross the border into the Russian Federation, and now it's part of the culture in Russian sport. It's like a common thing now."

CHAPTER 19

Sixteen for Sixteen

Slava Fetisov had nothing left to prove. After Olympic gold, all the World Championships and Canada Cup gold, he finally had succeeded in capturing the ultimate prize in the game: something silver, with his name etched on it. He was 39. All that remained was to take the Stanley Cup home to Moscow for a celebrated victory lap around Red Square, and he could call it a career.

Besides, the Russian Five was history. The limousine crash forever ended a story that, in retrospect, was so short as to seem ethereal. It lasted less than two seasons. But what joyous and memorable seasons they were.

So Fetisov felt ready to welcome a well-earned retirement from the game. Ready to get on to more important things, like making the world a better place to live. That plan lasted about two weeks. It was ending as he limped into Joe Louis Arena a few days following his release from the hospital after surviving the limo crash that left two teammates fighting for their lives.

The stirring reception from grateful, prayerful Red Wings fans got him thinking – or rather re-thinking – his retirement plans. Seeing his fallen friend's stall in the dressing room that day clinched it. A few minutes earlier, it was painful just to lean over to drop the puck for a ceremonial face-off in a charity game because he was recovering from broken ribs and a punctured lung. His limp was caused by nerve damage when he suffered a gash on his right leg. And all Slava Fetisov could think about, suddenly, after seeing Vladimir Konstantinov's name above his empty stall, was playing hockey one more year.

"I realize I am so happy I am part of this organization," Fetisov said. "It was probably deep in my mind then that I want to come back. Maybe another year, I am thinking. Maybe I can play for both of us. . ."

There began the defense of the Stanley Cup, three months before training camp opened for the 1997-98 season.

The mood was predictably somber during the four-hour ride from Joe Louis Arena to Traverse City, traveling north and west through Michigan's lower mitten to the resort town on Lake Michigan, a golf and fishing mecca and the new site of the Red Wings' training camp. The boys on the bus, heading back to work after a short but eventful summer. It was September 11th at a time when 9/11 was just another date on the calendar.

Each player returning from the previous season had enjoyed the customary day or two that all team members get with the Stanley Cup. Fetisov, Igor Larionov and Slava Kozlov pooled their time to take it home to Russia. Captain Steve Yzerman strapped it to his wave runner out on Lake St. Clair. All of them had a story or two, or a thousand, from their time with that big trophy. Now, however, duty called whether they were ready.

They were ready, and they were proud.

"We looked around and realized, 'Hey, we're all champions here,'" said Darren McCarty, the man who scored the Stanley Cup-winning goal against Philadelphia. "It was really cool. Just a bunch of guys, relaxing on a bus. Nobody's changed."

Yet nothing would ever be the same. Missing among those champions were three critically important players who helped get them there: forward Sergei Fedorov, the team's best player, was holding out in a contract dispute; goaltender Mike Vernon, the playoff MVP a few months earlier, had been traded in a bold first move by newly appointed general manager Ken Holland; and the man who weighed heaviest in the hearts of everyone on that bus – Vladimir Konstantinov, their most versatile and physically punishing defenseman who was learning how to stand on his own and move around again with the aid of a walker. Also missing was their beloved massage therapist, Sergei Mnatsakanov, adjusting to life confined in a wheelchair.

It cast a malignant pall over the group in what should have been a moment of joy – a brotherhood reuniting after weeks of separation. But it is hard to be cheerful when you're gripped by survivor's guilt.

"You just keep thinking about it, and it's hard," center Kris Draper said of his return to the game that summer. "It doesn't seem humane. . . You feel kind of guilty about what was going on. But the bottom line is we're hockey players. It's our job. We have to go out and play hockey."

And if they had to do that, they might as well win. That was the prevailing attitude every man brought to camp that September. But no one ever mentioned it.

"The truth of the matter is nobody brought it up. Nobody said anything," senior vice president Jim Devellano recalled. "The team just quietly went about its business, but you could just feel what they were all thinking right from the beginning of training camp."

Coach Scotty Bowman felt it, too. These guys weren't physicians or faith healers; they couldn't fix their fallen brothers. They were hockey players, and by then they knew how to win; they had a big beautiful silver trophy with their names engraved on it as proof. If they could bring a little joy into Vladdie's life again, if they could put that big smile on Natsa's face once more, then damn it, they were going to win it again. Who needed words?

"Just the fact that they thought so much of Vladdie," Bowman said, "especially the Russian players. He was their comrade. It was just something they all believed in."

They believed.

That became their mantra, and it took on a life of its own when Slava Kozlov quietly placed into the palm of Konstantinov's gloves a lucky rock a fan had sent him the previous May for his birthday. On the rock was written the word "Believe." The rock eventually wound up on a shelf in Konstantinov's locker, which remained organized with his uniform, his equipment and his skates hanging in place as a sober reminder.

"I remember our first game we played that season, and Vladdie's jersey was hung up there in his stall," Draper said. "Every game, as I was getting dressed, I'd check over my shoulder and see that jersey. It kind of made you want to dig down deep and give a little extra, you know?"

Nicklas Lidstrom remembered how at the start of the new season the team felt closer, if that were even possible, than a few months earlier when the Wings had won the franchise's first Stanley Cup in 42 years. They were hurting, collectively. But they were happy to be back on the ice together, playing a game that gave them joy. They were grateful, too, that Fetisov had decided to return for one more year; everyone had expected him to retire. Most of all, they desperately missed their friend and teammate – on and off the ice.

"I sat right next to Vladdie in the locker room," Lidstrom recalled. "His gear was hanging up there the whole season. That rock that said 'Believe' on it was right there next to me. Every day at practice, or before games, you're reminded of what happened. Slava Fetisov was sitting on my other side, and you could see him every day, looking at that empty locker and thinking about the guy who should have been with us.

"Every guy in the room saw it, and I think that motivated our team to have success again. Somehow, it kind of rallied us not to forget what Vladdie was going through, what had happened. . . and to try again to win another Stanley Cup."

When the regular season started, in fact, the Red Wings wore that sentiment on their chests. Associate coach Dave Lewis proposed a patch with the initials of each injured teammate: VK and SM, and the word "Believe" in Russian and English. The NHL approved the idea, and the Wings wore that circular emblem on their right chests throughout the season. Although they still didn't talk much about it, they were proclaiming their intentions to the entire hockey-watching world.

As it turned out, Vladimir Konstantinov arrived sooner than anyone had imagined, but he came in a wheelchair. Physical therapist John Wharton made his daily visits to his injured teammates at the hospital again. One day he took a long look at Vladimir and said, "Man, I think you're ready. We need to get you out of here. Let's take you to a practice."

By then, Konstantinov had recovered enough to respond to such suggestions. If he didn't like something, he'd shake it off with a sharp snap of his head. First to the right, then to the left, as if to say, "That's not happening."

But if it was something he liked – such as Wharton's suggestion to visit his teammates at The Joe, he knew how to express that, too: Thumbs up, a deep nasal inhale with wide eyes, as if to say, "Let's go!"

And on a mild, mid-November day, they did. With owner Mike Ilitch's security team arranging the details, Konstantinov left the hospital and arrived at the east gate of the arena a few minutes before practice was ending. Wharton, the only member of the team to know of this visit, raced to the gate as soon as he got the call and wheeled Vladdie into the dressing room, helping him sit in his stall with all his equipment still in place, his skates sharpened, his No. 16 sweater hanging, the "Believe" rock on a shelf over his nameplate a few inches about his head.

The scene that followed, Wharton said, "is hard to put into words." Players walked into the room, tired and sweat-soaked, and when they saw their broken teammate sitting there wearing his leather Red Wings jacket – a gift from the owner – smiling and giving them the thumbs-up sign, well. . .

"There were a lot of teary eyes in the room that day," Wharton said. Each player greeted Vladdie with hugs and handshakes. He seemed to react most noticeably to the Russian players who spoke his native language.

In some respects, it may have been the most important day of that season.

"Seeing him sitting there in his stall, with that 'Believe' stone. . . that was kind of a moment for the players on that team," Wharton said. "It wasn't just a rock anymore. He's here with us. He's home. That's when we all started to believe. You can do things with a stone, a patch on a uniform, a billboard, but until you actually see the living proof –

Vladdie was there in that dressing room with us – it was an epiphany moment: OK, we can do this."

From then on, Wharton would try to arrange those visits as often as possible. They were good therapy – for everyone.

They believed. But they also knew it wasn't going to be easy. Winning that trophy in consecutive seasons was becoming increasingly difficult, especially after the National Hockey League expanded from 21 to 30 teams. Now they were trying to win again missing three important pieces from their lineup. Although their playoff MVP goalie was gone, traded for two second-round draft picks, the players had plenty of confidence in a young Chris Osgood. And they knew that Fedorov would return when he finally came to terms on a new contract – although there was a bit of a scare when he signed a mammoth front-loaded contract with Carolina that the Ilitch ownership had to scramble to match to keep him.

However, there was no replacing Vladimir Konstantinov, and that was worrisome from the opening day of training camp.

"Not having Vladdie in our lineup leaves a huge hole," captain Steve Yzerman said before taking the ice that first day of camp. "He's one of the best defensemen in the league. Maybe the best. We've got to figure out a way to replace Vladdie, and I don't mean with one individual. As a team."

Other players would have to raise their games, Bowman said. And they did. Vladimir Konstantinov had finished second to the New York Rangers' Brian Leetch in the balloting for the Norris Trophy as the NHL's best defenseman in 1997. Leetch was a spectacular offensive defenseman and deserved the award that year. Even Konstantinov had said so after he'd found out he was a finalist for the award.

So Konstantinov's were some big skates to fill, and Lidstrom stepped into them.

"Nick was always a great defenseman. But in Vladdie's absence, he became an even greater defenseman," Brendan Shanahan said. "I think he just decided he was going to bring more. The assignments that Vladdie took were now Nick's. And Nick all of a sudden went on a run of winning Norris trophies."

Over the next 13 seasons, Lidstrom won the award seven times, finished second in the voting three times and placed third once. That would have been unlikely had Konstantinov stayed healthy.

Lidstrom and his teammates started strong that season in the fall of 1997, losing just twice in their first 15 games. They played like a team on a mission, inspired by their doting fans who packed Joe Louis Arena. And they all got a boost from an occasional visitor.

"When Vladdie came to the room, he sat in his locker and we all came up and gave him hugs," Draper said. "We'd be sitting there getting dressed, and the other Russians would be talking to him a lot more than we would, because now there was a real language barrier, but everyone was just so happy to see him there."

Later, in a break during the game, public address announcer Budd Lynch would report that Konstantinov was in the house, watching from the owners' suite. The screen on the scoreboard over center ice would show him smiling and waving. All eyes would turn in his direction as fans would stand and cheer wildly. Many of them would wave. Some would weep. Players on both teams would tap their stick blades on the ice or along the boards as they stood by their benches, the time-honored sign of respectful applause among hockey players.

"I'd always notice a little more life in the next few shifts," Wharton said.

"When you have 20,000 people and they stood up for an ovation of 2½ or five minutes, you know, that's when you get the signal that you gotta do it," Igor Larionov said. "If those boys are fighting for their lives, we've got fight for our lives, too. That's what we did."

At mid-season, however, those visits stopped. Konstantinov left in January for Florida, seeking treatment at a special brain center renowned for caring for those with closed-head injuries. It was difficult for the teammates he left behind, although Wharton, Doug Brown and Dave Lewis flew down to see Konstantinov when the league interrupted its schedule for the Winter Olympics in Japan.

"That was special, and we were amazed at the improvements he was making," Wharton said, noting that Konstantinov had been down there just a few weeks at the time.

On January 30, Konstantinov rejoined his teammates once more in a ceremony at the White House, where the Stanley Cup champions were welcomed by President Bill Clinton. In a private moment before the official ceremony began, Clinton mingled with the Wings players. New York Times sportswriter Joe Lapointe reported an anecdote told to him by coach Scotty Bowman. Apparently, the president sought out Konstantinov.

"I like the look in your eye," Clinton said to him.

Larry Murphy, a defenseman standing nearby, turned toward the president and said, "You should see him play."

No one would see him play hockey again, as the president sensed.

"I know how much Vladimir Konstantinov means to everyone here," Clinton said to applause that filled the East Room. Konstantinov smiled and gave the president a thumbs-up. Clinton returned the gesture.

In February, after missing 59 games in a contract dispute, Fedorov finally signed a $38 million deal after the Red Wings matched an offer from the Carolina Hurricanes. He would collect a whopping $28 million of that within about four months. He should have been on top of the world, but in fact he was on the verge of a meltdown within days after returning to his team. That's how hard the absence of Konstantinov hit him.

"I saw him get very emotional about it on a number of occasions. It really affected him," Wharton said. "I knew he struggled with it. We all struggled with it. But Sergei was more emotional about it, openly emotional."

At one point, Wharton felt obliged to confront Fedorov and offer some solace.

"I just miss him so much, you know?" Fedorov said, holding back tears. "I miss having him here. I miss him being around."

Wharton was at a loss for words until he grabbed Fedorov's jersey, No. 91, and held it upside down.

"I showed Sergei how his number could look like a No. 16, Vladdie's number," Wharton said. "And so I told him, 'Just look. Vladdie's on your back every day. Every time you put that jersey on, he's with you.' I think that helped him quite a bit. Vladdie wasn't there physically, but he was definitely always there in spirit. We made sure to keep him there."

Wharton, too, had his moments, pulling double duty taking care of his team and, every day when not on the road, visiting the injured teammates at the hospital.

"I found myself going through the motions because I was exhausted and I was missing a couple of my friends," he said. "For the first time in four years, Sergei Mnatsakanov was not there, helping me with massages. I had a new Russian, Sergei Tchekmarev, so there was an adjustment period. We hit it off well, but nobody's like Sergei Mnatsakanov and his personality, the way he called me 'Chief.' Things like that were special to me."

Teammates missed their hard-working, happy-go-lucky trainer every bit as much as they missed their best defenseman. "We had that 'Believe' patch on our shoulder, and it wasn't just for Vladdie," Shanahan said. "It was Sergei Mnatsakanov as well. He was loved, *loved* by the guys in our room. He's just a special, special man."

The players, while driven to succeed, were more workmanlike than emotional in the way they went about their business. They knew what they had to do, and when they had to do it, so they didn't overextend themselves. They lost their final three games of the regular season and finished second by six points in their division and in the conference to Dallas, a team proving itself to be every bit the equal of Detroit and Colorado atop the NHL pyramid. Then the playoffs began, and the Red Wings got serious. Even though they might not have been as dominant as they were in winning the Stanley Cup the previous year, there was something different about this group.

Shanahan noticed soon after the playoffs began. The team was in Phoenix during the first of four rounds it would take to win the trophy again, and he was having lunch with Yzerman.

"You know," Shanahan said, "I feel like we're even more determined than we were last year."

Yzerman nodded in agreement.

"We sort of had this sense that there was like an anger about us, an anger mixed with determination that we were going to win this thing again," Shanahan said. "We'd lose a game and someone in the press would write that we were complacent, that we weren't as good. And that would piss us off even more. There was no complacency. I just remember all of us having this feeling, just really driven to win it again."

Dave Lewis noticed it too, from the first day of training camp six months before.

"It just permeated our group, and as a coach I knew what was going to happen," he said, noting that those "Believe" patches the players wore were mostly for others. "When you're in Joe Louis Arena and you're in the locker room preparing for the game and you look up and see an empty stall, you don't need a patch, you know? You've got the memory. . . For me, the visual was that empty locker. Every day."

It inspired the poet in Lewis, and before the playoffs that spring he wrote something to share with his team, to remind heartbroken teammates, and perhaps inspire them.

BELIEVE IN 16

Life is measured by Time Lines.
The birth of a child, the death of a loved one,
the day you were drafted.
Your first car, the day you were married.
The age that passes by 20, 30, 40 years.
Time never stops, it never will.
The time spent in June of 1997
will never be erased from the memory of
those who were there.
The hearts of so many beat as one,
living each other's dream for more than 8 weeks.
The time was right, we made it right.
Sixteen victories in the Spring of '97,
look back. . . it seems like yesterday.
Was it easy? No.
Was it rewarding? Yes.
So many emotions ran through that June.
Only you know what you left back at that time.

It starts again where it ended.

JLA, Joe Louis Arena.

Some have gone, others have arrived.

Time and changes seem to have something in common.

The new are excited for a chance.

The old are excited for the same chance.

This time, the vision may be clearer

but the route will be different.

It will be as challenging.

There are no shortcuts on this journey.

You will be tested again.

YOU ARE THE CHAMPIONS!

There are 15 other teams,

360 players,

That want their time in June.

16 VICTORIES, 16.

If we could stop time, we would, that June day.

BELIEVE me when I say

that we have two extra hearts to add to our roster.

Their names aren't listed.

The number has great significance.

They will always be there.

Life is measured by Time Lines.

Don't let this time slip away.

© 1998, Dave Lewis; reprinted with permission

Detroit won each of the first three series in six games. The most difficult series by far, and easily the best series of the entire tournament that spring, was the Western Conference finals against the Dallas Stars, a skirmish that turned into a battle that became an all-out war. It was highlighted by a frustrated Dallas goaltender Eddie Belfour nearly emasculating Detroit's Martin Lapointe by driving his big goalie stick between Lapointe's legs in a matinee game at Joe Louis Arena. Detroit prevailed in the series to advance to the Stanley Cup Finals for the third time in four seasons. Dallas, which had beaten Colorado to advance to the Western Conference Finals, would have to wait.

The Wings faced the Washington Capitals in the spring of 1998 in a series that was considerably more difficult than the results indicated. Each of the first three games were decided by one goal. Detroit won the opener at home, 2-1, and needed an overtime goal from Kris Draper for a come-from-behind 5-4 victory in Game 2. The series shifted to Washington, and again the Wings prevailed 2-1 on Sergei Fedorov's game-winner.

That set up a Game 4 that coach Scotty Bowman had no intention of losing. Bowman wasn't much of a locker-room orator. He motivated his players in different ways, getting to know them so well that he understood which buttons to push to get the best out of each of them. That was Bowman's calling card throughout his redoubtable coaching career: When it came to getting the most out of his players, especially his star players, he was sheer genius.

But now he had something to say, so he gathered his team to remind them once more exactly what was at stake. Despite all the trauma and emotional hardships his team had suffered in the past year, it had come this far, earning 15 of the 16 victories it took to win the most challenging championship in sports. And as an orator, Bowman was on his game that day.

"It was like a poem," Slava Fetisov remembered. "Scotty said you should play now for Vladimir. We knew they were going to bring him to Washington for this game. We knew this could be special moment not only for Detroit Red Wings, but for NHL history. We played all year for this, and now we got to our last game to realize this.

"Of course, it gives us extra energy. Extra strength. Extra leaning on the shoulder of each other."

Kris Draper put it more succinctly: "No way were we losing that hockey game, no chance. Not with all the emotions we were feeling, and having Vladdie there with us."

And they didn't. On June 16, 1998, the Red Wings won in a rout, at least compared to the other three games. The score was 4-1, but it wasn't that close. It was over relatively quickly. Just 10:30 into the game, Detroit's Doug Brown scored the first of his two goals. Sergei Fedorov, in a masterful encore performance after recording the game-winner in Game 3, recorded two assists. The Russians weren't fooling around.

When the final horn sounded, Draper glanced toward his team's goal and has this memory seared into his brain: Goaltender Chris Osgood throwing his hands up in the air in jubilation, stick going one way, helmet and gloves the other. Draper felt what every player in a Detroit uniform was thinking at once: "We did it!"

Soon the ice was littered with equipment as the Wings poured over the boards from their bench to mob their teammates who had just staved off a furious final charge by the Capitals. But this happiest (and most heart-wrenching) of all Hollywood endings was just getting started.

Before a worldwide TV audience, "Hockey Night in Canada" broadcaster Ron MacLean was interviewing Bowman.

"This is really a dream-come-true after the tragedy of last season," Bowman said. "I knew our team would come through, the way they felt about Vladimir Konstantinov – and Sergei Mnatsakanov, too. They would give every bit they could to win this Cup."

MacLean's job in that moment was to ask questions, but he, too, was overcome by a moment churning with emotion.

"You can see the love in every eye here," MacLean said. "That's more important than the Stanley Cup itself, almost."

The traditional ceremonies followed, but they seemed to take forever.

"We just wanted it to go faster," Dave Lewis, the assistant coach, said. "It was like, 'Can't you just give us the Cup and get it over with?' And so we waited."

Captain Steve Yzerman was awarded the Conn Smythe Trophy as the playoff MVP. Then, finally, NHL commissioner Gary Bettman called him over – "Steve Yzerman, let's do it again. Come get the Stanley Cup!"

As Yzerman skated toward the commissioner and the trophy, Lewis recalled seeing something remarkable at one end of the ice. "I'll never forget this: The Zamboni doors opened and out comes Vladimir Konstantinov. Fetisov was pushing him, and there was a big smile on Vladdie's face."

That's what everyone remembers, the unmitigated joy.

Yzerman and the commissioner held the trophy together, posing for photos, then the captain took the Cup and held it over his head, posing for the all-important shot that the NHL and the Red Wings would use for much of their marketing material over the next year. What happened next was instinctive and unplanned. And it remained a blur to this day in the mind of the guy who orchestrated it.

"When they wheeled Vladdie onto the ice, he had this big smile on his face. He was really happy to be part of it," Yzerman said. "I know Igor and Slava were really happy. Well, I don't know if happy is even the right word. But to have him there to be part of it. . . Everyone on our team loved Vladdie, but those guys had a special bond with him. Everyone just felt very, very good that he could be there with us."

Yzerman couldn't even recall whether he skated with the Stanley Cup, the traditional lap around the rink the captain usually made with the trophy over his head. He didn't. Instead, he did the only thing that felt right at the moment. He did a quick 360-degree turn so that everybody with a camera could get their shot. Then took a couple of strides over to Konstantinov, and he lowered the Stanley Cup.

"I remember thinking I wasn't sure how we were going to do this, but we just put it right there in his lap," Yzerman said.

With Fetisov and Larionov on either side of the wheelchair and Yzerman skating shotgun, holding the Cup steady, the entire team skated a victory lap that had nothing to do with a sporting event and everything to do with the triumph of the human spirit. Everyone experiencing that transcendent moment seemed captivated. The ovation in the Capitals' building was long, warm and sincere.

"For the players right then, winning the Stanley Cup didn't matter to any of them," Lewis said. "They just wanted the Cup for this, the experience of putting it on Vladdie's lap so they could show him: 'We did this for you. All of our experiences this year, everything that happened, it was for you. You were our focal point. You're one of us, and you'll always be one of us.'"

Lewis remembered looking around the ice that night and seeing the raw emotion on the players faces, tears of passion and joy.

"They all lived through this together," he said. "Nobody knows what it's like to go back to your hotel room after taking a slapshot off the ankle during a game, and the pain is so bad you can't sleep at night. But you have to get up and go to practice the next day and play the next night. Nobody knows about that except for the athletes. Vladimir Konstantinov knew all about that. The players he played with knew the pain and suffering he went through to win that Cup the year before in '97. Those are some of the things that you only experience as part of that group in the locker room, and that's what they were giving back. All the pain. All the suffering. All the sacrifice – it's for you. And it made them feel better than it probably made Vladdie feel in getting it."

Nearly two decades later, Yzerman remained wistful when he talked about that moment.

"We were able to give him the Stanley Cup," he said. "It was like. . . that's what movies are made of, you know?"

"Hockey Night in Canada" TV analyst Harry Neale, a former Red Wings coach, spoke for everybody in hockey as he watched that scene unfold.

"What a joy to see Vladimir Konstantinov here tonight," Neale said. "The only greater joy would have been to see him play."

By the time the Wings finished their team victory lap behind the wheelchair, stopping at center ice for more photos, everyone in the building was reaching for a Kleenex. "This is the moment when you are not shy of your tears, this kind of man tears, you know?" Fetisov said. "You cannot be ashamed of that."

Shanahan has that center-ice memory hanging on his wall at home.

"It's just a great photo," he said. "That moment when the Cup gets placed in Vladdie's lap. . . It was a release for all of us. And all of us crowding around as he's being wheeled around the ice – that's one of my favorite moments – of my life."

Yzerman handing the trophy over immediately to Konstantinov was something Igor Larionov wouldn't soon forget, either.

"Another very human gesture by the captain to recognize the team's spirit, what this team is all about," Larionov said. "It was about Vladimir Konstantinov, the guy who was supposed to be with us for many, many years – but he's not anymore. He's with us on the ice, but in a wheelchair. So Stevie hands him the Cup and we push Vladdie on the ice for like 35-40 seconds. That was an amazing feeling, for the family, for Vladdie and for the whole team."

Draper said he experienced no finer moment in his career. "One of the greatest memories I have of being a Stanley Cup champion was being there at center ice when Stevie got the Cup and gave it right to Vladdie," he said. "It was something that meant so much to all of us to be able to do that. When we say we did it for Vladdie – we *did it* for Vladdie. That was something that makes us all proud. Everything that we had gone through was nothing compared to him."

That moment came just over a year after the limo crash that put Konstantinov in the hospital for months with massive brain injuries. But it was still early enough for some optimism.

"I think we still had a lot more hope then," Shanahan said in a conversation in the fall of 2015. "The story still has an unhappy ending, but in that moment we felt hope. We were happy that we were able to do that. And we felt that when we won the Cup he was still on our team."

"You see Sergei (Mnatsakanov) and Vladdie now – you know what these guys were," Yzerman said. "Vladdie was an athlete. Sergei is a special human being, absolutely fabulous, beloved. What those guys had to go through and what they did for our organization. . . and as players, to come back and win and then be able to celebrate with the Stanley Cup and have Vladdie on the ice, I think it gave him some joy. And I would say that for the other Russian guys it had to be a moment of serenity for them, too."

Especially the two older ones. Every player in the Detroit Red Wings' locker room that season gave a little extra – and sometimes a lot – inspired by their two fallen teammates. But Fetisov and Larionov, were special all year.

"They're both Hall of Famers, but considering their ages they probably performed better than what anybody thought they could, particularly in the playoffs," Lewis said. "They were the diesel that led the train that pulled everybody else with them. And everybody followed. Stevie was the captain, but Fetisov and Larionov had a closer connection to Vladdie, where he came from and what he went through. They were the driving force."

And when the Wings finally won that second Cup in Washington,

Fetisov felt conflicted, engulfed at once by great joy and overwhelming sadness.

"It was mixed emotions," he said. "We did what we promise to each other we would do. We got great support from the fans all year, and we knew this moment would be special for all of us. We did not realize how much it was going to be special for Vladimir, how he would understand what's going on, in his condition.

"You start to realize life's situation, that this could happen to anybody. It's hard to explain how this happened. Why this happened. What we did as hockey players, as a team, we just built up another victory for our friend who would never play again."

In the visitors' locker room of what was then the gleaming new MCI Center in Washington, the Detroit Red Wings toasted their victory and quenched their season-long thirst by drinking freely again from the Stanley Cup – a concoction of sheer bliss and heartbreaking blues.

"I will never forget being in the dressing room, and Vladimir was with us," Fetisov said. "He tries to drink champagne from the Cup. It was probably the toughest moment for me. He was in the room there with us, but he was not in uniform. He was in the wheelchair."

CHAPTER 20

Twelve Giant Steps for Hockeytown

He stood and walked. Wobbly as he was, balanced on either side by teammate Slava Fetisov and trainer John Wharton, Vladimir Konstantinov rose from his wheelchair took a dozen deliberate steps to his place on the platform at Hart Plaza, where most of the 1.2 million people who lined the parade route down Woodward Avenue had gathered on a luminous Thursday afternoon.

The roar began as soon as Konstantinov stood. As he began to walk they really let loose, cheering and screaming, whistling and applauding, laughing and crying, they cheered with all the love and respect and admiration and appreciation as if it were he who scored the goal that won a second Stanley Cup in as many years.

"Vlad-die! Vlad-die! Vlad-die!" They screamed it along the entire parade route as he rode alongside Sergei Mnatsakanov, the massage therapist and trainer who was critically injured with Konstantinov in that limousine accident a year and six days earlier. The chants and applause only grew louder when the two were wheeled onto the platform at the end of the parade on Detroit's riverfront.

"The two biggest cheers that you gave, that were much-deserved, were for Vladdie and Sergei," center Kris Draper told the crowd, drawing an even louder roar.

Those steps Konstantinov took were his first in public since the accident that ended his career. I wasn't there to see it, but my former colleagues at the Detroit Free Press, as usual, had the event well-covered.

A small army of great journalists represented the newspaper, including writers Mitch Albom, Drew Sharp, Jason La Canfora, Helene St. James and Nicholas Cotsonika, and photographers Julian Gonzalez, Mary Schroeder, Kirthmon Dozier, Pauline Lubens and Gabriel Tait, among others.

"He is so excited, he absolutely loves it," Konstantinov's wife, Irina, told the Free Press. "He understands everything that's going on. I believe Vladdie became one of the vessels of the heart of the team. I didn't realize before the accident how important a role he was playing in hockey life in Detroit.

"You know what? Within one week, two different people, completely different backgrounds, different areas of the country, tell me, 'Vladdie is always going to be for Detroit like Elvis Presley was for the country. He is going to be remembered as a legendary player for years. Another person tells me, 'I bet you 10 years from now he's going to be as popular and beloved in this town as he is today.'"

That was an understatement. More than two decades later, Vladimir Konstantinov remains one of the most beloved athletes in Detroit sporting history. But on that day, Michigan Gov. John Engler summarized Konstantinov's importance to his team perfectly: "I think the Wings proved that they didn't lose a star when Vladdie got hurt; they gained a guiding star. We pay tribute to him here today. Michigan *believes* and Michigan thanks you, Vladdie."

And coach Scotty Bowman similarly characterized his team and what it meant to a city whose heart was broken a year earlier: "The Red Wings, to me, are what life is all about – sharing and caring and believing. This group of players and all the support staff have shared something this year to really get to the top of the mountain once again."

The next night, the champions gathered for a final public appearance at Joe Louis Arena in a "Thank You" rally for season-ticket holders and suite holders. It included a video celebration, speeches by players and coaches – and the Stanley Cup. Again, Vladdie and Sergei were feted as guests of honor in an emotional outpouring of support from a crowd of about 13,000.

At one moment during the celebrations, a reporter asked Sergei Fedorov how the team planned to celebrate over what everyone hoped would be a more joyful summer.

"No limos this time," he said. "We'll drive our own cars, or we'll walk. We want to celebrate more than six days this time."

And they did.

CHAPTER 21

〜⫷⫸〜

When Loyalty Matters

Mike Ilitch was the ultimate closer. Long before he and wife Marian opened their first Little Caesars Pizza joint in Garden City, Michigan, he mastered the most essential of all sales techniques while peddling pots and pans door-to-door along the streets of suburban Detroit. He perfected the art of closing deals.

Years later, after he started buying sports franchises and building stadiums with the billions he made in his pizza empire, Ilitch still handled many of the most important deals himself. And few things were more vital than signing the players he felt he needed to win. So it was when he and his top two hockey lieutenants, senior vice president and chief confidante senior vice president Jimmy Devellano and general manager Ken Holland, met with Sergei Fedorov in the summer of 2003. Fedorov's contract had expired, and Ilitch had no intention of letting his most dynamic player get away.

Fedorov proved his value to the franchise from the moment he stepped onto the ice in his first training camp in 1990. In the next 13 years, he became the Red Wings' most decorated hockey player since Gordie Howe was winning scoring titles and MVP honors two generations earlier. In fact, Fedorov's Hart Trophy as the NHL MVP in 1994 was the first for a Red Wing since Howe won the last of his six Hart trophies in 1963. For long stretches during his peak years between 1993-98, Sergei Fedorov was the best hockey player in the world.

"Probably the most talented player I've ever played with, the most gifted naturally," teammate Brendan Shanahan said. "There was really nothing he couldn't do when he put his mind on it. Sometimes Scotty would say, 'Go shadow Mike Modano,' and Sergei would just skate with him the whole game. Whatever Sergei wanted to do on the ice, he could. He was strong, he was quick, he had a great shot. Our power play breakout, no matter what we drew up, we all sort of knew our power play breakout was to give the puck to Sergei and get out of his way. Just let him carry it in, and then we'll setup.

"And he was a fabulous person."

Joe Kocur, who spent parts of six seasons with the New York Rangers between two stints with the Wings, played with some of the finest players in NHL history. He ranked the captains of both teams, Steve Yzerman in Detroit and Mark Messier in New York, near the top in terms of their star quality. "But Sergei Fedorov is the best player I've ever played with," Kocur said. "He could dominate a game in one shift. When he was at the top of his game, he was one of the top five guys who ever played the game."

Ilitch had all the proof he needed of Fedorov's value in the 1993-94 season, when Yzerman went down with a serious injury that kept him out more than two months. In a game on October 21 against Winnipeg, Yzerman was hit from behind into the boards, suffering a herniated disk.

"It was a crazy year in the sense that I was so sad, as most of the fans in Detroit were, that Steve went down with a heavy injury," Fedorov said, "and we don't know when he is coming back."

That's when coach Scotty Bowman went to the whip on his best player.

"Out of bad always happens some good," Fedorov said. "I started receiving lots of ice time. I remember the first three or five games, I couldn't catch my breath. I didn't understand at the time how much I was playing. I didn't really look at it. We were successful, but it was heavy on the body and heavy on my mind. I start to think, 'Is it ever going to stop?'

"Then I realized after five games when I started playing those heavy minutes that no matter what pressure I received from opponents, everything was standing still. I'm moving much quicker, much faster, doing a lot of things to help the team win the game. I get 29-30 face-offs every game. In the NHL, that's heavy stuff. That's a lot of work. But I realized that I started getting better, and even the film shows that everybody else is standing still – but I was moving. It was an amazing feeling. Then I started to look at the ice time, 28, 29, a couple of times over 30 minutes. I played every two shifts."

Suddenly, Fedorov felt as though he could do no wrong. He had entered that condition that athletes frequently describe as "the zone" where they seem to be able to anticipate a sequence of events so that they're exactly where they need to be. In a word, they feel invincible. Psychologist Mihaly Csikszentmihaly described it in his book "Flow: The Psychology of Optimal Experience." According to his study, "flow" was a state in which people "are completely absorbed in an activity, especially an activity which involves their creative abilities." During this optimal experience, they feel "strong, alert, in effortless control, unselfconscious, and at the peak of their abilities."

To those watching, it was something to behold. For opponents, it was maddening. For the Wings, it was a blessing. When Fedorov was on the ice, which was half the game, opponents rarely touched the puck. But even as it became a routine, Fedorov couldn't imagine it continuing beyond three weeks or so.

"It wound up being almost all year," he recalled. "But eventually, Stevie came back and it was a huge help for our team, and my minutes went down. Then my video starts slowing down, too. All of a sudden, everybody started keeping up with me."

That mojo put Fedorov into a good-natured tussle with his buddy, Wayne Gretzky, for the scoring title that season.

That battle ended prematurely, however, on April 5, 1994, in an 8-3 victory at Vancouver. Fedorov collided with teammate Shawn Burr. Fedorov spent a few days in a Vancouver hospital with a concussion. He finished the season with 56 goals and 64 assists for 120 points. Gretzky finished with 130 points (38 goals, 92 assists) for the last of his 10 scoring titles.

"We were all just thinking about winning that year, but it was fun to race Wayne," Fedorov said. "Every game he would get 3-4 points. And then I would get 3-4 points. Unfortunately, I had to spend 3-4 days in the hospital in Vancouver – thanks to my buddy Shawn.

"But it was a lot of fun to experience that moment as a hockey player, when you're really flying. It was an unbelievable experience."

At the end of the season, Fedorov needed a new trophy case. He won the Hart Trophy as the NHL's most valuable player, the Lester B. Pearson Award (now known as the Ted Lindsay Award) as the league's outstanding player as voted by his peers in the NHL Players Association, and the Selke Trophy, awarded to the best defensive forward in the league.

Sadly – and unfairly – that was the level of play by which Fedorov always would be compared. "People wanted more for the next five years," he said, "but it didn't happen. We needed to win the Stanley Cup. I had to learn how to play, instead of 28-29 minutes, 18-20."

A few years later, Bowman again showcased Fedorov's immense talent when he put his star forward on defense. The Wings had suffered a spate of injures on the blue line, and Bowman sensed that Fedorov could help fill the void because of his defensive expertise as well as his skating acumen. Fedorov could skate forward and backward at nearly equal speed, but he had mixed feelings about the move. He resisted it at first, but he enjoyed the extra ice time that came with being one of the top defensemen. Bowman had been playing the team's four forward lines almost equally, which didn't sit well with top players who were accustomed to playing many more minutes. But the players understood later that their coach was trying to keep everyone as fresh as possible for the playoff run.

On defense, Fedorov again would be playing 20-plus minutes a game – though he thought he would be filling in for just a few games. He stayed on defense for a month-and-a-half before he returned to playing forward, but Bowman liked what he saw of his star.

"He was the best defenseman in the league for about a six-week period," Bowman said. "He could have been an all-star defenseman. Really, I think he could have won a Norris Trophy."

Eventually, Sergei Fedorov would help lead the Wings to not one but three Stanley Cup crowns from 1997-2002. In 1997, he led the Wings in playoff scoring with eight goals among 20 points in 20 games. In 1998, he was second in team scoring, but scored the most goals, 10, among 20 points in 22 games. In 2002, he was tied for second in team scoring with 19 points in 23 games. In his 13 seasons with the Detroit Red Wings, Fedorov played in 162 playoff games and scored a remarkable 163 points.

This is why Mike Ilitch was so intent on closing that deal with his luminous star.

For the full year before Fedorov was to become an unrestricted free agent, which would have allowed him the freedom to sign with any NHL team of his choosing, Devellano made numerous overtures to Fedorov's handlers to forge a new deal.

"But no matter how hard I tried to get something done with his agent, Michael Barnett, we just couldn't come to an agreement," Devellano wrote in his book, "The Road to Hockeytown," which chronicled his then 40 years in the NHL. "We just couldn't seem to get anywhere. There was no real argument between us, nothing really nasty transpired during our talks. . . They never admitted it directly, but I got the distinct impression during our talks that Fedorov just wanted to play somewhere else at that point in his career, whatever his reasons may have been."

Interestingly, in an interview with The Hockey News just a few months earlier, Fedorov described as a non-issue the very suggestion that he might sign with a team other than the Red Wings.

"I'm confident that with my new representation from (Barnett) that a deal to keep me in Detroit will be able to get worked out," Fedorov said.

Ilitch was confident, too, when he stepped in to put an end to the protracted negotiations. Money talks, had always been his mantra. So, after a brief exchange of pleasantries, the Red Wings' owner made his final, nonnegotiable offer: $50 million for five years, $10 million a season. It was a staggering proposal, considering that Fedorov was 33 years old, his performance already beginning to decline – according to his statistics. He would be an awfully expensive 38-year-old asset by the time the deal expired.

But that deal also generously reflected what Fedorov had done for the franchise since the Wings had orchestrated his defection 13 years earlier. Fedorov had posted 400 goals among 954 points in 908 career games with the Wings. He scored at least 26 goals in every full season.

In other words, his credentials were impeccable.

The 2002-03 season had ended horrendously when the Red Wings, with a lineup studded with future Hall of Famers, were unceremoniously swept by Anaheim in the opening round of the playoffs. Ilitch, though, had designs on winning more, and it would be a lot easier with Fedorov in the Detroit lineup.

Fedorov thanked Ilitch for the offer, but he remained non-committal.

"I'm going through some personal issues with Anna," Fedorov said to his bosses, according to Devellano. "I need some time to think about this."

Anna, of course, was the young Russian tennis star Anna Kournikova, nearly 12 years his junior. The two had been family friends since Kournikova was a young teenager. Their mothers were best friends. Eventually, the relationship between the two athletes grew romantic, though they acknowledged little publicly about their relationship. It wasn't until they were divorced that Fedorov even conceded they had been married. Fedorov disclosed the marriage – and the divorce – in that March 2003 interview with The Hockey News.

Maintaining a relationship between two world-class athletes with demanding schedules in different sports wasn't easy. Nicklas Lidstrom, Fedorov's roommate when the Wings were on the road, remembered frequently being awakened in the middle of the night while Fedorov was beneath the covers speaking quietly in Russian.

At one point, Wings coach Scotty Bowman, in a rare move, released Fedorov from the team for a few days so that he could travel ahead to Los Angeles and spend some time with Kournikova to work on their fragile bond. Fedorov confessed years later that he always would be grateful to Bowman for that very human gesture, acknowledging after that he played even harder for his coach. Bowman eventually retired from coaching after the 2002 Stanley Cup season, replaced by Dave Lewis.

And then, with $50 million on the table, Fedorov left the meeting with Ilitch, saying he'd think it over. Ilitch knew better. He turned to Devellano and said: "You know what? He's leaving."

"How can you be sure?" Devellano asked.

"Because you don't need time to think about an offer like that."

Ilitch was right. On July 19, 2003, Fedorov's career in Detroit came to an end when he signed a shorter deal for less money with the Anaheim Mighty Ducks. He had accepted a four-year deal worth $40 million, which irked the Wings even more.

"His decision to leave was bitterly disappointing," Devellano said. "No matter what we said or did, he just seemed intent on leaving us – and he did."

Sergei Fedorov, gone Hollywood. Red Wings fans felt betrayed, but few who paid any attention shouldn't have been surprised. This was one of the brightest stars in the NHL constellation, and he lived the high life. Flashy cars, starlets, models and world-class tennis players on his arms. The guy seemed naturally destined for life in Southern California.

That certainly was the perception, but Brendan Shanahan suggested anyone who knew Fedorov understood there was more to him than that. A lot more.

"Sergei was this sort of cool, Hollywood guy, into the new cars, the sports cars, the slick suits and the long, highlighted hair, all that stuff," Shanahan said in a November 2015 interview a few hours before Fedorov was inducted into the Hockey Hall of Fame. "But he was actually this very sensitive, very kind, and in some ways almost this childlike person. His approach to hockey was like a kid. He just enjoyed being out on the ice and skating. While some of us saw it as a business or a responsibility, I think Sergei just sort of had fun playing the game."

Fedorov insisted when he left Detroit that he harbored no bitterness, saying he would miss the fans, "who were great to me." It had been a wonderful ride, he said, "but everybody in life at some point has to change direction or place or time, and this is absolutely normal for me to change and move on."

In other words, Fedorov was willing to take $10 million less for a change of scenery.

Could there have been more to it than that? Arguably, yes. Fedorov had a long and trusting relationship with Bryan Murray, who had been his first coach and general manager in Detroit. Murray was GM in Anaheim in 2003. His team that had beaten Fedorov's Red Wings so resoundingly that spring advanced to the Stanley Cup finals.

The perception among some around the league was that the franchises appeared to be headed in different directions, and Fedorov decided to go to the team whose arc was clearly rising.

Another widespread perception was that as much as Fedorov admired and respected his teammate and Red Wings captain Steve Yzerman, Fedorov wanted a team he could call his own. He wanted to be the guy, like Yzerman had been the guy in Detroit since he was drafted by the Wings in 1983.

"I think role might have had something to do with it, his importance to the Anaheim team at the time," Murray told me later. "Because of that, I'm not sure I had to talk very hard. Contract was part of it, but I knew him and he knew me. I think we felt we could trust each other, and those are sometimes the kinds of issues you have to deal with when you recruit a player."

That trust was established over many long conversations in the coach's office, when Fedorov was a rookie in the NHL struggling with multiple issues.

"He was in my office fairly often as a young player, talking about not only things on the ice, but off-ice as well," Murray said. "I think with any young player, and in particularly a young player whose language was an issue, whose style of play was an issue, whose newness to the NHL was an issue – it's our obligation as management and coaches to deal with young players on an individual basis.

"Sergei was a good guy. He really wanted to be good. He knew he could be good. He was a good listener and a good learner. And of course, he became a great player."

Murray deflected a question about how he managed to pry Fedorov from Detroit.

"I don't know this for sure," he said, "but maybe Sergei just felt it was time to have a change and try his ability elsewhere."

But why would he leave when he had such a good thing going in Detroit – and leave $10 million on the table? He's been asked that untold times in myriad ways, especially when he comes home to Detroit – where his mother still lives.

"I didn't really want to do it for any kind of reasons. After all, I spent 13 seasons playing for the Red Wings," Fedorov said when the

Wings honored him the night after he was inducted into the Hockey Hall of Fame. "I said numerous times I would like to be a Red Wing for the rest of my career. For some reason at these times, you got advisers. So, I'm gonna blame the agents and what they advised."

The line was meant to inspire a laugh. But how Fedorov ended his career was more depressing than funny. Or just wrong for someone of his stature in the game. He scored 31 goals in his first season on the West Coast, but the Ducks collapsed and missed the playoffs. A lockout wiped out the next season. With Murray replaced in Anaheim, Fedorov was traded five games into the following season to Columbus, a struggling expansion franchise. He finished as a shadow of his former self in Washington before leaving the NHL to play three more seasons in Russia's Kontinental Hockey League, until age 42.

For someone who had done so much in his tenure in Detroit, Fedorov didn't get anything close to a hero's welcome when he returned to The Joe as a visiting player. In the first few years, especially, fans would boo him each time he touched the puck. The first time was on Dec. 3, 2003. He scored a goal – but the Wings won, 7-2.

The way he took care of himself, Fedorov could have played out that five-year contract in Detroit, signed on for a few more years and called it quits after 20 years. And it's a good bet that his jersey No. 91 would have been hanging from the Joe Louis Arena rafters before he was inducted in the Hockey Hall of Fame.

Woulda, coulda, shoulda. The look on Sergei Fedorov's face grows pensive when he fields the inevitable questions about why he left speaks volumes when he's run out of clichés in two languages. Then there is the public dilemma that has become somewhat of a delicate PR issue for the Red Wings. A staple topic in sports-talk radio around Detroit is whether Fedorov's number, indeed, should hang next to the other Red Wings icons throughout their nine-decade history in the National Hockey League: Gordie Howe, Ted Lindsay, Terry Sawchuk, Alex Delvecchio, Sid Abel, Steve Yzerman and Nicklas Lidstrom.

When the subject is broached for Fedorov, he walks a fine line between talking about what a great honor it would be and what, if anything, he might have to build bridges with ownership, the ultimate authority in these decisions.

"I don't know. Maybe. Possibly," he said. "I've got to be careful what I'm saying. If it happens, it's great. When it happens? I don't know. But if it happens it will be one of those moments you cherish for the rest of your life.

"I don't want to put any pressure. If it doesn't happen? Still, to be part of 13 seasons here, three Cups and celebrations, victory rallies. What else could you wish for?"

For Sergei Fedorov, that might have to be enough. Retiring his number figured to be an awfully heavy lift as long as Mike and Marian Ilitch owned the club. The Ilitches valued loyalty every bit as much as they do winning – and making money. And for all the splendid highlights and moments that Fedorov brought fans out of their seats with the kind of hockey skills this town had rarely seen, in the end he remained loyal only to himself. At least that was the perception of ownership and management. It remained to be seen whether this equation changes since Mike Ilitch's death in February 2017 – and the club's stewardship turned over to son Chris Ilitch.

After the 1997 Stanley Cup, Fedorov refused to sign a contract for more than a half-season before agreeing to that staggering front-loaded $38-million contract with Carolina. Without question, he helped the Wings win their second straight Stanley Cup that spring. Scotty Bowman has said he doubts his team would have repeated as Stanley Cup champions without Fedorov. So yes, it's arguable that the Ilitches got their money's worth. Then five years later, despite that $50 million offer from Mike Ilitch, Fedorov walked away to sign with Anaheim. The Ilitches have long memories, and the smart money around Detroit said it would take a small miracle to get Marian Ilitch to change her mind about this.

As compelling an argument Fedorov supporters might have for retiring No. 91, and as strong a rebuttal as the Ilitch family could counter, there may be room for a reasonable compromise: Hang a banner to honor one of the most memorable eras in Wings history – and five fabulous players at once. Design a banner with the names and numbers of all the

Russian Five who were so instrumental in helping the Wings end their Stanley Cup drought – and the "Believe" logo that inspired their second straight championship in 1998.

Invite them all for a banner-raising, with Scotty Bowman – the Hall of Fame coach who assembled them and put them together as a unit. Three of those players have joined Bowman in the hall: Slava Fetisov, No. 2; Igor Larionov, No. 8; and Sergei Fedorov, No. 91. The others: Vladimir Konstantinov, No. 16, and Slava Kozlov, No. 13.

Based on their career resumes, each one of those players has a decent argument about having their numbers raised, though to be sure Fedorov has the best case.

"I came here, 20 years old, in 1990. Best summer ever," he said when the Red Wings honored him at The Joe the night after his Hall of Fame induction. "Now I am here, in different circumstances. I owe the Red Wings everything. They believed in me. They drafted me. They accepted me. They gave me the opportunity to play. I had the best years of my life here."

Only one of those Russian Five numbers remain in service: Justin Abdelkader wears No. 8. No. 13 was back out of service after Pavel Datsyuk returned to Russia following the 2015-16 season. No one wore No. 2 after Brendan Smith was traded to the New York Rangers in early 2017. No one has worn No. 16 since Konstantinov took off his sweater on June 7, 1997, the night the Wings won the Cup.

It's time. Hold the ceremony. Honor them all. Raise a single banner with all their numbers, but keep them all in service. One of the best marketing franchises in the league can make millions in a merchandizing campaign.

Everybody wins. Precisely the way Mike Ilitch preferred to close his deals.

CHAPTER 22

Smashing Myths, Bridging Cultures

As individuals, they fulfilled the heritage bequeathed to them by the masterful and commanding doctrines of the Soviet Union's Central Red Army. When they were united in North America with the Detroit Red Wings, the Russian Five left their own incandescent legacy for generations to follow, carved in the hearts and minds of all those who not only love and respect the game of ice hockey but yearn for a more peaceful and united global community.

Scotty Bowman said it best; they were game-changers – Sergei Viktorovich Fedorov, Viacheslav Alexandrovich (Slava) Fetisov, Vladimir Nikolayevich Konstantinov, Vyacheslav Anatolevich (Slava) Kozlov, and Igor Nikolayevich Larionov. Their footprint on the sport, especially in the National Hockey League, is massive and undeniable. In global politics, they mattered, too.

What began in the late 1980s, at the apex of *perestroika* when the Red Wings started drafting Soviet players and began plotting to steal them from behind the rusting Iron Curtain, has reverberated throughout the NHL.

"Everyone is copied. We're no different than any other business," said Jim Lites, president of the Dallas Stars. Lites was the executive with the Wings and the mastermind behind bringing Fedorov, Konstantinov and Kozlov to Detroit. "Whatever is successful is emulated. Why buck the system?

"Detroit has the best scouts in Europe to this day, and we are the beneficiary in Dallas by having Jim Nill as our general manager. He came from that system in Detroit. He gets it. We don't hesitate to draft Russian players. They've been doing it in Detroit since 1989. . . The Russian Five were a big part of the first completely amalgamated foreign team in Detroit. They had great North Americans, a great Canadian leader in Steve Yzerman, one of the greatest defensemen of all time in Nick Lidstrom, a Swede. But the icing on the cake was what the Russians did and how they did it – and the level and depth that they gave."

As Lites noted, the first wave of Russians and Europeans helped Detroit win three Stanley Cup titles in a six-year span from 1997-2002. With all that infrastructure built in, a second generation of imports helped the Wings win another championship in 2008.

"All of us in the National Hockey League were impacted by the great work the Russians did collectively as part of the Russian Five," Lites said. "It sure didn't take long to figure out what those guys were doing and how they were doing it. They were unique. They played keep-away. It became a possession game.

"You watch three-on-three now in our overtimes. Who wins? The teams that possess the puck. The Red Wings were playing five-on-five that way. They had the puck all the time. Everybody used to dump the puck in and chase it down behind the net. The Russians changed that. They changed our game."

The Russian Five did more than influence how the game was played on the ice. They transformed how the sport was taught in North America, according to Bryan Murray, the Wings' coach and general manager when the Russians started arriving in Detroit.

"I remember talking to some people around the league," Murray said. "We loved what we saw. It opened all of our eyes, and we saw these people as guys who were going to have a big impact on winning teams."

It also provoked the governing ice hockey organizations in North America to take a long, hard look at how they were teaching the game to youngsters, Murray added.

"You saw that when the Russian Five were playing together," he said. "They weren't afraid to go back and regroup because of their puck skills. They knew there weren't going to be many miscues. It literally changed our game."

They also changed misguided and parochial perception that competing for the Stanley Cup was somehow the exclusive domain of North American players. The Russian Five obliterated that silly myth.

"Their legacy should be. . . it's historic, it really is," said assistant coach Dave Lewis. "To bring that kind of performance, not just in a regular-season game but in the playoffs at the highest level – to win a Stanley Cup, multiple Stanley Cups. And to prove to the world that you can win with Russians – not just one, but with five of them.

"It was a revolutionary thing to even have one or two on your team. We had five, and we haven't seen it since. And to influence and marvel your teammates like they did, guys like Steve Yzerman and Nick Lidstrom. Those guys aren't dumb hockey people. I really think it should be talked about in terms of the history of the NHL, and how they changed our game."

As grateful as Jim Devellano was for how the Russian Five transformed his team, he and other NHL executives also understood that the European imports were vital to the growth of the league.

"When the NHL under (then president) John Ziegler decided it was going to put a footprint across the United State of America and go from a 21-team league to 30 – well, that's a big expansion," Devellano said. "And it could never, ever have been accomplished without European-born players. The Russians were a big, big part of it. Without them, you couldn't expand this league. I was here. I know what player personnel was like across the league. We needed Europeans who could come over here and play – and the Russians did it, big time."

Nevertheless, the Russian revolution wasn't exactly embraced by North American players, some of whom would wind up losing their jobs just the way American and Canadian autoworkers lost theirs when the market was flooded with cheaper, and often better-made, vehicles from Asia and Europe. Detroit teammates of the Russian Five, however, were quick to see how talented these players were, how likely they were to improve the team. Their perceptions about lost jobs quickly vaporized, as well, and they quickly realized that having their names engraved on the Stanley Cup was as important to the Russians as it was any Canadian kid who fell in love with the game on a frozen slough.

"One thing about the Russian people in general that I've learned from being around them in hockey is that they're very, very proud," Steve Yzerman said. "We were in the room with them, we're living with these guys every day, and they clearly showed us how important it was to them. And this was really important.

"In particular the older guys, Igor and Slava. They came over under a different system, and they had accomplished a lot. They had won a lot. They were proud hockey players, but they were also proud of where they had come from. Whether they had to defect or negotiate with the government to get over here, they were still proud to be Russian. And you can see now, they all go back home – and they speak proudly of Russia.

"But I think what they all went through and in the way they conducted themselves, the way they played for our team – that has changed the tone for European players in general. After the Russians, we had the Swedish players all come in. We had Nicklas Lidstrom here, winning the Conn Smythe (Trophy, as playoff MVP) being the first European captain to lead his team to the Stanley Cup. The perception of European players just evolved, and it was probably that first group, the Russian Five, who were the biggest leaders in that change."

But for Devellano, who turned 74 in January 2017, the great Russian experiment in Detroit had far greater implications. He was raised during the Cold War, when his fellow Canadians, like most Americans, had a distorted opinion about Russians.

"For me, I have to be honest here, it was a little bit political," he confessed. "I mean, holy cow, I grew up with all this propaganda about how the Russians were our enemy. Now here we were, bringing the enemy over here. Then they were so good – the last missing piece for us to win. And they became our friends. I think I learned something about propaganda and how it gets our minds working against different people."

For all the Russian Five did to elevate the game and quality of entertainment on the ice, their influence on geopolitics mattered even more to them.

"I think any sport, when international events happen, can be a great bridge for cultures to understand each other," Fedorov said.

The elder Russians, Fetisov and Larionov, helped to build that bridge between two cultures that desperately needed one after enduring nearly a half-century of the Cold War.

"In the old days of the Soviet Union, when we played against Canada, the U.S.A., against Germany or the Swedes, we had to show the might of the Soviet Union – how big we are, how powerful we are," Larionov said. "At any cost, we have to win."

Failure to win might mean the loss of what few freedoms and privileges were afforded elite Soviet athletes. And what they experienced when they arrived in North America at about the time the Berlin Wall came down made them as qualified as anyone on Earth to compare the cultures.

"When we are going to North America, we are a part of a group. It's international. That's what's so good about North America, about the U.S.A.," Larionov said. "You have the freedom to express yourself, but you have to make it yourself, by your talent, your work ethic, to be part of the group.

"That's what we did, and we showed the world what we can do. But it wasn't about promoting the lifestyle of mighty Russia, or the mighty Soviet Union. It's more like all about showing how the people of Russia, they have a soul and they have a heart. And we show that we are all the same, we just speak a different language and we were brought up in a different system."

Their success, Larionov added, gave the Russians powerful tools to build that bridge. At every stop on the NHL tour, Detroit's Russian Five were an item of great interest and curiosity. And the players – again, especially the two veterans, gave generously of their time to the media. They understood how important it was; they were acutely aware of their place not only in the history of the game but even in the politics of two great empires beginning to warm to each other.

"By playing the games, and then talking to the media, we can talk about the rich culture of Russia – about the poets and the architecture and all kinds of things that happened in the rich history of Russia," Larionov said. "We show that we are all the same and we're willing to make life better, and maybe hockey better, too.

"And that's what we try to do. If you touch anybody, their souls and hearts, that's the goal. There's no politics, no propaganda. It was just a way to communicate and socialize and make the life better."

Perhaps no one is better positioned to continue the normalization between the two superpowers than Fetisov, who returned to Russia and spent seven years as its minister of sports before becoming a senator in its parliament – and a longtime political ally of President Vladimir Putin. Any influence Fetisov may be able to wield could be critical at a time when Putin is being blamed for pulling his country back to a time when the world feared a nuclear holocaust between the Americans and the Russians. While proudly and stubbornly Russian, Fetisov professed great admiration for America when he played and coached there for the better part of 15 years. He has seen and experienced the best and the worst of both nations – and he speaks as if he's committed to ensuring long-lasting, peaceful and friendly relations between the two. It begins with the power of sports.

"It is more than a game. The sport is even bigger now. Especially now, do you hear me?" he said, raising his voice to make sure his interviewer was tuned in and understood his message. "Sport is one of the instruments that can unite the people, bring the people together. I know this because it happened during this period of *perestroika* years ago. We start to build the bridges again.

"Now, as a senator I say to my counterpart in the American Congress: We should build an exchange program for sports. I will never forget my international experience, being part of the National Hockey League success as part of an international family. And of course, Detroit was the best example of that.

"So I know for a fact if our kids become friends then we have nothing else to do, just follow their steps. We need to do this for the kids. This is what sports can do for the world right now."

When it really needs it. Fetisov sensed this a year ahead of Donald Trump's surprise election to the American presidency in November 2016, bringing with it unprecedented handwringing around the world. Relations between Russia and America have rarely been more worrisome, simply because of the many unanswered questions a Trump administration raised.

"For me, it's kind of strange to even talk about," Fetisov said, choosing his words carefully. "What we did in the past should give us a different perspective on the relationship between the two countries. The more friendly we are gonna be, the safer the world will be."

Fetisov offered an historical analogy to help explain Russia's position on the world stage: "Russians are not aggressive. Read our history. We are never the aggressors. You know, Napoleon tried to get us. Hitler tried lots of stuff. . . But we know how to defend ourselves. And a good example is the roughest sport in the world, hockey. In North America, you have to play aggressively. But you can play artistically, too. We tried to bring something different, and the result was good. The people around the world, they appreciate it."

The Russian Five built the bridge to a better, more beautiful and entertaining brand of ice hockey. But that was just a start, Fetisov said, and it's important to learn from that experience.

"We need to build more bridges than weapons," he said. "That's my deep feeling about what should happen between our countries. Like we did in Detroit, you know?"

Like Steve Yzerman and Nicklas Lidstrom, Brendan Shanahan is one of the most cerebral among North American teammates of the Russian Five. He is as comfortable discussing fine wine, theories at the chessboard and Soviet history as he is hockey's left-wing lock defensive system or other strategies related to the game at the NHL level. But when he speaks of his five Russian teammates, he does so out of a profound respect for them as people as well as the players they were and what they brought to the league. They all came from the same school of hockey in the Soviet Union, but they weren't cookie-cutter players, or people.

"They're all different, different guys," said Shanahan, who found himself frequently on Larionov's wing when the Russian Five unit was broken up. "They showed there could be success playing a different style. But it also showed a lot of people in the NHL that these guys were also warriors, that they had the passion and the respect for winning the Stanley Cup, and how much it actually meant to them. They broke a lot of stereotypes.

"But I also want to respect them all as individuals. All had their own interesting story about how they got to the NHL, and they're all amazing stories. . . but somehow they all got here and they all melded together. And I want to make it clear: There were some games and some shifts when they were the Russian Five and we just all sat on the bench and giggled as we watched them go out and do what they did. When they were the Russian Five, it was so much fun to watch. But it wasn't like we were a team of 15 guys plus the other five on their own. They were one with us. They were teammates. Great teammates."

To a hockey player, there is no greater legacy.

EPILOGUE

Five stories above ice level, in the owners' lavish suite at Joe Louis Arena where Mike and Marian Ilitch had witnessed too many years of second-rate hockey, the air was heavy with a sticky mist. Standing in the doorway, I watched as champagne flowed freely. The quality of the bubbly, however, was a few octaves above what the athletes were spraying around in their overcrowded locker room after the Red Wings ended a 42-year Stanley Cup drought.

Here, the vintage was 1982, the year the Ilitches bought the Detroit Red Wings for $8 million from Bruce Norris. The founders of the Little Caesars Pizza chain had set aside cases of it for this singular moment, their first Stanley Cup championship on June 7, 1997, and now they were sharing it with family, friends and business partners. Clouds of smoke from expensive cigars mingled in the mist with unbridled laughter as the Ilitches made their way through the crowd like joyful parents of the bride at a fairy-tale wedding reception. The story that was unfolding in this luxury suite was the one of several that I would share with readers in the next edition of the Detroit Free Press, and I was surprised that I was the only reporter to come knocking.

The Ilitches were cautious around the media, rarely granting an audience, and usually only after an interview was arranged well in advance through layers of their handlers. But when they conceded to such meetings, Mike and Marian were delightful, engaging and thoroughly interesting people – honest, well-spoken – and often brutally, refreshingly blunt. It was easy to like this family. Even easier to respect them.

Denise, the eldest of the seven Ilitch children, greeted me at the doorway of the suite. An attorney who would rise to president in the family's vast business empire before her brother, Chris, took over and who later was elected as a regent for the University of Michigan, she often foresaw the opportunities in certain events that the rest of the family could not. She promised me she'd get me some time with her father. After talking briefly, we were joined by her (then) husband, Jim Lites, the former Wings executive vice president who had left the organization a year earlier to become president of the Western Conference rival Minnesota North Stars, who eventually became the Dallas Stars.

After a few minutes spent reminiscing about how all the bad times of the previous 15 years suddenly seemed so worth it, Denise went to fetch her parents while Jim spoke affectionately and respectfully about how happy he was for his in-laws and what this Stanley Cup championship meant to them.

"They've worked so hard to bring this town a winner," Lites said. "Mr. Ilitch spent what he had to, spent what it took when the other owners around the league brutalized him for it. He changed the league, the way he did things. He deserves this. And so does this town."

Suddenly, Mike Ilitch was approaching, his arms open, smiling like I'd never seen him smile before. A former minor-league shortstop for his hometown Detroit Tigers – a franchise he purchased in 1992 – Ilitch was neither tall nor short, but vigorous in the way that you know his Marine Corps uniform from 45 years earlier would still fit him. He wore a mop of curly hair always cut and styled in a way that reminded his wife, Marian, of a Roman emperor. So when they opened their first pizza shop and needed a name, it seemed only natural to her that they call it Little Caesars – without the apostrophe.

As Ilitch approached, I held out my hand, but he grabbed me and embraced me instead. A big bear hug that surprised me. I tried to laugh, but found that I was nearly breathless.

"Here's the guy," Ilitch said, looking at Lites and pointing at me. "This is the guy who started it all."

"Congratulations, Mike," I said, "but. . ."

"But nothing," he said. "You're the guy who went out and got me those Russians. Without them, we wouldn't be here."

"Come on, Mike, I. . ."

"Listen to me," he said in a tone oozing with fatherly warmth and unbridled authority, "I mean it. You helped make all this happen. You're a big part of all this. And I want you to know: I'll never forget it. Ever."

That championship celebration was the first of four. The Ilitches won Stanley Cups again in 1998, 2002 and 2008, and Mike was inducted into the Hockey Hall of Fame in 2003. He said he couldn't believe the selection committee let "a pizza man" in such a place of honor. When he died on February 10, 2017, at 87, his Red Wings had reached the playoffs for 25 straight seasons, and were valued, according to Forbes magazine, at $625 million. They also were poised to move into a new $863-million downtown home, Little Caesars Arena, in a 50-block entertainment and residential area dubbed The District Detroit, the result of decades of vision by a minor-league shortstop, pizza man and beloved benefactor to the city he adored.

Jim Devellano, the man primarily responsible for drafting three of the young Soviets and hiring the man, Scotty Bowman, who traded for the other two to form the Russian Five and end a four-decades-long Stanley Cup drought, celebrated 51 years of service in the NHL in 2017. He remains the Red Wings' senior vice president and alternate governor – the post he's held since 1990. He also served 13 years as vice president of the Detroit Tigers, the baseball club also owned by the Ilitch family.

Not bad for a guy who dropped out of high school in the ninth grade because he hated algebra, a guy who went to work in Toronto's garment district for 80 cents an hour, a guy whose hockey career started as a "bird dog" scout for NHL teams, working for nothing out of the purest love for the game, a guy who not long ago donated his seven Stanley Cup rings to the Hockey Hall of Fame. He was inducted into the hall in 2010 for building dynasties with the New York Islanders and Red Wings – which included one of the longest playoff streaks in NHL history.

No one in hockey disputes that. But Devellano doesn't get nearly enough the credit for helping to groom numerous others who went on to enjoy their own success after serving as front-office understudies during his 35 years in Detroit, including: Ken Holland; Jim Lites (president of the Dallas Stars, which won the Cup in 1999); Neil Smith (a Stanley Cup with the New York Rangers in 1994); Bryan Murray (Stanley Cup finalist with Anaheim and Ottawa); Jim Nill in Dallas; Don Waddell in Atlanta and Carolina; Doug MacLean in Columbus; Jacques Demers, and later Steve Yzerman, in Tampa Bay (a Stanley Cup finals in 2016). Most of them were direct hires by Devellano.

Devellano was also known to take young or inexperienced reporters under his guidance. He was an uncommonly kind, patient and generous man – and I tested every one of those attributes in my early years as a beat reporter for the Free Press, when I was getting my butt kicked daily by Vartan Kupelian, at the Detroit News. Devellano understood the importance of good, positive publicity for a franchise that needed it badly – and his team wasn't getting much of either from the News when I was assigned the Wings' beat in 1985. Jimmy D. spent an inordinate amount of time with me, helping me to bring me up to speed not only with his team but with the entire league, and occasionally spoon-feeding me a few scoops. For that I was and remain eternally grateful.

Scotty Bowman isn't an easy guy to be around sometimes – and he does it to us on purpose.

As one of his Montreal players, Steve Shutt, used to say: "You hated him for 364 days, and on the 365th day, you collected your Stanley Cup rings."

Reporters who covered Bowman's teams didn't get Stanley Cup rings. So we had an extra day.

It went the other way, too. One of my brothers in the hockey-writing fraternity once relayed a friendly missive from Bowman: "Red Fisher, Jim Kelley and Keith Gave are the three biggest assholes in the media." (I may not have that exactly right; "assholes" might be too nice a description.) Either way, I took it as the highest compliment I could ever expect to receive. Fisher, of the Montreal Gazette, and the late Kelley, of the Buffalo News, are two of the most respected writers in

NHL history. Both are in the Hockey Hall of Fame.

To be sure, Scotty and I had our issues, sometimes more public than either of us might have wanted. There were a couple of times when I was sure he was going to hit me, and I'm glad he didn't. He was in his mid-60s then, 17 years older than I. But I would have been no match, I'm sure, for the power he could wield in those fists. He might have killed me.

For the record, though, I had my moments with other coaches, too. Jacques Demers and I had many door-slamming conversations. Same with Bryan Murray, who could get right in your face if he felt you'd done him wrong by what appeared in the newspaper or was said on the air.

The relationship between the coaches and reporters, at least the ones who travel with the teams and are around every day, is like many marriages. There tends to be a fair amount of screaming and yelling, some door-slamming. But almost always you find ways to get through it and move on, and be stronger for it. So it was with Scotty, who could also be guilty of some incredible random acts of kindness. One day, after we hadn't spoken for a week or so following one of our tiffs, he saw me passing by his office as I made my way into the dressing room.

"Hey, Keith," he said. "I've got something for you."

And he handed me a copy of his 1974 Topps hockey card, #261, inscribed: "To Keith" at the top with his signature at the bottom. That sucker is worth $40. Unsigned. The same card signed by Bowman was going for $123.99 on some Internet memorabilia sites. It is not for sale.

Best of all, Scotty Bowman gave us championship teams to cover in Detroit, like he did in Montreal and Pittsburgh before. He coached nine seasons in Detroit, compiling a record of 410-193-88-10. His Red Wings teams finished first in their division six times and second twice, and they averaged an unthinkable 109 points per season. They also won three Stanley Cups. He retired from coaching in 2002 and spent another five seasons as a consultant for the club before taking a similar assignment with the Chicago Blackhawks, where his son, Stan, was the general manager. With the Hawks, Bowman added three more Stanley Cup rings to his collection, giving him 14 for his career.

The truth about working with Scotty Bowman, as anyone who has ever played hockey for him will confirm, is that he never made it easy.

Some coaches, like Demers, will fill a notebook for you and keep talking. Others, like Murray, were extraordinarily generous with their time and honest to a fault. Bowman didn't have much time for us – at least those who covered his team. But he loved the visiting writers because he'd get them in his office and turn the interviews around, badgering them with questions about the teams they covered. Scotty Bowman gathered intelligence; he sure didn't share much of it regarding his teams.

That was OK, too. When I re-examine my years working with Scotty, I cannot help but admit he made me work a lot harder. And in the process, he made me better at my job. I know a lot of hockey players who would say the same thing about him. (I'm guessing Red Fisher and Jim Kelley would as well.)

Sergei Fedorov always knew how to make a lasting impression, on or off the ice. He is still in my mind's eye as he was the first time I saw him play, on that sheet of ice on a warm summer evening in Helsinki, shortly after the Wings drafted him in 1989. There were moments it seemed like he was the only skater on the ice. All the other players were mere spectators, like those of us in the stands.

Sergei Fedorov mesmerized us with his immense talents – all of us, fans, members of the media, teammates, coaches and front-office executives. And we held him to ridiculously high standards. Nothing he did – and he did more than any Red Wings player since Gordie Howe dominated the National Hockey League 40 years earlier – was ever quite good enough. Nevertheless, when he left Detroit in 2003 to sign a free-agent contract with Anaheim, it felt – to fans, not to mention an owner who did so much to get him and was willing to pay dearly to keep him – like a punch-in-the-gut betrayal. To Sergei, though, it must have felt like a jailbreak. Finally, he was free of all those unreasonable expectations. Free from the shadow of his friend, Steve Yzerman, the brightest star among stars on that Red Wings team. Free to enjoy life in a part of America that had always captivated him, where he could be the star of his own team.

After 13 wildly successful seasons in Detroit, Sergei Fedorov was gone. But so was his mojo. There followed six forgettable NHL seasons with three clubs, two of which traded him away, followed by three more seasons in the KHL with Mettalurg Magnitogorsk. His career NHL statistics were beyond reproach: 1,248 games, 483 goals, 696 assists, 1,179 points, a .94 points-per-game rate; in the Stanley Cup playoffs he was even better, scoring 52 goals among 176 points in 183 games, or .96 points per game. Sergei Fedorov did what most other players merely talk about. He elevated his level of play when it mattered most. It earned him a place in the Hockey Hall of Fame.

In November 2015, we interviewed Sergei for the "The Russian Five" documentary in Moscow at the headquarters of the "Big Red Machine," where he was serving as general manager of the Red Army Club. And talk about impressions. Here was a man so proud of his place in the game it showed in every stitch of his clothing. He wore a dark blue suit with red pinstripes and a red tie trimmed with blue and white stripes. In lieu of a pocket square, he wore the Cyrillic letters for CSKA beneath a red star stitched onto the pocket on his left chest. And the foundation of this beautiful wardrobe: A pair of black wing-tipped shoes – with red shoelaces. This was his uniform as a proud, Red Army Club executive.

In more than two hours of filming, Sergei Fedorov reminded us again that he was so much more than a great hockey player. He was just as he arrived in Detroit, a defector on Mike Ilitch's corporate jet, a kind, caring, sensitive man, and one of the great thinkers in the game. After the interview, we talked of those good times in Detroit, as well as a few of those rare, not-so-good times.

"Nothing personal, right Keith?" Sergei said as put his hand on my right shoulder. It was a gentle jab, a reminder of those infrequent times when my analysis of his performance was less-than-glowing in the morning newspaper. Whenever I criticized a team or a player, a coach or general manager, it was based on copious reporting. I tried to be careful in the extreme. My policy was to never write something I wouldn't say to someone's face. It may have been presented as my opinion, but it was shaped by voluminous interviews with other hockey people, scouts, players, coaches and team executives – the real experts. As I often told Sergei and many others, it was never personal. But it was something I felt was worth sharing with readers and fans who were so emotionally invested in the team I was covering.

That said, in retrospect I understand now that some of the criticism I had heard about Sergei from players and coaches was wildly unfair. Perhaps it was based on the kind of professional jealousy that exists in many workplaces. Maybe it was simply misguided, or even mean-spirited. But it was also rather ironic, the criticism from his teammates. Whenever they get the opportunity, players like to mention that they are human, too, not machines. No one should be expected to bring an A-plus performance to each of the 82 games on the schedule. Coaches understand that as well, though they are loathe to admit it. Yet there were those who sat on the bench with Fedorov who were perfectly willing to judge him the way fans and media unfairly judged them. They expected an A-plus performance every night. So, for much of the time he spent in Detroit there was a whispering campaign: Teammates and coaches never knew which Sergei was going to show up from night to night – the guy with MVP credentials, or the guy just going through the motions. Someone even suggested how wonderful it would be if we could get a player with Sergei Fedorov's talent and Steve Yzerman's heart.

All of that is patently, undeniably and absurdly unfair. Sergei Fedorov is one of the finest players in the history of hockey and one of the greatest Red Wings of all time. He deserves to see his No. 91 hanging from the rafters of the Wings home arena, too.

It was never personal. In fact, knowing what I know now, I regret writing some of that garbage. We didn't know how truly lucky we were until Sergei Fedorov left. And now that I think about it, that might have been his point.

Slava Kozlov was, and remains to this day, a certifiable rink rat. The son of a widely respected hockey coach in Voskresensk, Slava made a promise to his father, Anatoly, that when his playing days were over he would try coaching as well. It's a way to honor the man who taught him the skills that would rank him among the best players in the world, and to give something back to the game that had provided so much for their family. But it was humbling to start all over again.

"I am a rookie again. So much to learn," Kozlov said when we visited him at the headquarters of Spartak, one of the Moscow teams in the Kontinental Hockey League.

Kozlov spent nine seasons in Detroit. He was unquestionably the proudest and most grateful member of the Russian Five. He was also the most humble, always somehow avoiding the spotlight even when he scored all those clutch goals. It crushed him when the Wings traded him in the summer of 2001 to Buffalo for goaltender Dominik Hasek, who helped the Wings win another Stanley Cup in 2002.

Kozlov was limited to 38 games in Buffalo because of injuries, and the following summer the Sabres traded him to Atlanta, where he had seven more productive seasons before leaving the NHL to finish his career with five more seasons in the KHL. Kozlov played 1,182 games in the NHL, scoring 356 goals and 496 assists for 853 points. He also had 44 goals among 88 points in 139 Stanley Cup playoff games.

In the Wings' dressing room, they called him The Grump, a nickname he played along with but, in my experience, never displayed. Slava Kozlov was one of the kindest, warmest, soft-spoken and respectful people I've ever met in or out of sports. I have countless pleasant memories of the time we spent together, but the one most seared into my memory is the night he came to my home in Dearborn after a hockey game. I had arranged a surprise retirement party for my good friend, Len Hoyes, who had covered the Red Wings for the Booth Newspapers chain throughout Michigan. I had invited the entire team, all the players, the coaching staff and GM Jim Devellano, and nearly everyone showed up even though a few hours earlier the Wings had lost a game to the New York Rangers.

Kozlov hadn't been in North America long, and when I greeted him at the door he was rather wide-eyed as he looked around. We had a nice home in the blue-collar suburb built around Henry Ford's motor car company. It was a large and comfortable home, but hardly extravagant. As we stood in the foyer, Kozlov whispered to me in Russian.

"Is this a private home?"

"Yes, of course it is."

"Who lives here?"

"Just my wife and me and a couple of dogs," I said.

No doubt that was the first and last time I'd ever made that kind of impression on a National Hockey League player. And soon, Kozlov was living by himself in a home in the exclusive suburb of Bloomfield Hills, where my home would have been woefully out of place.

But I am most grateful to Slava Kozlov for inviting me to his home in Russia, not once but twice. He took me to Voskresensk during the NHL players lockout in the fall of 1994, where he introduced me to his beautiful family. And when I returned to Moscow with a film crew in December 2015 to interview him for the Russian Five documentary, Slava opened his home to us again. Although he was living in Moscow during the hockey season while his wife and children were in Spain, Kozlov maintained his boyhood home even though his parents and grandfather had passed away. Now that house exists as a shrine to both Slava's playing career and his father's coaching career.

Kozlov sat in front of the camera for more than two hours answering questions about his career in Detroit and his time playing with the Russian Five. When it was over, he quietly approached one of the producers and said he would understand if everything he had just shared with us wound up on the cutting-room floor. He couldn't imagine anything he shared was worthy of being in the film.

That tells you all you need to know about Slava Kozlov, except for this: He couldn't have been more wrong

Igor Larionov stood on a makeshift stage at one end of Joe Louis Arena, his head bowed as thousands of season-ticket-holders stood and pleaded with him, chanting, "One more year! One more year! One more year!"

Two nights earlier, he and his Russian Five comrades had helped the Detroit Red Wings to their first Stanley Cup title in 42 years. Larionov was 36 years old and had just played out his contract with the Wings. He was free to sign with any club that would have him. Since his victory lap with Slava Fetisov and the Stanley Cup, Larionov had been riding one emotional wave after another. He was overwhelmed by the parade down Woodward Avenue that drew more than a million people; there was never anything like that in Red Square for all those gold medals he helped those Soviet teams win. Now this: "One more year! One more year!" It felt like all of Detroit, the hardscrabble town that reminded him so much of his own hometown, smaller, but with the same kind of hardworking people with the same kind of love for their hockey team, was showering him with its affection. They wanted him to stay, at least a little while longer. They wanted one more dance.

Larionov stood there alone at the center of that stage. His head remained bowed. Suddenly, he felt exposed and ill-equipped for the moment.

"You go on that stage and you got no stick, no helmet, no skates, and you're standing there facing thousands of fans, and you have to say a couple of words," Larionov recalled. "You know they love the team and they want the trend we have taken to go for a few years to come, so they start chanting, 'one more year!' I'm just standing there, and there is management behind me. What can I do? I want to tell the fans, 'You must talk with them.'"

He laughs as he points over his shoulder, recalling the moment. But he was right. He couldn't return unless the club wanted to re-sign him. But this may well have been the moment Igor Larionov fell madly and truly in love with Detroit, and he couldn't imagine leaving. Not then. Perhaps not ever. He could get used to this feeling every bit as much as the city's hockey fans could get used to winning, especially with the beauty, grace and panache that he and his comrades brought to their performance.

"I was only there for about a year-and-a half, and now they want me to stay, so it was nice to be recognized, to be part of their lives," he said. "If I touched their hearts, these people and the fans, by my game and my contribution. . . It was a very nice moment. Something special and amazing, like a reception of love for our fans."

Larionov had already come to appreciate the significance of playing in Detroit, a city with a long hockey history, on a team that drew intense media coverage. Almost overnight, he had become a household name – and not just in Detroit. When the Wings traveled to places like Phoenix, Los Angeles and Florida, the arenas were filled with fans wearing Wings paraphernalia. They knew his name, too.

And he appreciated how those fans were able to separate politics from sports, how they seemed to understand the difference between

Soviets and Russians, and how hard those five imports from the Red Army Club played for their team.

"When you put your heart and soul into every night, in every shift, in every game for the people coming to watch you play, they appreciate that," Larionov said. "You want to give it all for them because you want them to come back. That was my approach. You have to entertain. You have to play your game. All the rest of the stuff is going to take care of itself. For me, it felt good to be accepted, and I just wanted to give back to the city.

"We showed the pride and we showed the character and we showed the heart to play for the Detroit Red Wings. And we made some success. We could see that when there were slogans at the parade like, 'I want to name my son Vyacheslav!' It was nice to see that."

The Detroit Red Wings' management received the message loudly and clearly at the rally that night, and the reception Larionov nervously enjoyed probably added a few bucks to a new contract that would keep him in Detroit for three more seasons. In the summer of 2000, though, Larionov signed a free-agent contract with the Florida Panthers, where he would be reunited with Pavel Bure, who was a rookie in Vancouver during Larionov's earliest days in the NHL. It didn't work, and the Panthers traded Larionov back to Detroit, where he played for another 2½ seasons, helping the Wings earn another Stanley Cup in 2002. He spent his final season with the New Jersey Devils, where his friend and former Red Wings teammate Slava Fetisov was an assistant coach.

In 14 NHL seasons, Larionov played 921 games, scoring 169 goals and 475 assists for 644 points. He also scored 97 points in 150 playoff games and won three Stanley Cup rings in Detroit. A resume that also included 457 games in a 12-year career in the Soviet league earned him induction into the Hockey Hall of Fame in 2008.

In an active retirement after his playing days, Larionov spent time as director of hockey operations for SKA Saint Petersburg in the KHL. He also was a professional wine broker, creating several wines under the labels "Hattrick," "Slapshot" and "Triple Overtime" – an homage to the game-winning goal in the third overtime of Game 3 of the Stanley Cup finals in 2002.

Today, he is a well-respected player agent. He has made Detroit his year-around home. He has become one of us.

Slava Fetisov is standing at his locker in the Detroit Red Wings dressing room, quietly changing out of his uniform after practice. He cannot help but overhear the conversation taking place at the locker next to his, and his face is starting to turn the color of the red crest on his hockey jersey. He doesn't say a word, but he's getting angrier by the second.

When I think about it now, it seems almost cruel. But I was an American sportswriter, and the guy in the locker next to Fetisov's was Mike Ramsey, a defenseman on the U.S. Olympic team of college kids who upset the mighty Soviets at the 1980 Winter Games in Lake Placid, New York. Ramsey was on the ice, helping to quell a furious Soviet rally in the final seconds of the game as broadcaster Al Michaels was screaming into his microphone, "Do you believe in miracles? Yes!"

This wasn't Fetisov's favorite subject. He was on the losing team that day in one of the most stunning upsets in sporting history.

"Fucking lucky," Fetisov would mutter under his breath, unable to control his wrath.

Funny how things work out in life. Fifteen years later, in that 1995-96 season, Mike Ramsey and Slava Fetisov were occasional defense partners on a team widely predicted to win the Stanley Cup. And the two of them agreed on a couple of things: If that U.S. team played that Soviet team 100 more times, the Russians would probably win all of them. So yes, all agreed, Al Michaels was right: It was a miracle.

In the Soviet Union, naturally, that loss was an unthinkable embarrassment. Fetisov often tells a story of the pre-Olympic reception for the Soviet athletes, the entire delegation, at the Kremlin.

"They told to the hockey players we can lose to anybody except the Americans," Fetisov recalled. "It was a joke. Everybody was laughing."

And then there was that game in Lake Placid, a monumental loss that shadows Fetisov wherever he goes. He was a young man then playing a sport and dominating in a way that personified Soviet power and might. Matches played by the Soviet National Team were effectively surrogates, underscoring Soviet supremacy in the global community.

The players, most of them officers in the Red Army, were often feted like returning war heroes, their exploits providing a focal point for Soviet propaganda at a time when that nation faced worldwide criticism for its invasion of Afghanistan.

Because of that, Fetisov said, the game against Team USA might have been one of the most important, from a political point of view, in the history of Olympic sports. And that Soviet team should have dominated those American college boys. It was, in Fetisov's view, the best Soviet team ever assembled.

The Americans won, 4-3, after a controversial move by Soviet coach Viktor Tikhonov. He pulled legendary goaltender Vladislav Tretiak after the first period, an inexplicable move that Tikhonov never explained or effectively defended.

"That was the question all the players were asking: 'Why does this happen?'" Fetisov said. Of greater concern, at least to his players, was that Tikhonov managed to keep his job after that catastrophe in Lake Placid, especially considering the heightened expectations at the highest levels of Soviet authority.

"That's the big, dark secret," Fetisov said, "maybe in the whole history of sports."

His first Olympics was a dream-come-true just to be part of that team, but the silver medal Fetisov took home is a reminder of his most burdensome nightmare nearly four decades later. He would survive, however. And thrive. Slava Fetisov went on to win two gold medals in a treasure trove of honors that includes: seven world championship gold medals and one silver; nine-time Soviet league All-Star and two-time NHL All-Star; two-time USSR Player of the Year; three world junior championships, one Canada Cup championship, five-time IIHF Best Defenseman award; the Soviet Order of Honor award; the Order of Lenin award; three Stanley Cup finals appearances; two Stanley Cup championships rings; induction into the USSR Hall of Fame; induction into the International Ice Hockey Hall of Fame; induction into the Hockey Hall of Fame; and much more. He even has an asteroid named after him.

Slava Fetisov played in 546 games over nine seasons in the NHL with New Jersey and Detroit. He scored 36 goals among 192 points. In 478 games in the Soviet league, he scored 153 goals among 374 points.

But his value as a player was measured by more than numbers. He was one who could dominate a game by sitting on the bench, by virtue of his leadership acumen alone. And that's why he's a Hall of Famer.

I first met Slava during the NHL player lockout in the fall of 1994, when he took a group of Russian NHL players back home for a series of games for Russian hockey fans who were missing their star players. The series helped to raise money to fund sports programs for Russian youngsters. Near the back steps of the Red Army sports complex, Slava was arriving as I was leaving. I stopped him and introduced myself as a journalist from Detroit. He was surprised to see a Western reporter there, but I explained that I was there to cover the games because they included Sergei Fedorov, then a star in Detroit. Fetisov greeted me warmly, and from that moment made sure I had everything I needed to do my work and send my dispatches back home for hockey fans there who were starving for scraps of news and tidbits and gossip in the absence of games because of the labor dispute.

Fetisov's post-playing career included a stint as an assistant coach in New Jersey, general manager of the Russian National Team for the 2002 Olympics in Salt Lake City, president of the Central Red Army Club, and Minister of Sport, an appointment by Russian President Vladimir Putin.

More than 21 years later, when we traveled to Moscow to interview Senator Viacheslav Fetisov for the documentary film, nothing had changed even though now he was among the highest-ranking political leaders in his country. Slava was just as kind, accessible, gracious and accommodating as he was at that first meeting. And when he called me his friend, I knew he was sincere.

He has even come to terms in a positive way, with the "miracle" that went the wrong way on him in 1980. In his years living in Detroit and New Jersey, he became well aware of what that singular moment meant to Americans.

"I like to think that I contributed to the growth of hockey in the United States," he says. And by the way he smiles, it's clear that's plenty good enough.

Vladimir Konstantinov played just 446 games in his six-year career with the Detroit Red Wings. He scored 47 goals among 174 points and amassed 838 penalty minutes, making enemies in every NHL outpost with the way he competed. The world is left to wonder what might have been had he completed a career that surely would have included at least 10 more productive seasons if he had stayed healthy.

Vladdie was just beginning to emerge as one of the best players in the NHL when his career was cut short in that limousine crash that ruined everything just a week after he raised the Stanley Cup over his head

It's pure conjecture, of course, but I like to think the Wings would have won even a few more Cups before he reached the natural end of his career. It's also safe to say that Nicklas Lidstrom, as deserving as he was, might not have won all those Norris Trophies, seven of them in a 10-year span from 2001-11. Konstantinov may have spun off enough votes in some years to spoil his teammate's chances. And this: By now, Konstantinov would have been retired long enough to be eligible for the Hockey Hall of Fame. Much like his role model and former defense partner in Detroit, Slava Fetisov, Vladdie may not have had all the fancy statistics, but he was the kind of dominant, game-controlling player the Hall seeks to honor.

Konstantinov had a kind of aura about him, the way he competed, that made people curious about him. Opposing coaches asked about Konstantinov more than any player Lewis has been around.

"It happened all the time. They wanted to know what makes that guy tick. What is he afraid of? Does he ever get intimidated?" Lewis recalled. "And I would always answer, 'None of the above. And I can't tell you how or why. He's just a special breed.'"

His transformation from the latest Armani fashions (nobody on that team dressed better) to hockey uniform was nothing short of remarkable.

"If you saw Vladimir Konstantinov get off a bus and walk into the rink, you would probably think he was not a regular player, that he might be an extra guy, like maybe a seventh defenseman," Lewis said. "But once Vladdie put on his skates, pulled a jersey over his head and stepped onto the ice, you knew this guy was a warrior. He was fearless.

You didn't see that when he wore street clothes. The only place you can really identify a hockey player is on the ice, in the game. Because then there's no place to hide. You can't hide your character. You can't hide your skill. You can't hide your focus and you can't hide your determination because you're performing against players on the same level. A guy might lead an ordinary life away from the rink, but once he steps on the ice, his character is exposed – and this is who he is as an athlete and as a player. . . When Vladdie slipped on his jersey, it was almost like he became like a Batman character."

After the game, after the shower and a change back into those elegant suits, Vladimir Konstantinov once again became the quiet, humble and unassuming man that made him so comfortable to be around. He didn't require the accolades, the idolatry from fans, the media interviews. In fact, I cannot recall him ever referring to himself in a conversation. Most athletes at that level cannot complete a sentence without using "I" three or four times. Can't blame them, really. The world revolved around most of them for their entire lives en route to stardom and the multi-million-dollar contracts. With Vladdie, it was always "we," always about somebody else he thought was more deserving. But if you're like me and believe that the silence between words says more than the words, then Vladimir Konstantinov always had a lot to say.

I've always tended to judge other men by who I'd want in the foxhole with me when the bullets are flying. In those days in the mid-1990s when the Russian Five were helping to reshape the landscape in the NHL, there was someone in nearly every stall of the Red Wings' locker room I'd feel safer with in that foxhole. But if you had put a gun to my head and made me pick just one, I'd want Vladimir Konstantinov with me. And so would his teammates.

Since June 13, 1997, when that limousine with the sleeping driver left the roadway and crashed into a tree on Woodward Avenue north of Detroit, Vladimir Konstantinov has led a different kind of existence. Every day since has been a battle for a quality of life that most of us take for granted. He lives in suburban Detroit and continues to spend many hours a week working with his longtime therapist, Pamela Demanual, who accompanies him on his frequent visits to Joe Louis Arena, where his locker room stall was always there for him.

I have many wonderful memories from the time I spent around Vladdie, most of them away from the rink. I'll never forget the unmitigated joy on his face when I showed him his name on the Red Wings' list of draftees, that night in Helsinki in 1989; how proud he was – of his family, his wife Irina and daughter Anastasia – when he invited me into his first home in America, the high-rise apartment near Joe Louis Arena; and the handshakes that exuded not just strength but honor and integrity with the way he made eye contact at the same time, hands interlocked until that incomparable connection was fulfilled.

Vladimir Konstantinov always represented the very best in us.

He still does.

Acknowledgments

I always thought that putting out a newspaper was one of the greatest team sports mankind had ever invented – until I tried writing a book. Both, it turns out, require a legion of immensely talented people requiring a variety of extraordinary skills. In other words, just as I needed the support of so many to survive as a news and sports reporter during my various career assignments, so too were so many essential hands required to turn this pile of pages into something resembling a book worth reading.

Any list of acknowledgments for this project must begin with my colleagues at the Detroit Free Press, starting with sports editor Dave Robinson, the man who hired me to cover the city's very bad professional hockey club in 1985. Eventually, he was succeeded by Gene Myers, who in his active retirement was one of the final readers of this manuscript and, as he did for so many years at the Freep, saved me from myself on several occasions.

I am grateful beyond words for the faith Dave and Gene put in me and for their guidance and support. During those Free Press years, the assistant sports editors, notably Owen Davis and Steve Schrader, a platoon of faultless copy editors and my writing colleagues all helped in myriad ways to make me look better in those morning editions than I had any right to claim.

Because of their unbridled encouragement, Genevieve and the late Dr. John Finley were as responsible for moving me forward on this project as anyone. It was while serving as editor on Jack's book, "Hockeytown Doc" (Triumph Publications, 2012), that I began to think I could finally bring to fruition what I began more than two decades ago. Words fail to describe how monumentally important that beautiful couple and their family came to mean in my life in recent years.

Mentors Craig Childs, Mark Sundeen, Richard Adams Carey in the Mountain View Grand MFA program at Southern New Hampshire University are wildly successful authors whose careful and constructive readings, edits and suggestions improved the manuscript immeasurably. Nancy Martindale, a writer-in-waiting and an eagle-eyed copy editor, helped to find and fix many typos and stylistic inconsistencies.

I'd be remiss in not thanking Red Wings ownership, the late Mike Ilitch and his wife, Marian, and everyone involved in building a remarkable hockey club. From the front office to the public relations staff to coaches, players and the people who managed the building and sold beer and pizza in the stands, it was and remains a marvelous organization, and I was lucky to call Joe Louis Arena my office for so many years.

There may have been other options to get this book published, but I'll never know. As soon as Dan Milstein expressed an interest in committing his Gold Star Publishing Co. to the complex task of printing and marketing it, I was all in. A successful author himself, Dan is also the executive producer of the documentary film, "The Russian Five," through his new film company. His generous support made it possible for a young director, Joshua Riehl, and his team to put this amazing story on film. The interviews we conducted for the documentary were essential in augmenting a lot of the legwork that took place starting in 1989. I'm grateful and indebted to Joshua for reaching out and asking me to help produce and write this story for the screen.

Finally, and most importantly, I thank my wife, Jo Ann, who endured so many readings of these pages in their many incarnations that her eyes glazed over. But she never complained and never said a word, other than to suggest where I might give certain passages some additional thought or to offer a word of encouragement and support when I needed it most – which was often.